The Champ

MAINSTREAM *SPORT*

THE CHAMPION HURDLE
1927–2002

MICHAEL TANNER

EDINBURGH AND LONDON

Copyright © Michael Tanner, 2002
All rights reserved
The moral right of the author has been asserted

First published in Great Britain in 1989 by the Penguin Group

This edition published in Great Britain in 2002 by
MAINSTREAM PUBLISHING COMPANY
(EDINBURGH) LTD
7 Albany Street
Edinburgh EH1 3UG

ISBN 1 84018 678 X

This edition, 2002

No part of this book may be reproduced or
transmitted in any form or by any means without written permission from the publisher,
except by a reviewer who wishes to quote brief passages in connection with a review
written for insertion in a newspaper, magazine or broadcast

A catalogue record for this book is available
from the British Library

Typeset in Perpetua
Printed and bound in Great Britain by
Cox & Wyman Ltd

Contents

	Acknowledgements	7
1	George, Jack and Tony	9
2	Enter the Peacock Blue	22
3	'Something of an enigma'	30
4	The Sport is Cut to Shreds	36
5	The Two Peter Pans	47
6	'Well done, you ould divil'	57
7	HRP and the Shropshire Lads	64
8	Pot Pourri	81
9	The Ultimate Champion	97
10	Uplands versus Kinnersley	106
11	Six of the Best	120
12	Three Lively Ladies	142
13	Lambourn Supreme	154
14	Toby Takes on Newmarket	166
15	Pipe Über Alles	181
16	'O-le, O-le, O-le, O-le . . . '	203
	Epilogue: 2002	216
	Appendix 1 – Results	219
	Appendix 2 – Records	243
	Appendix 3 – Timeform Ratings	247
	Appendix 4 – Bibliography	248
	Index	250

Acknowledgements

I should like to reiterate my gratitude to all those individuals and organisations whose time and co-operation helped me during the production of the original work; and for additional assistance this time round I extend special thanks to: Gerry Cranham, for the photographs of See You Then and Istabraq; Mrs Henry Alper and Peter Curling, for permission to reproduce the paintings of Persian War and Dawn Run respectively; and to *Timeform*, for permission to include the ratings contained in Appendix 3.

Michael Tanner,
Sleaford,
October, 2001

1

George, Jack and Tony

Hurdle races originated, so the story goes, when the Prince Regent and his royal party amused themselves by racing over sheep hurdles on the Downs near Brighton. Be that as it may, the first officially recorded hurdle race took place at Durdham Down, Bristol, on 2 April 1821, run in three heats of one mile with five hurdles in each heat, some eleven years after the first official steeplechase. Over a century would elapse before hurdling was rewarded with its own undisputed championship.

Although both branches of the sport enjoyed public interest neither was immune from criticism. 'The very horses have a peculiar air about them,' wrote Robert Surtees, 'neither hunters nor hacks nor exactly racehorses. Some of them doubtless are fine, good-looking, well-conditioned animals but the majority are lean, lathy, sunken-eyed, woebegone, iron-marked desperately abused brutes, lacking all the lively energy that characterises the movement of the up-to-the-mark hunter.'

Charles Apperley – better known as the essayist and hunting correspondent Nimrod – was even more scathing, particularly with regard to the junior branch of the winter game which, though not so cruel as steeplechases, he deemed, 'childish and silly exhibitions . . . serving to show the cruelty of steeple-races by the numerous falls of the horses that contend them'.

But at least steeplechasing possessed the magnificent, if dangerous, spectacle of the Grand National. Hurdling had no such figurehead and suffered as a result. The much respected Arthur Coventry, an extremely successful amateur rider who afterwards became the official starter to the Jockey Club, approved of hurdling because it had, he maintained, no pretensions to be anything other than an admirable medium for gambling. In this respect opportunities abounded. The hurdlers may have lacked a Grand

THE CHAMPION HURDLE

National but a hundred years ago, for example, there were as many decent hurdle races as steeplechases, some 66 with a prize in excess of £100, headed by Croydon's Grand International Hurdle worth £766 and Kempton's Grand Handicap Hurdle at £594. In fact, nine hurdle races existed worth £400 or more compared to only a single chase, the Grand National at £1,035. However, by the turn of the century, the relative position began to resemble that of modern times. The ratio of £100-plus races now stood 63 to 43 in chasing's favour and there were twice as many chases (ten) exceeding £400 as hurdle races. The National, at £1,975, was supported by Manchester's Lancashire Chase (£1,725), whereas hurdling could only muster the Jubilee Handicap of £875, run at Manchester in April, and Gatwick's International Hurdle (£825), inherited from Croydon, in March.

Accordingly, there were few specialist hurdlers of real repute since they were either obliged to double up on the Flat or take their chances over fences. Those who did shine often did so at Croydon, home of the Grand International and Grand National Handicap Hurdles until its closure in 1890. Charles I won both events in 1880 and the former on a second occasion in 1881, while Sir William Nugent's Clonave actually won both the big hurdle and the Great Metropolitan Chase at Croydon's December meeting of 1874.

The career of Bellona was even more onerous. 'A great, raking brown mare with the grandest head you could ever wish to see,' according to her owner, the Hon. George Lambton, she cost £300 when bought out of Mat Dawson's yard in the autumn of 1886. Put to jumping, and ridden by her owner, 'she took to the game like a duck to water', so that the impecunious Lambton resolved to win some money on her first time out in the Grand National Hurdle. 'She did her part gallantly, strolling home ten lengths in front and the race put me on my legs for a short time.' Lambton and his trainer Joe Cannon considered her such a superb fencer that, five-years-old or not, she was aimed at the Grand National. However, by the spring of 1887 Lambton was again 'out of funds' and the pair decided to let the mare run for the Grand International Hurdle even though Aintree was only three weeks away. Despite jumping big, Bellona got up in the very last stride of a fast-run race in desperately deep ground to pip Silver Sea by a head.

All Bellona's courage and class could not help her in the National. The pace at which she had been forced to take hurdles

THE CHAMPION HURDLE

proved her undoing because she attacked Aintree's fences a little too wildly, overjumped the second and fell, much to Lambton's chagrin since he had backed her to win £10,000. Subsequently sold, Bellona never did manage to negotiate the National course, the 1890 race finally claiming her life when she got badly staked after her jockey had fallen off at Becher's.

Although a race carrying the title of Champion Hurdle was run at Liverpool between 1841 and 1844 (won on its last two renewals by Mr Raworth's Cattonian), the twentieth century opened with valuable weight-for-age races over hurdles conspicuously absent from the calendar. In 1907, Sandown Park instituted the Imperial Cup, another handicap which, along with the Liverpool Hurdle, offered just over £800 to the winner. However, one notable modification to the National Hunt scene came via the elevation of Cheltenham's Spring Festival in the years after 1902. The National Hunt Chase soon became the season's third richest race and the Gloucestershire Hurdle, once worth £67, became, by 1914, the richest in the calendar at £827.

It was therefore fitting that the prize went to Lord Rosebery's Wrack because he could claim to be the best hurdler active during the years preceding the First World War. From one of his owner's most productive families (his grandam was the 1,000 Guineas winner Chelandry), Wrack was a bay entire, small but broad for his height and very powerfully built. On the Flat he won ten races including consecutive Newbury Spring Cups. In between he won six of his seven hurdle races, culminating with the Shamrock Handicap Hurdle under 12st 7lb at Newbury in March 1915. Later that year he was sold to the United States as a stallion, the money being used to renovate the church at Mentmore. Though Wrack was not destined to be crowned Champion Hurdler, one of his descendants would eventually earn that esteemed title.

The other prince of twentieth-century hurdling denied his heritage was Trespasser. He, too, was an entire horse, bay in colour and more than useful on the Flat, the Queen's Prize at Kempton in 1921 being one of his seven victories. Over hurdles he was unbeaten in six races which included a tremendous treble in the Imperial Cups of 1920–22, the last twice carrying no less than 12st 7lb. (In 1921 he won by ten lengths, conceding the second horse 35lb.) Also, like Wrack, one of his daughters would breed a Champion Hurdler.

11

THE CHAMPION HURDLE

Although Trespasser retired a shade too early for his name to be inscribed in the annals of the Champion Hurdle, he did at least win at the Festival, namely the County Hurdle in 1920. Furthermore, his jockey in all those six victories, who had also partnered Wrack, went on to win the inaugural Champion Hurdle on 9 March 1927. George Duller deserved to be the first jockey on the roll of honour because he was arguably the greatest hurdle-race rider of them all.

Son of 'Hoppy' Duller, who initially trained trotters but later switched to the Flat, George junior was apprenticed to Schwind at Streatley before transferring to his father. Short and strongly built, with features politely described by Roger Mortimer as 'homely', he was fascinated by speed in all its forms, joining the Royal Flying Corps in the First World War (he often flew himself to meetings) and lapping Brooklands at 100 mph in racing cars. This familiarity with speed, allied to the lessons he absorbed from watching his father train trotters against the clock, made Duller an uncanny judge of pace. As the majority of hurdle races were then run in muddling fits and starts, Duller was instinctively able to dictate the terms on which the race unfolded and regularly illustrated the difficult art of waiting in front. Moreover, he revolutionised the very style of riding. When he began riding most sat well back in the saddle but, sitting up the horse's neck, he was quickly dubbed the 'Croucher'. Not for an instant did his centre of gravity alter over a hurdle, thereby enabling his mount to resume its stride immediately. As one anonymous rival put it: 'George loved to make his own pace if possible, but if someone else wanted to go on and George thought he was going too fast, he was quite content to tuck in behind him. He had a tremendously strong seat and no matter how hard his horse hit a hurdle he never budged an inch in the saddle.' Duller seldom rode over fences (though he did accept the mount on Silver Ring in the 1920 Grand National) and he was probably not so adept a finisher as Frank Wootton, who had been a leading rider on the Flat, but for all that he was a master craftsman.

Despite almost uninterrupted success, Duller remained a modest man. He rode six winners of the Imperial Cup, seven of the International, three County Hurdles and two Liverpool Hurdles. Since his number of rides was limited he only won the jockey's title once, with 17 winners in the war-restricted season of 1918, but during the seven years leading up to the first Champion Hurdle Duller's strike rate stood at an astonishing 26.8 per cent. It was

THE CHAMPION HURDLE

widely believed that whatever Duller rode in the inaugural Champion Hurdle would win. His choice was Blaris.

The Cheltenham Festival which greeted Blaris and Duller was a far cry from the struggling infant of 1902. 'The fact that so many people look forward each year to the meeting is not in the least surprising for, try how you will, you can find no parallel to this fixture through the racing year,' said the *Sporting Life*. 'There is nowhere quite like Cheltenham. It has been called many names and perhaps the most common term is the Ascot of steeplechasing. Though meant as a compliment, as indeed it is, the phrase does not go nearly far enough and certainly misses in its wording all that is really most charming about Cheltenham. Here there is something that Ascot cannot show nor any other fixture through the length and breadth of England – the real love of racing for its own sake and the embodiment of that much-abused phrase "the sporting spirit". At Cheltenham nothing matters quite so much as the sport.'

Although the creation of the Gold Cup three years earlier had in no way endangered the financial superiority of the Grand National, or for that matter the four-mile National Hunt Chase at the Festival itself, the establishment of such a valuable conditions race for staying chasers was already viewed as a success. Consequently, the inception of a similar 'championship' for hurdlers over the classic distance of two miles was an obvious step, especially as the 'timber-toppers' had no alternative target like the Grand National in the offing. In point of fact, hurdling badly needed a shot in the arm because many of those decent pre-war prizes had fallen away lately. The Imperial Cup (£882) and Liverpool Hurdle (the first '1,000 pounder' at £1,250) remained the two lucrative end-of-season objectives but the Jubilee had dwindled to £349 and, worst of all from a traditionalist's standpoint, the International to a paltry £390. Before Christmas there was no remotely decent handicap to aim for other than Liverpool's November Hurdle, and that of only £132. The conditions of the Champion Hurdle Challenge Cup – four-year-olds to carry 11st, five-year-olds 11st 10lb and older horses 12st – would obviously prove attractive to the sport's acknowledged stars like Blaris who otherwise had to risk fencing or the prospect of top weight in the hotly contested County Hurdle. On the debit side, the new blue riband offered a mere £365 to the victor compared to the £830 of the latter and was the least remunerative of the Festival's four hurdle races. It thus came as no surprise to see only

THE CHAMPION HURDLE

four runners stand their ground for Wednesday's championship contest but, significantly, Blaris was among them.

A six-year-old bay gelding, Blaris belonged to the redoubtable Mrs H. Hollins, who once chased 'Tuppy' Bennet round the Aintree paddock after he had continually, and injudiciously, remounted her horse Turkey Buzzard in the 1921 National. Blaris was trained at Burgh Heath, Epsom, by Bill Payne who, after becoming champion jockey in 1911, mixed riding with training.

Blaris made his hurdling début during the 1925–26 season, quickly recording two victories in maidens before graduating into handicap class to complete his hat-trick in Newbury's Berkshire Hurdle, all with Duller aboard. He began the current season at Sandown just as successfully and then defeated the previous County Hurdle winner Checktaker in Liverpool's November Hurdle. Unfortunately, overnight rain prior to Manchester's Victory Handicap saw him all at sea in the resultant heavy ground. As Cheltenham approached, a morale-boosting run seemed essential yet Payne withdrew Blaris from the General Peace Hurdle at Lingfield in favour of a two-mile steeplechase. The horse thanked Payne in no uncertain manner, trotting up by 20 lengths. Naturally, Duller did not ride him that day (in any case he was recovering from a foot injury) and even though he had partnered Blaris in all his seven hurdle wins his presence on him in the Champion Hurdle was not guaranteed.

Two of the gelding's opponents had clashed the previous Friday in the Lingfield Hurdle Cup and Duller partnered the winner, Boddam. However, his six-length victory proved inconclusive since his main rival Harpist was brought down by a swinging hurdle. Until then Frank Hartigan's horse was unbeaten over timber and on known form Harpist had the beating of Boddam. Moreover, Hartigan cancelled his customary holiday on the Riviera to supervise his final workout.

Once it was announced that Duller would partner Blaris any reservations concerning his unorthodox preparation were forgotten and his price hardened to 11/10 at the off. A fine day and a large crowd, which included the Prince of Wales, welcomed the history-making quartet as they came onto the course and cantered towards the start, away to the left of the stands. Ahead of them lay a taxing two miles and nine flights of hurdles, 'not less than 3 feet 6 inches from the bottom bar to the top bar'. The first two came on the run

THE CHAMPION HURDLE

past the stands. Then, as the runners bore left beyond the winning post, another awaited them at the top of the rise, followed by two more along the back straight. The sixth marked the furthest point of the course, at the top of the hill, whereupon the ground falls away sharply as they turn back towards the stands. Two hurdles down the hill preceded the ninth and final obstacle (the first on the first circuit). Bar the occasional elimination of a flight in bad weather the course remained more or less the same till 1980 although the actual race distance varied from two miles to two miles 200 yards.

The 20/1 outsider Labrador immediately expressed resentment at his no-hoper tag by promptly bolting. Once under way, Duller took Blaris straight into the lead. Billy Speck, however, well aware of Duller's penchant for orchestrating a race, drove Boddam alongside. The pace was palpably slow. Harpist was swishing his tail ominously and the further they travelled the more it appeared he would play no significant part in the finish.

The two leaders were still upsides at the penultimate flight but, now, in a few strides, the championship was settled. Duller gave Blaris the office and away he sailed, over the last and up the hill, relentlessly putting eight lengths between himself and Boddam. Only two Champion Hurdles would ever be won more authoritatively.

Blaris returned to defend his title yet his endeavours were dwarfed by the presence of a horse whose subsequent history is of sufficient magnitude to fuel suggestions that he was the greatest horse to compete in, let alone win, any Champion Hurdle. Put quite simply, Brown Jack was unique.

Not many horses are partial to a bit of bread and cheese. Brown Jack was – though only the cheapest American Cheddar. Not many horses receive telephone calls. Brown Jack did. At Steve Donoghue's retirement dinner a receiving set was placed in Jack's box in order that the jockey who shared the glory of those six consecutive Queen Alexandra Stakes might send his old friend a message. Not many horses have inspired a church sermon on all that is good in life. Brown Jack has. Not many horses have their shoes carried by the local bus service as a good luck charm or give their name to a village football team. Brown Jack has. When he died in 1949, at the age of 25, his heart was found to weigh 19lb compared to the 11 to 12lb of an 'average' racehorse.

THE CHAMPION HURDLE

Brown Jack arrived at Aubrey Hastings' Wroughton yard in July 1927. He was bred by Mr George Webb of Kings County, Ireland. Mr Webb had sent his mare Querquidella to Jackdaw, a young sire of great promise who won the 1912 Queen Alexandra. Unfortunately, the resulting colt foal had a weak heart, but a second mating with Jackdaw bore sturdier fruit when a good-looking brown colt was born on 5 April 1924. Brown Jack was somewhat mettlesome during his preparation for the yearling sales, and when he was led out unsold Webb began to wonder whether his colt was as promising as he believed. However, Marcus Thompson saw something he liked, bought the colt privately for £110 and took him home to Tipperary, where he was soon gelded. Fate then interceded. Charlie Rogers was scouting the district for possible jumpers. Passing close to Thompson's house, his car ran out of petrol and when Thompson kindly agreed to give him a lift who should Rogers spot grazing on the lawn but Brown Jack. The price on this occasion was £275.

Rogers determined not to rush Brown Jack, preferring to give him six months at grass rather than run him as a two-year-old. Jack grew fat and docile. In his first race at Navan in May 1927 he surprised no one by finishing last. A month afterwards he again ran unplaced but Rogers noted he was becoming lively and interested: 'He became a lion instead of a lamb.' Consequently, Rogers contacted the Hon. Aubrey Hastings, one of whose owners, Sir Harold Wernher, he knew to be looking for a maiden with which to eventually win the newly inaugurated Champion Hurdle. Hastings was a respected judge. He had trained and ridden the 1905 National winner Ascetic's Silver and subsequently trained three more. A deal was done at £750 with a £50 contingency should Brown Jack win a race. On the gelding's arrival at Wroughton the staff failed to see what their guv'nor had perceived. Nobody was anxious to 'do' Brown Jack. Young Alfie Garratt only had one horse so the job was his. Alfie soon had to earn his wages because Brown Jack fell sick with a chill and high fever. A diet supplemented by hot beer, eggs and whisky pulled him through the crisis.

Brown Jack gradually matured into a well-made horse, a little over at the knee but possessing a great sloping shoulder and wonderful, albeit curiously bowed, forelegs. Behind the saddle he had plenty of power. He quickly showed he could jump and neither during his schooling nor his races did he make the hint of a blunder.

THE CHAMPION HURDLE

A month's hard work up on Barbury Hill prepared Brown Jack for his hurdling début over one and a half miles at Bournemouth on 16 September. Third place seemed to teach Jack all he needed to know and ten days later he won a similar event at Wolverhampton. The animal he defeated was ridden by Duller who, significantly, asked Hastings whether he might have the mount in future. Though understandably cheered, Hastings could not comply for his stable jockey was Lewis Bilby Rees, the talented older brother of Frederick Bilbo. Coincidence or not, Duller did not ride in any race contested by Brown Jack until the Champion Hurdle.

Brown Jack sought further experience to lend credibility to his assault on the championship. He ran, and won, four more races before Christmas, all characterised by fluent hurdling and a late, devastating challenge on the Flat. 'He was always very calm and did not seem interested,' said Rees, 'but once he got going he would bowl along, taking his hurdles beautifully and gaining two or three lengths at every jump. As soon as he hit the front he would cock his eye and have a look at the stands.'

Just as everything was progressing nicely, Brown Jack was struck by a recurrence of the fever. Laid up for two months he did not reappear until 16 February when, not fully tuned, he ran disappointingly. Less than a fortnight later, however, he comprehensively turned the tables on the second, Rolie, a decent horse who won the County Hurdle, to win the Leicestershire Handicap Hurdle (his first victory over two miles) and prove he was back to his best.

One race remained between Brown Jack and his Cheltenham goal. Though worth only £219 and invariably run on the Friday before the Festival, the Lingfield Hurdle Cup was fast becoming a dummy-run for the Champion Hurdle, owing to its weight-for-age conditions, a rarity outside the championship. Here Brown Jack would really be tested by the likes of Zeno, Peace River and Royal Falcon.

Zeno was considered invincible. He had won the Imperial Cup and was fresh from a six-length victory over Peace River in the General Peace Open Hurdle, which was also assuming pre-Cheltenham significance, at the last Lingfield fixture. Peace River received 7lb; Brown Jack 17lb.

Zeno attempted to make all the running but early in the straight Brown Jack caught him and looked certain to win until Peace River

THE CHAMPION HURDLE

burst through on the rails and, catching him unawares, beat him a length. Zeno was a further four lengths back and had suffered some interference. On 7lb better terms, many believed he could reverse the result in the Champion Hurdle itself.

Once again only a handful of contenders lined up for the race but, as the *Sporting Life* suggested, 'It must be regarded as a real championship as Blaris, Zeno, Peace River and Brown Jack are probably the best four hurdlers in training.' Blaris had been specially prepared for the race, which in his case meant the odd combination of a steeplechase in January and a National Hunt Flat race in February. He won both and opened 6/4 favourite, drifting to 2/1 as more money came for Zeno at 5/2. Brown Jack was next at 4s, with Peace River at 5s.

For the only time in its life the Champion Hurdle was run on a Thursday. Heavy snow had fallen that week and a bitterly cold wind limited the attendance. Zeno set his usual strong gallop, closely tracked by Blaris and Brown Jack until the latter moved up to dispute the lead at the second last. As at Lingfield, Zeno quickly capitulated and the old champion could find no more. Where was Peace River? On this occasion Rees was ready for him and Brown Jack was still full of running. In the air together at the final flight, Wroughton's rising star found the superior speed on the level to win by one and a half lengths in a time eight seconds faster than the previous year.

Wernher was in Egypt and missed the speedy realisation of his ambition. His horse's hurdle record now stood at seven wins from ten starts. Surely there would be other years. But, unbeknown to the crowd thronging the winner's enclosure, Brown Jack's future was sealed. Before saddling him for the race Hastings asked Steve Donoghue to weigh up his chances of winning on the Flat. 'Well?' said the trainer when they met after the race. Donoghue nodded emphatically. 'Yes, he'll win on the Flat, and I'll ride him.'

Thus did Brown Jack vacate the stage for immortality elsewhere. So did Blaris. Although only seven, his attentions were henceforth concentrated upon fences, over which he won 13 times including the Coventry Cup at the 1930 Festival. Poor Peace River died shortly after the championship and of the cast assembled for the 1929 race, the principal boy seemed to be yet another four-year-old in Clear Cash.

Despite preparations for Cheltenham being ruined by a lengthy

THE CHAMPION HURDLE

period of frost and snow, Clear Cash came to the Festival possessing credentials so impressive that his supporters would not hear of defeat. On the final day's racing before the month-long freeze, 8 February, Sir John Grey's bay colt defeated Zeno and two other Champion Hurdle candidates in the General Peace. Not for the last time, Cheltenham came off worse in its dice with the winter weather. Racing was impossible on 5 March and the meeting was postponed for a week. Some pundits wondered whether the stoppage would induce a wholesale reversal of earlier form. *The Times'* correspondent wrote: 'It has been impossible for any trainer, unless he could use the sands at the seaside, to give any horse in his stable a gallop for several weeks.'

Royal Falcon had been well beaten by Clear Cash at Lingfield. After winning the previous season's Imperial Cup he changed ownership and stable and, though twice successful on the Flat, his only recent form over hurdles was that Lingfield outing. However, the six-year-old's new trainer was the veteran Irishman Bob Gore, who just happened to train at Findon, near the Sussex coast, where numerous sandy beaches provided perfect gallops throughout the lay-off. Gore knew his onions. He'd taken General Peace and Jerry M to Paris and won big races with both, besides winning the 1912 Grand National with the latter. When Royal Falcon walked into the Cheltenham paddock, chestnut coat gleaming and with his tail plaited in the inimitable Gore style, the message was not lost on several judges who scurried off to back him. Having F.B. 'Dick' Rees on his back did his chances no harm either.

Nonetheless, Clear Cash started 7/4 favourite, any waverers merely recalling the weights for the Imperial Cup in which he was set to receive only 5lb from Royal Falcon, whereas in the championship he received a stone. Of the others, Rolie's form appeared superior to Blancona's, and Fenimore Cooper, whose only attribute was the presence of Duller (taking this opportune moment to announce his impending retirement), also seemed well held. This left only Helter Skelter – and the Champion Hurdle was his very first race over hurdles!

Run for the first time on its traditional Tuesday, the race was a *tour de force* by Bilbo Rees. 'The manner in which Rees kept the winner always just in behind the leader until he challenged between the last two hurdles was admirable,' commented *The Times*. Blancona tried to bring his stamina into play by setting a fast pace

THE CHAMPION HURDLE

(the time was surpassed only once pre-war) but he had shot his bolt with three to jump. To the immense distress of favourite backers, Clear Cash surrendered without a fight and it was Rees, lurking in the shadows of Rolie and Fenimore Cooper, who held all the aces. Relishing the hill, as he had at Sandown, Royal Falcon stormed home by four lengths.

For the winner and his connections a number of notable milestones were established. Royal Falcon was the first entire to win the championship and was the first horse owned by Miss Victoria Williams-Bulkeley, the youngest person ever to own a Champion Hurdler, having bought him privately two months earlier. No one can say how much he owed his victory to the Sussex beaches because after winning on the Flat in April he was exported to America.

Thirty-five minutes after the Champion Hurdle, Rees employed totally different tactics in the Gold Cup, making every yard on Easter Hero to win by 20 lengths. Rees therefore became the first of ten jockeys to achieve the championship double at the same Festival. F.B. was entitled to call himself the finest all-round jockey of the inter-war period. Tall and powerful, with an elegant seat and the smoothest of hands, he was champion jockey five times during the 1920s (in 1924 with a record 108 winners from only 348 mounts) and it was said that he even fell off gracefully. Few, if any, post-war champions could be argued his peer.

In the 1930 Champion Hurdle, Rees partnered Lady Curzon's Arctic Star who, as a two-year-old, shared one of Charlie Rogers' paddocks with Brown Jack. Indeed, Arctic Star initially looked the better prospect and, although he could never match his old playmate, he won a Cesarewitch and was pretty decent over hurdles. Clear Cash beat him in the 1930 General Peace Hurdle but a month previously, at Newbury, he had trounced a useful novice called Brown Tony. In Brown Tony's defence, this was only his third race over timber. A four-year-old by Brown Jack's sire, he won a Kempton maiden on his second appearance and was trained by Jack Anthony. The youngest of the three Anthony brothers to distinguish themselves on the Turf (a fourth ended up a major-general), Jack rode his first winner aged 16 and won three Nationals and was champion jockey before he even bothered to turn professional. Brown Tony's rider was Tommy Cullinan, a young Irish ex-amateur. All in all, the Brown Tony team were not without

THE CHAMPION HURDLE

hope, for as *The Times* said on the morning of the race: 'He is a young hurdler of possibilities who might cause a surprise.'

Since his victory over Arctic Star, Clear Cash (trained by Owen Anthony) had returned to Lingfield for the Hurdle Cup only to suffer another defeat. Yet, for the second year in a row, he started favourite for the title. His closest market rival was Peertoi, owned and trained by the Wootton brothers, and ridden by Staff Ingham. Until a spread plate cost him his chance in the Lingfield Hurdle Cup, Peertoi had waltzed through four races unextended. If the betting was any guide, a close race was in prospect because two and a half points covered four of the five runners.

The bookmakers' assessment was shrewdness personified because, in the words of *The Times*: 'It would be very difficult to imagine a finer or more exciting finish.' A head and a short head was all that separated the placed horses – the tightest finish of the championship's entire history.

A contributory factor in this heart-stopping conclusion was undoubtedly the snail's pace at which the initial three-quarters of the race was covered. The race proper hardly began until the field entered the straight. Peertoi, Arctic Star and Clear Cash were in line abreast but Cullinan, tucked in behind, was being 'nearly pulled out of the saddle' by Brown Tony. At the last, Peertoi held a fractional advantage over Clear Cash and the race seemed to rest between them. Up the hill they battled, hammer and tongs, oblivious to the fact that Brown Tony was being wound up by Cullinan for a race-winning surge. Inexorably the young duo closed the gap and with barely a stride remaining led for the only time in the race. Clear Cash was beaten into second place again – the first of 11 unlucky animals to be placed twice without winning. Cullinan's day was not yet over. He went straight back out and won the Gold Cup on Easter Hero, which also gave Jack Anthony the coveted trainer's double. Three weeks later Cullinan went one better, winning the Grand National on Shaun Goilin. No other rider has achieved this unique treble. It marked the summit of Cullinan's career and he later felt compelled to take his own life.

The story of Mrs de Selincourt's Brown Tony also ended painfully for, although running bravely in handicaps under big weights, he never won again, and after falling in the Sandown Open Handicap Hurdle of 1931 he had to be destroyed.

2

Enter the Peacock Blue

The loss of the 1931 championship to persistent frost provided an opportunity to evaluate the impact of the Champion Hurdle during its formative years. In four renewals the race had attracted only 21 runners, a lack of patronage in comparison to the major handicaps which reflected the disparity in reward. On the other hand, the *Sporting Life* declared: 'The race is designed to attract only the best available talent and thus fields are more select than numerous.' This defence, however, lacked conviction because the 'best available talent' remained horses en route to more remunerative careers on the Flat and over fences. It was not lost on the race's critics that two championships had fallen to four-year-old novices and that only Blaris, for one reason or another, had defended the title. The Champion Hurdle badly needed an outstanding winner whose reputation was forged over hurdles and essentially maintained over hurdles. Although Insurance defeated only six opponents in his two victories, he satisfied those criteria and the event came of age as a result. Furthermore, he introduced to the championship's history one of its most intriguing human personalities, Dorothy Paget.

Seldom has the English Turf seen a character like the Hon. Dorothy Wyndham Paget. Enormously rich, impossibly difficult and invariably eccentric, no one more deserved the oft-used epithet 'living legend'. Thousands of words have been written about her – some contradictory, a few downright libellous. Yet much bears repetition in this particular work since altogether she won four Champion Hurdles with three different horses – a record – and bred the winners of two more.

Spoiled rotten by her mother, she grew up morbidly shy, finding male company openly distasteful and, although a beautiful slip of a girl, became stout and ungainly by middle age, an appearance not helped by her habitual uniform of an ankle-length tweed coat.

THE CHAMPION HURDLE

Capping the ensemble would be a beret pulled firmly down over the severely cropped brown hair that contrasted starkly with her large and rotund pallid face. As a young woman she received excellent reviews as a performing musician. Then, inexplicably, a conscious decision was made to eliminate all actively aesthetic pursuits from her life. A period as an accomplished horsewoman – showing, hunting and pointing – gave way to a brief flirtation with motor racing which cost her over £40,000. Money, of course, was no object. She had always gambled and it was only a matter of time before horseracing began to consume her life. It's impossible to calculate how much money she spent, won or lost over 30 years. At the end of one season she was said to have taken £60,000 from the ring but her losses were not so well documented. Once described as the world's best loser, she remarked, 'I ought to be, I've had plenty of practice.'

If this public side of Dorothy Paget did not generate sufficient racecourse gossip, rumours of her reclusive existence at the appropriately named Hermits Wood offered scandalmongers plenty of scope. She slept all day, rose at midnight, worked for three hours and then played bridge until dawn. A cook was always on duty to answer calls for banquets though she frequently touched little more than a morsel; she seldom drank anything other than Malvern water, her sole indulgence being an addiction to Turkish cigarettes, a hundred of which she would consume daily in her distinctive holder. She harboured all kinds of superstitions: green was a detestable colour, multiples of three her favourite numbers (Insurance had nine letters). Everything and everybody acquired a nickname; her tweed coat was 'speckled hen', her Rolls-Royce was 'Hilda', Charlie Rogers, who managed her Irish stud, was 'Romeo'. Herself she called 'Tiny'.

Not surprisingly, she was notoriously tricky to work for and went through trainers like sliced bread. 'Training Dorothy Paget's horses is child's play,' opined Basil Briscoe, 'but it's a hell of a bloody job trying to train Dorothy Paget.' She could be infuriating, yet as Fulke Walwyn, who trained for her after the war, says, 'She would drive you bloody demented, but the next moment she would say something endearing and you would forgive her.' Firmness, allied to a devilish sense of humour, was paramount in all dealings with Miss Paget. Once, she unwisely told Walwyn that he and his jockey had somehow conspired to bring about the defeat of one of

THE CHAMPION HURDLE

her horses. 'If that's what you think,' the angry trainer retorted, 'you know where you can put your horses, all 35 of them – and I've no doubt there'll be plenty of room for them!' The horses stayed with Walwyn. When Dorothy Paget died in 1959, aged 54, her peacock blue-and-yellow hooped colours had won 1,532 races, including seven Gold Cups, a Grand National and a Derby in addition to the quartet of Champion Hurdles.

A phone call to Old Etonian Basil Briscoe in the autumn of 1931 secured Miss Paget's place in the story of the Champion Hurdle. She asked the 28-year-old trainer if he knew of any good chasers and hurdlers. 'For the only time in my life I was able to tell an owner that I knew of the best steeplechase horse in the world and also the best hurdle-racer in this country.' The former was Golden Miller; the latter, a big four-year-old bay with a smear of white between his eyes, named Insurance.

Both horses belonged to Mr Philip Carr, for whom Insurance had won his last three races in brilliant style, eliciting the comment from the *Sporting Life*: 'We believe that nothing would induce Mr Carr to sell Insurance.' But Carr knew he was dying and accepted Miss Paget's offer which, though variously reported, was generally regarded to be £12,000 for the pair. An alternative version of the transaction given by Clive Graham (long-time 'Scout' in the *Daily Express*) to John Oaksey, which is more in keeping with the raffish image of the period, has Miss P and Briscoe burning the candle at a posh *chemin de fer* party in London. The trainer successfully banquo'd the owner three times running. Almost in the same breath he offered her 'Golden Miller, Insurance and Solanum (another decent chaser) – £13,500 the three, provided they stay with me'. When in gambling mode, Miss P was loath to say 'no'.

Insurance had been a successful performer on the Flat, numbering the 1930 Welsh St Leger among his four successes. By Blaris's sire Achtoi out of a mare called Prudent Girl, he quickly proved a superior convert to hurdling and chalked up that treble in the care of Vic Tabor before Carr transferred him to Briscoe at Longstowe, near Cambridge. In the third of those, Insurance scored a resounding victory over the year-older Song of Essex, an exceptional hurdler owned and trained by Sir Hugh Nugent. During the ensuing three seasons these arch enemies clashed seven times, and Insurance's three defeats over English hurdles were all inflicted by Song of Essex. Prior to the 1932 Festival, Insurance led two to

THE CHAMPION HURDLE

one, having also won at Kempton in January when Song of Essex met with considerable interference, but failing by two lengths to concede 5lb in the Lingfield Hurdle Cup. Remembering the 9lb turnaround in the weights at Cheltenham, the bookmakers had good reason to send Insurance off the first odds-on favourite in the race's short history. With Arctic Star dropping out on the day, the only other horse to stand his ground was Jack Drummer, whose slim chance was signified by a 33/1 quote. If Insurance was to be upset, the iron-hard going seemed the likeliest culprit since his forelegs were none too sturdy.

Billy Parvin pushed Song of Essex into the lead but the gallop he set was not severe enough to exert any pressure on Insurance's doubtful legs. Ted Leader never allowed him more than two lengths' daylight all the way round and merely had to twitch the reins at the bottom of the hill for the favourite to lengthen and accelerate 12 lengths clear by the post, the most emphatic margin in any championship. 'I am not saying that he is a very great hurdler, fit yet to be classed with Trespasser and others,' said *The Times*, 'but he seems to me to be the best hurdler in training at the present time.' Miss Paget may not have accumulated another fortune at the expense of the bookies for the Tote (Insurance paid a princely win dividend of 3s 3d for a 2s stake) but even Midas could not have bought the look of pleasure she wore when Golden Miller provided Briscoe, Leader and herself with the championship double by taking the Gold Cup immediately afterwards.

The weather was in total contrast 12 months later when Insurance defended his title. The sky was full of showery clouds and the ground was holding, just right for the champion. However, so much snow had fallen around Longstowe that Briscoe experienced difficulty getting Insurance fit. He began by running in two Newbury steeplechases either side of Christmas, winning the second. A fortnight later he took on Song of Essex at levels in the General Peace and was beaten two lengths. This constituted a hat trick for the Nugent horse and, at the same weights, his connections went to Cheltenham hopeful of a similar result. Insurance, meanwhile, showed he was back at his best, giving Wenceslas a thrashing round Hurst Park. The two principals (Insurance 11/10 on, Song of Essex 3/1) would not have the race entirely to themselves. Tom Coulthwaite's Windermere Laddie was a durable blighter who had won his last two races under enormous weights.

THE CHAMPION HURDLE

The ride on Insurance that March went to the small, tough, five-times champion jockey Billy Stott. He soon had reason to thank his imperturbability, for down at the start Song of Essex grabbed his right arm and tried to make a meal of it. Delaying the start for a minute or two, Stott temporarily bound the wound with his handkerchief.

Understandably the five runners went no gallop in the tacky ground (there has only been one slower time) and remained tightly bunched for the first one and a half miles. Descending the hill, Insurance passed Tees Head and Stott commandeered the inside rail for the final, vital turn into the straight. Though quite legitimately executed, the move effectively put paid to Windermere Laddie who was challenging on that side. In expectation of a threatening run from Song of Essex, Stott drove Insurance over the final flight for all he was worth, to be comforted by a roar from the crowd announcing his bitter rival's collapse. 'We were coming again at great speed when we toppled over,' moaned Parvin, although many jockeys in the stand reckoned Song of Essex was already a beaten horse. Insurance strode resolutely up the hill to withstand Windermere Laddie's renewed effort by three-quarters of a length. Stott's manoeuvre thus proved critical.

Still only six-years-old, and approaching the height of his powers, Insurance's grip on the championship looked set to continue for as long as Miss Paget desired. But Nemesis was not far away. That summer he made an abortive trip to Auteuil for the French Champion Hurdle. The ground was firm and he travelled badly. Those fragile forelegs sustained damage and Briscoe was continually thwarted in his attempts to get the horse race-ready throughout the following season. Target after target was sidestepped until, on race morn itself, Briscoe admitted defeat. Seasonal retirement became permanent. He won eight of his twelve hurdle races, only one English horse having beaten him. In due course Insurance found himself installed at Miss Paget's Elsenham Stud in Essex alongside Golden Miller. The two became inseparable companions and were a star turn at the 1950 International Horse Show. Insurance survived his friend by three months and eventually collapsed, aged 30, in the spring of 1957 while drinking from the brook which ran through his meadow. Two large headstones mark their graves.

The hard ground prevailing throughout the spring of 1934 claimed another distinguished victim in the American horse Flaming,

THE CHAMPION HURDLE

who was bred to be a Champion Hurdler, being by Wrack out of Flambette and therefore a full brother to Flambino, the dam of American Triple Crown winner Omaha. Bought out of a selling plate by the noted American polo player and amateur rider G.H. 'Pete' Bostwick, Flaming finished the 1932–33 season by winning the prestigious handicaps, the Imperial Cup and Lancashire Hurdle; performances (at Sandown he had three of the Champion Hurdle field behind him) which stamped him championship class. However, he was not the soundest of horses and nearly a year passed before he reappeared over hurdles. He won all right, giving 23lb to a winner of the Liverpool Hurdle, but walked away feelingly. He then took the International and in another handicap was rated 5lb superior to Insurance. The Champion Hurdle lay at his mercy if he could stand training. Bostwick's trainer was Ivor Anthony, who took control of Wroughton upon the sudden death of Aubrey Hastings in 1929. Like brother Jack, Ivor had been champion jockey and once, at Pembroke, actually rode all six winners in an afternoon. As a trainer his hallmarks were endless patience and meticulous attention to detail. He loved 'problem' horses and would do everything in his power to get them right. In his opinion Flaming could not do himself justice in the Champion Hurdle and he counselled withdrawal. After all, he and Bostwick possessed a more than competent substitute in Chenango and the opposition appeared flimsy. Insurance was unlikely to compete, Song of Essex had lost his confidence after a number of falls, and the best of the young hurdlers, Free Fare, who finished ahead of Chenango in the Lingfield Hurdle Cup, was also out of the race after working poorly. In consequence, Chenango started as red-hot favourite to defeat his four opponents. Only Sir Ken would start at more cramped odds. Bostwick could not come over from America and the mount was offered to the 22-year-old Irishman Danny Morgan.

The same age as his stablemate, Chenango was also sired by an ex-English stallion in the guise of the Eclipse winner Hapsburg. In contrast to Flaming, who was an entire, he was a bay gelding and had been a leading steeplechaser back in the States during 1931 when his victories included the Temple Gwathmey Memorial. Before that Lingfield reverse, he had put together a sequence of three good wins at Wolverhampton, Hurst Park and Newbury.

With Free Fare's defection the race lost most of its interest. Song of Essex fell at halfway and Chenango galloped home to win

THE CHAMPION HURDLE

unopposed by five lengths and six lengths from Pompelmoose and Black Duncan. Such a substandard, poorly contested race added nothing to the championship's lustre.

Chenango's attentions were redirected to fences in the main and the 1935 Champion Hurdle was left to Flaming. However, he had not jumped hurdles in public for a year and his legs could not stand the strain. He was soon tailed off and Bostwick pulled him up before halfway. It was an unhappy week for the American. The following afternoon Chenango failed in the County Hurdle, and later in the summer he died.

Eleven competitors had faced the tape on a cold but bright day, only three of whom started at less than 10/1. An extremely open race seemed in prospect. The uneasy favourite was Gay Light, beaten in the Lingfield Hurdle Cup and, at nine, getting a bit long in the tooth. Moreover, his action suggested he would be unsuited by the track. Briscoe provided the second favourite, Hill Song (a full brother to Song of Essex), who had won the Irish St Leger after being beaten by a head in the Irish Derby and came to the championship the winner of two out of his last three races over timber. Next best was the four-year-old Victor Norman, who had made every yard to win the International. Little heed was paid to last season's Imperial Cup hero Lion Courage. Subsequently sold, he moved stables and had not won since. His trainer, Frank Brown, preferred to wait for the Imperial Cup again rather than take on the cracks at levels. The elder brother of champion amateur Harry, and another Old Etonian overflowing with charm, Brown enjoyed nothing better than pitting his wits against opponents, be they in the ring or on the track, and laying one out for a big handicap. It was only on the insistence of Lion Courage's jockey that the horse took his place in the line-up.

Already twice champion jockey (with four more titles to come), Gerry Wilson was fast developing into the decade's foremost rider. The strongly built son of a horse-dealer in the Whaddon country, he was dubbed the 'Oyster' by his family since he rarely came out of his shell. He was fiercely competitive and tremendously brave. Both these priceless qualities were needed in abundance if Lion Courage (a 100/8 shot) was to play more than a supporting role because his form was poor and Wilson was carrying a painful shoulder injury.

Hill Song tore off at a tremendous clip, leaving all bar Victor

THE CHAMPION HURDLE

Norman toiling and even the grey conceded defeat coming down the hill. At this moment, eagle-eyed observers spotted Wilson driving Lion Courage through the field and by the turn the pair had got to Hill Song's girths. After one and a half miles at this speed (the time was a new race record of 4 minutes 00.20), Hill Song threw in the towel without much of a struggle but Lion Courage soon had to live up to his name as Staff Ingham urged Gay Light in desperate pursuit. Crossing the last the two were locked together but Lion Courage out-fought his adversary to win by half a length. Wilson's effort had been monumental. He gave his horse a breather down the hill and, injured shoulder or not, had outridden one of the best hurdle jockeys (which he was judged not to be) in the finish. Straight after the race he left for London and treatment on the shoulder, returning on the Thursday to ride Golden Miller in the Gold Cup.

Having provided Jackdaw with his third individual winner of the Champion Hurdle, an unparalleled achievement, Lion Courage never ran over hurdles again, though he did win a couple of chases at Gatwick and Uttoxeter the following season.

3

'Something of an enigma'

The Champion Hurdles of 1936 to 1938 were dominated by Free Fare. Starting favourite for all three, he triumphed only in 1937, though a fall at the last undoubtedly cost him a second title a year later. Bruce Hobbs, his partner in 1938, reckons he was 'head and shoulders above the rest that year – he'd have been passing the post when the rest were jumping the last because I had four double-handfuls! The faster they went, the better he went. He was a great jumper and would often take off outside the wing, but he had to be held up or he'd pull himself to the front. He was a very, very good horse – you don't win a big hurdle race going away, with 12st 7lb, after a ten-month lay-off without being a bit special.'

That Free Fare should gain only one title from his four attempts (he was brought down in 1939) was very much in character. 'He is something of an enigma,' said the *Sporting Life* in the spring of 1936. 'His owner, were he less phlegmatic, would be either ecstatic or in despair. Twice he has swerved away a winning chance in the Manchester November Handicap, a race which he won in a canter at the third time of asking when not so greatly fancied.' The owner in question, what's more, was a man not averse to a wager. It is not on record whether Mr Ben Warner missed the boat when Free Fare finally won the Manchester race by five lengths at odds of 22/1, but he certainly lost a well-publicised four-figure sum when his horse was beaten in the 1934 Lingfield Hurdle Cup. Before that setback Free Fare had won three in a row. Subsequently withdrawn from the Champion Hurdle to await the Liverpool Hurdle (in which he carried top weight into fourth, less than two lengths off the winner), he saw one of those behind him at Lingfield rub salt into the wound by lifting the championship.

Free Fare inherited his wiry, sparely-made chestnut frame from his sire Werewolf, a moderate performer on the track. He first

THE CHAMPION HURDLE

attracted attention over timber when winning the 1933 Liverpool Hurdle as a five-year-old. His career on the Flat began less auspiciously – he finished down the field in a Leicester seller – but after missing the whole of the 1931 season he won seven races in the next. Those two costly stabs at the November Handicap in 1933 and 1934 resulted in defeats by half a length and two lengths and he was never a contender for Lion Courage's championship after a brief flirtation with fences, but his victory in the 1935 November Handicap and another in a Sandown bumper paved the way for a return to hurdling.

He could not expect to have matters all his own way in 1936. Mrs Michael Stephens' grey, Victor Norman, at five, three years younger than Free Fare, followed his fourth place in the previous year's championship with two excellent victories before failing to concede 27lb to Styx River at Newbury. His trainer, the American Morgan Blair, maintained he had been short of a gallop that day. Known as 'Bam', due to his habit of uttering that exclamation whenever he entered the weighing room (his original name was Bamberger), Blair would have made a fine cavalier. He completed the course in the 1921 National after no less than four falls in order to land a substantial bet and got round again in 1925 activated by similar motivation. This second adventure involved considerable pluck for he rode with a scar still raw from an appendix operation and had sweated off 18lb in 48 hours to make the weight. Blair was unconventional but no fool. Victor Norman was an extremely modest animal on the Flat yet Blair detected the conformation of a jumper, a view reinforced by the female side of the grey's pedigree since his dam Tickets was a daughter of the mighty Trespasser.

Despite any recent form over hurdles, Free Fare waltzed to an eight-length victory in the Lingfield Hurdle Cup and became all the rage for the Champion Hurdle at 5/2, although in the weights for the Imperial Cup he was assessed a mere one pound superior to Victor Norman and only 2lb superior to Dorothy Paget's Wheatley among his championship rivals. Miss Paget's seven-year-old had won the International from Swift and True, Cactus II and Armour Bright, all of whom reopposed at Cheltenham.

At Tuesday lunchtime there seemed little prospect of the race even being started. Fog rolling down from Cleeve Hill was making visibility all but impossible. Next to nothing was seen of the first race but sunshine and a strong wind fortunately came to the rescue.

THE CHAMPION HURDLE

Otherwise one of the truly outstanding performances in the Champion Hurdle's history would have been lost.

After the antics of Swift and True had delayed the start, Victor Norman (Frenchie Nicholson) went straight to the head of affairs and gave a display, in the *Life*'s opinion, 'worthy to rank with Trespasser, winning in the style that stamped him as the best timber-topper since that great horse's heyday'. *The Times* was no less eulogistic: 'His crossing of the hurdles was effortless and at almost every hurdle he gained on his opponents. He is a natural jumper and how few of them do we see?' Free Fare, coming late on the scene as usual, was three lengths back in second.

He made no such error in 1937, by which time he had exacted revenge on Victor Norman at Lingfield. The grey lacked condition, his supporters averred, due to the vagaries of a weather-interrupted preparation. They preferred to savour three splendid efforts either side of Christmas. At Kempton he narrowly failed to concede two stone and a week later he collected Sandown's Annual Handicap Hurdle with 12st 7lb on his back. Then, in January, only the concession of 19lb enabled Our Hope to beat him by three-quarters of a length at Newbury.

However, hard on the heels of the Lingfield defeat came another disappointment when he ran deplorably at Gatwick. Nor would he relish the heavy ground, the legacy of a desperate winter. When snow and rain caused the race's inevitable postponement from 2 March, his connections' slim hopes of a reprieve were even then dashed as the ground became dead and wanted a lot of getting. These conditions would not inhibit Free Fare, although he had not worked for five days because of the snow. Of far greater significance to the statistically minded was his age. No nine-year-old had hitherto shown the necessary speed to win the championship.

Victor Norman set off with the intention of repeating his successful tactics of 1936, closely pursued by this season's Paget representative, Menton. The favourite lay handily in third. The order remained unchanged until Victor Norman cried enough coming to the second last, allowing Menton to hug the rail into the straight. Now the drama commenced because, once unleashed by Georges Pellerin on the outside, Free Fare shot past the Paget horse and instantly crossed to the fence before jumping the last with a comfortable advantage. He may have distracted Menton momentarily as he clattered the hurdle unceremoniously, losing all

THE CHAMPION HURDLE

hope of renewing his challenge. In fact, Our Hope, revelling in the mud, finished fastest of all and reduced the favourite's lead to two lengths at the post. Free Fare's erratic behaviour had very nearly cost Ben Warner another major prize. The consensus of opinion, however, was that the incident occurred too far from the finish to have affected the outcome. Crack Belgian-born hurdles jockey Georges Pellerin thus secured his only championship and 62-year-old Lambourn trainer Ted Gwilt his greatest success. Mind you, his Saxon House yard will be heard of again.

Free Fare's second title seemed such a foregone conclusion that something was bound to go wrong. His reappearance was left till January. Carrying 12st 7lb top weight in the competitive Weyhill Handicap at Newbury, he started at the remunerative odds of 100/8 and trotted up by four lengths. Then came a stunning display in the General Peace which he won by a contemptuous 15 lengths from Lobau. The latter took his chance at Cheltenham even though he fell in the International and was humbled by Beachway in the Lingfield Hurdle Cup in between. With Victor Norman having gone chasing, opposition to the champion dwindled and was given interest by the first challengers from Ireland and France.

Several Irish-bred horses had contested the Champion Hurdle but Arthur Morrow's Up Sabre was the first to be trained in the Emerald Isle. After being placed at Manchester he won a small race at Haydock – not, at face value, championship form. The French challenger was a more intriguing proposition. Chuchoteur began his career in England under Atty Persse, actually winning a race and running unplaced in the Royal Hunt Cup as a four-year-old. Now six, he belonged to the Vicomte de Chambure and arrived fresh from a victory at Auteuil. His French rider, Michel Plaine, had taken the trouble to familiarise himself with English hurdles, partnering Diogenes into second place at Shirley the day before the Champion Hurdle. The fifth and final runner was Our Hope.

The 1937 second had experienced mixed fortunes this season. He fell in Free Fare's Newbury comeback race and could only finish fifth at Sandown a week afterwards. The nine-year-old then returned to try something approaching his best when beating Le Maestro at Newbury. A grey by Son and Heir, Our Hope was owned and trained by Roderic Gubbins. Initially, Gubbins leased Our Hope from his breeder, the Warwickshire art dealer Mr W.E. Robinson, but since the latter's death in 1937 had owned the

THE CHAMPION HURDLE

gelding outright. Aboard his horse was the distinguished amateur Capt. Reginald Peregrine Harding of the 5th Royal Inniskilling Dragoon Guards, who had already illustrated his worth at the Festival by winning the 1933 National Hunt Chase on Ego.

Cotswold mists again made their presence felt, delaying numerous special trains so that the programme was put back 15 minutes. However, as the sun gradually won its battle the scene was transformed into one akin to high summer. Neither Free Fare nor Our Hope were expected to appreciate the very firm ground, yet opposition to the former seemed so weak he wound up as tight as 2/1 on, with Chuchoteur at 9/2. Our Hope, the pick in the paddock, came next at 5s.

Few spectators beside Gubbins and Our Hope's loyal band of supporters could have enjoyed the race which unfolded before them. Everything went according to plan to begin with. Free Fare led the way but at little more than an exercise canter for the first mile or so. Then things began to happen alarmingly fast. The favourite had not been hurdling particularly well – he made a hash of the first and hit another low – and with the race apparently at his mercy he made a total mess of the penultimate flight. Taking off one stride too soon, he put a foot through the top bar and turned over. 'He was only cantering at the time and I could have won easily enough,' recalled Hobbs disconsolately. 'He would have hacked up but I'd been so tied up with orders – "hang on, hang on, don't let him go too soon" – that he was tripping over himself.' In addition, Free Fare's departure interfered with Lobau and so unsighted poor Up Sabre that he also came to grief. At a stroke the race was realistically reduced to a match between Our Hope and Chuchoteur.

Lady Luck had one more card to play, one eerily reminiscent of the previous year. Approaching the final hurdle, Harding glanced over his left shoulder to check on the whereabouts of the French challenger, on whom Plaine had been giving a passable imitation of the Duller crouch. In a flash the grey veered to his left, violently impeding Chuchoteur's progress up the inside rail. Gathering his wits, Plaine switched to the outside and for a moment, as the hill beckoned, it seemed the gap might close. But Chuchoteur's endurance had been sorely tapped at a vital juncture and Our Hope clung on for a one-and-a-half-length victory.

Although Plaine had a perfectly justifiable axe to grind he declined to lodge an objection for foul riding, 'a sporting gesture

THE CHAMPION HURDLE

from the Frenchman', according to the *Sporting Life*. Gubbins' prayers were answered. This lucrative success would help fund the new house and yard he had recently built in Lambourn. For Harding, this victory – the first by an amateur – was but one more rung up the ladder of fortune which ultimately saw him complete his military career as a major-general with DSO and bar.

For Our Hope and Free Fare (who holds the dubious distinction of being the hottest-ever losing favourite) the 1938 Champion Hurdle marked the beginning of the end. Both returned for the championship of 1939 but, at the age of ten and eleven, they represented a very old guard when set against a talented rising generation of hurdlers.

4

The Sport is Cut to Shreds

Miss Paget had not exactly abandoned the Champion Hurdle since the retirement of Insurance. As befitted National Hunt's premier owner, one of her hurdling battalions was usually considered worthy of participation. Wheatley carried the blue and yellow in 1936 but suffered the misfortune of being struck into, while Menton ran third to Free Fare. However, her candidate in 1939 looked extra special.

In the autumn of 1938 the Paget chequebook was again produced, this time to purchase a seven-year-old bay gelding by Soldennis out of the Swynford mare Margaret Beaufort named Solford. Bred in County Limerick by Jack Hartigan, he was bought as an unbroken three-year-old by Dan O'Brien, father of Vincent, who won three races on the Flat with him at four and five. Indeed, the young Vincent rode him to be second at Mallow in 1936 but unfortunately Solford broke down and missed the following season. After breaking his duck over hurdles at Naas in March 1938, Solford was nicely sharpened up for the Flat and proceeded to win six races, culminating with the Irish Cambridgeshire under 9st 9lb top weight. Clearly, he was just the sort to attract the attention of Miss Paget's 'Irish eyes', Charlie Rogers.

Solford crossed the Irish Sea to join the majority of Miss Paget's jumpers in Owen Anthony's stable at Letcombe Bassett, near Wantage. The least known of the Anthony brothers, the flamboyant, no-nonsense Owen had replaced Basil Briscoe in 1935. Solford promptly fell on his English début but wins at Hurst Park and in the International confirmed the rich promise shown in Ireland. On the strength of these displays he was installed favourite for the Champion Hurdle and on the morning of the race was as short as 100/30. Nevertheless, with 13 runners, the largest field to date, an abnormally competitive race was in prospect.

Before the tape rose, Solford had lost his market position to Lord

THE CHAMPION HURDLE

Sefton's four-year-old Iceberg II, winner of his last three outings. There was also money for Lobau, who had recently shown much improved form to win both the big Lingfield 'trials', the General Peace and Hurdle Cup. Among his victims were Apple Peel, Vitement, Prudent Achtoi, Mask and Wig and Lord Cadogan's highly rated Bahuddin, all of whom contested the championship. The one blot in Lobau's copybook was a January defeat at Newbury by Ard Macha. It was not lost on keen students of the game that the blinkered mare African Sister had been travelling awfully easily in the lead when she tipped up at the final flight and skidded along the ground on her nose. The first of her sex to compete in the championship, African Sister could be backed at 10/1, and as she belonged to a bookmaker and came from a betting stable it is safe to assume those odds were gratefully accepted.

African Sister was trained by Charles Piggott, whose stables on Cleeve Hill overlooked the course. An exceptionally shrewd man, who bought wisely and gave short shrift to any inmate unlikely to earn its keep, Piggott took endless care with their placement, an inestimable quality if two of your biggest patrons, Fred Sedgwick and Horace Brueton, happened to be bookies. 'He was very quiet, but if he said to me when I got up that I could win, he was nearly always right,' said his nephew Keith Piggott, the father of Lester.

Keith Piggot's father, Ernest — younger brother of Charles — had been the leading jump jockey of his era. His mother was a Cannon, his grandmother a Day, racing blood through and through. Not unexpectedly, his first winner over obstacles, a Manchester hurdle in 1922, was for Uncle Charlie, for whom he later partnered Vaulx (a £10 bargain buy) to win the Welsh Grand National, and Kiwi (240 guineas) to win the Welsh Champion Hurdle. African Sister was another cheap purchase though it was Brueton himself who bought her, for 220 guineas, out of a selling nursery. She was running unsuccessfully in sellers as a four-year-old when Brueton sent her to Piggott to see if he could make a hurdler out of her. Ridden from behind, she gradually adapted and after a Newbury seller Keith Piggott was able to report that she had 'flown' the last two hurdles and shown definite potential. A Brueton gamble on the mare at Uttoxeter came unstuck when she came in season, but six weeks later all was recovered by a facile victory at Stratford.

The chestnut daughter of Prester John improved to an extraordinary extent as a six-year-old, winning four consecutive

THE CHAMPION HURDLE

handicaps and finishing 1938 by defeating Champion Hurdler Our Hope at a difference of only 4lb. Sights were now firmly fixed on the Champion Hurdle. Then came that fall. For three weeks Charlie Piggott bathed her nose four times a day and she did no work to speak of until shortly before Cheltenham. However, African Sister was made of stern stuff. Only the previous summer she lay at death's door after suffering internal injuries during a race at Wolverhampton. Nursed round the clock for three days, she pulled through, but racing seemed out of the question. Two months later she finished second at Birmingham! Nor was Keith Piggott a stranger to adversity. As a toddler he was thrown from a pony into a pond and nearly drowned, he had a screw through his right elbow, reminding him of a badly broken arm, and a broken right thigh had left him slightly lame. The patched-up combination of African Sister and Keith Piggott was now about to play the phoenix.

If one found shelter from the biting wind it was a lovely day for watching steeplechasing, clear and sunny. Solford and Vitement (for sale at £1,000 throughout the last fortnight) disputed the lead, tracked by Bahuddin with African Sister occupying her customary early position right at the back. Coming down the hill it was obvious the favourite would not be troubling the leaders, especially Solford, whom Sean Magee dashed clear at the third last. As soon as the cheers rose for Owen Anthony's horse they were matched by those exhorting brother Ivor's Bahuddin. The pair drew away from the chasing bunch which included Mask and Wig and Free Fare, but not African Sister, who entered the straight stone-cold last.

One obstacle remained, for Solford and Bahuddin one too many. Astonishingly, both fell – quite independently – and what's more, hampered Mask and Wig. The carnage did not stop there because Mask and Wig swerved into Free Fare, causing the old champion to land in a heap on the prostrate Solford. As the leaders went down like ninepins, African Sister found herself accelerating into a challenging position with no one left to challenge! 'She did not seem to want to go to start with,' said Piggott, 'but when we turned for home she suddenly started to pick up. Although the two up front fell, she was going so well I would have won in any event.' The mare passed the post with three lengths to spare over Vitement.

Solford, Bahuddin and African Sister all seemed as good as ever the following season. Solford's campaign gathered momentum before Christmas with a six-length success at Gatwick and his

THE CHAMPION HURDLE

reputation easily survived two honourable defeats. Soft ground and the concession of nearly three stones proved his undoing at Leopardstown, while he failed by two lengths to give Carton 13lb in the International, where Bahuddin, victorious at Windsor on Boxing Day, could only finish seventh after clouting a swinging hurdle. Carton finished full of running at Gatwick and Fred Winter deliberately adopted a low-key preparation with him, intent on peaking at Cheltenham. Carton had been trounced by Solford in their December clash at Gatwick but he was now looking stronger and fitter by the day. The reigning champion illustrated her good health by humping 12st 4lb to victory round Cheltenham. Nevertheless, serious punters only wanted to know Solford who, according to the *Sporting Life*, 'was supported for a small fortune at 5/2 and 9/4'. After all he was 9lb better off with Carton for that two-length defeat and had looked the winner the previous year before his tumble.

The outsider Patrimony cut out the pace from Bahuddin and Solford at no more than a fair gallop, which resulted in African Sister taking noticeably closer order this year, and as the tempo quickened she snatched the lead from Bahuddin between the last two flights. Perhaps stunned by this comparatively novel experience, she may have hung fire a little when Solford swooped because the favourite went by to win unchallenged by one and a half lengths. In third place, some four lengths adrift, was the unfortunate Carton, whose saddle began slipping at halfway and ended up on his flanks. Solford, too, did not complete the course without mishap – the brushing boots he wore to prevent cutting into himself had somehow been torn off. A month afterwards, Solford confirmed his status as a champion by winning Manchester's Jubilee Hurdle. It was a memorable Festival for Miss Paget and Anthony since they also won the Gold Cup with Roman Hackle, thereby repeating the championship double of Insurance and Golden Miller. Such reward was no more than Miss Paget deserved as she entered 48 horses at the two day meeting.

The 1941 Festival was likewise curtailed by wartime restrictions. Only a limited number of tracks were granted dates, the *Sporting Life* was reduced to a weekly and Owen Anthony even briefly shipped his string to Ireland. The value of the Champion Hurdle naturally suffered. Solford's victory was worth £410 as against £745 won by Our Hope, the biggest prize to date. However, continuity

THE CHAMPION HURDLE

was provided by the presence of the last two champions. Solford's retinue were confident the 'double' could be repeated. They were not alone. Both Solford and Roman Hackle started favourite, the Champion Hurdler representing a 'three-star wager' as far as the *Life* was concerned. He won at Cheltenham on 19 February with ridiculous ease despite the burden of 12st 7lb and had been pre-race favourite at various shades of odds-on ever since. The handicapper now rated him 12lb superior to African Sister, who had been hard pressed to dispose of a mediocre opponent at Southwell in her final prep race. On the debit side, Solford had recently celebrated his tenth birthday, and African Sister was only a year younger. What kind of threat did the youngsters pose?

The best of them was generally assumed to be Lord Rosebery's Luncheon Hour, who had beaten African Sister at Cheltenham and, on the formbook, seemed little behind the champion. Another five-year-old was Ephorus, formerly a useful sprinter on the Flat and a February winner at Worcester. A quick, clever jumper, his trainer Fulke Walwyn had just received him as a wedding anniversary present from his wife Diana. The six runners were completed by two four-year-olds, Anarchist (the Paget second string) and the once-raced Seneca, an entire, handicapped elsewhere some 24lb below Solford. In the Champion Hurdle he would receive a stone, hardly sufficient to tip the scales in his favour. Punters could obtain 7/1 or better about Seneca and the other youngsters as the market sided with the hurdling establishment. Solford, the subject of some massive bets, was sent off 7/4 on, over seven points clear of African Sister.

Anarchist did his donkey-work superbly. Two hurdles out the race burst into life, though not in the manner anticipated. As the whips flew, neither champion could find anything. African Sister's excuse was a broken blood vessel. For Solford's downfall no reasons were forthcoming. Up the hill Seneca eventually wore down the plucky Anarchist to win by a head.

Seneca's victory was a triumph for the Smyths, jockey Ron and his uncle Vic, who trained the horse at Epsom for Sir Malcolm McAlpine, because they had amazingly repeated the family achievement of the Piggotts. Vic had been a skilful jockey himself in the years following the First World War, landing the Oaks on Brownhylda. His training career started with a bang when he was successful with his very first runner, Dragoon. Most of Smyth's

THE CHAMPION HURDLE

principal winners sported the McAlpine tartan and ultimately included the 1952 1,000 Guineas heroine Zabara. Ron Smyth had experienced weight difficulties similar to his uncle's and was obliged to forsake the Flat. In no time at all he transformed himself into a very polished and effective rider over hurdles, having his first mount in the championship on his father's Lemanaghan in 1940. Six of Ron Smyth's seven rides in the Champion Hurdle were for uncle or father and he won three of them. Although the last of this trio became a public idol, Ron Smyth, to this day, remains adamant that Seneca was the best of the three.

In fact, the Champion Hurdle was the first occasion Smyth partnered Seneca. On his only other start he carried a mere 9st 9lb at Cheltenham and won by six lengths thanks to a tremendous burst of speed on the run-in. A chestnut bred by his owner, Seneca was one of the few successful products of the 1920 St Leger winner Caligula, who proved virtually impotent at stud. However, a Newmarket victory before he began hurdling suggested Seneca had inherited some of his sire's stamina and less than a week after the Champion Hurdle he emphasised his class by winning the Yarborough Plate at Lincoln. It's highly improbable that any horse will equal Seneca's feat of winning the title on its second race over hurdles.

To those who argued that a championship contest over Cheltenham's severe track inflicted irreparable damage on four-year-olds, Seneca's subsequent history yielded further ammunition. He broke down and continually dodged those engagements available to him in a war-torn programme as Smyth struggled unavailingly to get him race-fit for 14 March 1942. Even so, with the Champion Hurdle expected to attract a large field and formlines scarce and unreliable, several scribes, like Meyrick Good, chose to stick with Seneca who 'has speed, endurance and weight-carrying ability'. Five days before the race – run on a Saturday for the first time – Smyth bowed to the inevitable. No racing had taken place since 10 January and it was impossible to get Seneca ready.

Although Smyth's stables housed barely a quarter of the horses it did in 1941, it still sheltered a capable substitute in Forestation, yet another four-year-old possessing impressive credentials on the flat. A bay gelding by Felicitation, he too inherited considerable stamina from his sire, in this case an Ascot Gold Cup winner. After winning twice on the Flat as a three-year-old, his relentless galloping

THE CHAMPION HURDLE

soon gained a hat-trick at Cheltenham over hurdles. Then, on what transpired to be the last day's racing before the Festival, he failed miserably to cope with Worcester's tighter, flatter track and was a soundly beaten fourth to Miss Paget's Easy Chair. No one doubted Forestation's stamina but did he possess the necessary turn of foot?

There was certain to be a new name on the roll of honour since neither Solford nor African Sister were intended runners. Miss Paget's 11-year-old had actually made the transition to fences, jumping fluently on his début, but an hour before Easy Chair's victory at Worcester his owner was reminded of racing's darker side when Solford broke his back in the Evesham Novices Chase. Presently, 1941's second, third and fourth — Anarchist, Ephorus and Luncheon Hour — returned, along with another previous combatant in Carton, yet none of this quartet had shown much sparkle in their pre-Cheltenham races. By process of elimination, favouritism thus fell to the newcomers, Southport, Verbatim, Milk Bar and Interlaken. The former pair of five-year-olds had clashed in January, victory going to Verbatim by a neck. Southport, a winner twice previously, was now 2lb better off. Milk Bar, a 70 guineas reject from George Lambton's yard, had also won twice, beating Interlaken on the first occasion, and looked every inch a champion in embryo. With a record 20 runners standing their ground, a strong betting market was assured. Southport and Interlaken were bracketed at 9/2 followed by Milk Bar and Verbatim at 7s. One shrewd *Life* reporter observed that Vic Smyth had trained four of Forestation's rivals so he 'should know where he stands'. Interestingly, Ron Smyth elected to ride Forestation (10/1) rather than his father's Southport.

The race was run to suit Forestation to a tee, as Poetic Licence set a strong gallop through the first mile. Three hurdles out, Tommy Isaac made his move on Anarchist and quickly went four lengths clear. The exacting gallop had taken its toll of the rest and he appeared certain to hang on to his advantage until Forestation came on the scene between the last two flights. Though the Paget horse led up the run-in, Forestation easily overhauled him to win, going away by three lengths. The Cheltenham hill had once again played a crucial role in the championship's destination and Forestation's love of it was borne out in his perfect score of four wins from four starts. By owning the winner the Smyth family had gone one better than 1941 and Ron Smyth became the first jockey

THE CHAMPION HURDLE

to win consecutive races – on different horses too. He went on to take the jockeys' title with 12 winners, an achievement which prompted his father to comment that he was evidently 'the best of a bad lot'. Naturally, the war was largely responsible for that small total (only 18 days' racing were possible) and its impact was never far away. Smyth himself was in the Royal Veterinary Corps and gave up his leave to go race-riding, while uncle Vic even donated his £495 prize to Lady Kemsley's War Relief Fund.

In some ways the government announcement on 10 September to the effect that it was 'unable to sanction National Hunt racing in 1942–43' was a blessing in disguise. The war had, in Meyrick Good's opinion, 'cut the sport to shreds'. Jumping's value as an entertaining release from the rigours of war no longer outweighed the difficulties of its staging.

The Champion Hurdle's three-year hibernation ended on 31 March 1945, the final day of a limited National Hunt season. It cost 30 shillings (£1.50) for admittance to the reserved enclosure, 10 shillings (50p) to the public enclosure and 4s 6d (less than 25p) to the course, with 'forces in uniform' at half price.

At seven years of age, the reigning title holder Forestation was still spry enough to provide a link with the past while the enforced break also gave his stablemate Seneca the opportunity of recovering from his leg problems. However, although Seneca (now gelded) did resume active life, once he was beaten in the Cleeve Hill Hurdle Smyth withdrew him from the championship.

The junior of the Smyth champions had fared much better, especially round Cheltenham where two more successes raised his track record to six wins from eight starts. Nevertheless, the *Sporting Life* advised caution: 'His lines have been cast in easy waters this year and if only he was a couple of years younger . . . the recruits to hurdling are well up to average, even if they cannot be graded up to the standard of Trespasser.'

The brightest of these shining lights was Triona, a four-year-old trained by Walter Nightingall. Not very big but an agile jumper, he had twice impressed with victories at Cheltenham, especially when accounting for another useful youngster in Vidi at the beginning of the month. When Vidi endorsed the form by winning on Gold Cup day (17 March) Triona's odds tumbled. As the lateness of this year's championship gave the six competing four-year-olds a unique weight advantage, he was dispatched a 2/1 favourite, ominously a position

43

THE CHAMPION HURDLE

no four-year-old had occupied since Clear Cash in 1929 or ever would again.

Second favourite at 9/2 was the five-year-old Brains Trust, one of two candidates from Gerry Wilson's yard, close by the course at Andoversford, the other being Radiance, an eight-year-old. Both were maidens when acquired by Wilson back in January, but the former champion jockey worked some magic or other because they were subsequently unbeaten, each recording a hat-trick. Even Wilson was unsure which was the better. Brains Trust, he told the press, was a 'stout-constitutioned horse' who had flourished and put on muscle with every gallop. In January, Brains Trust had received a 12lb beating from Forestation, yet by Gold Cup day he was able to slam him by a comfortable three and a half lengths in the Marle Handicap Hurdle despite being worse off at the weights. How Miss Paget must have been kicking herself, for she bred the chestnut son of Rhodes Scholar but after displaying no ability as a three-year-old she sold him 'for a mere bagatelle' to two local Cheltenham farmers, Messrs Burrows and Blakeway.

Although his public form was less inspiring, rumour insisted that Radiance was superior to Brains Trust at home. However, in his two most recent outings his principal victim was Seneca, clearly no longer in the top echelon. Faced with a choice between his brother-in-law's Brains Trust and Radiance or his father's Pythagoras, dual champion jockey Fred Rimell chose Brains Trust.

According to *The Times'* correspondent the Champion Hurdle had comprised 'perhaps the most exciting event of the week' but his expectations received a severe blow when the field set off at a dawdle. To the confirmed stayers like Forestation this was the kiss of death, yet Smyth did nothing to rectify the situation, while the imposed restraint caused Triona to become so agitated that Farmer had to let him go on at halfway. Entering the straight, Triona had opened a six-length lead but in consequence of that funereal early pace several others were queuing up to challenge.

The young leader had visibly exhausted his reserves of physical and nervous energy by the last flight, leaving Brains Trust and Red April to dispute the spoils. Rimell had plenty in hand and Brains Trust ran out a cosy winner by three-quarters of a length from Vidi who deprived Red April of second place at the death. Wilson thus became the first man to ride and then train a Champion Hurdler and Fred Rimell (who would emulate this feat eventually)

THE CHAMPION HURDLE

completed a four-timer during the afternoon to draw level with Frenchie Nicholson at the top of the jockeys' table on 15 winners to share the title. After his death in December 1968, Wilson's ashes were scattered along the Cheltenham track he had graced with such distinction.

It was no real consolation to Miss Paget (whose Prince Florimonde finished fourth) that she bred the winner. That was no way to cane the bookmakers. But she could not be kept out of the limelight for long. Back in Ireland she had a promising four-year-old called Distel who would pose a very live threat to Brains Trust in 1946.

Distel was a small handsome bay with three white socks, trained by the veteran Maxie Arnott at Clonsilla, County Dublin. He was bred by two stalwarts of the Irish scene, Arthur and Isadore Blake, from their 1938 Irish Derby winner Rosewell. Distel's dam, Laitron, a miler, had a mixed yet ultimately rich stud career. Altogether she bred seven winners, but two years after foaling Distel she was sold as a barren 11-year-old to Sir Percy Loraine for whom she bred Dairymaid (dam of 1,000 Guineas winner Abermaid), Silver Thistle (dam of world five-furlong record holder Indigenous) and Nella (dam of the inaugural Timeform Gold Cup winner Miralgo and the Irish St Leger winner Parnell). Distel, then, was bred in the purple. What's more, he was all Irish and the Emerald Isle had been waiting for a long time for a Champion Hurdler.

Scoring three times on the Flat, and finishing third in the Irish Cesarewitch, Distel rattled up seven victories from eight outings over hurdles prior to the 1946 Festival, giving Brains Trust a 16lb thrashing at Nottingham on 8 February. In the champion's defence, it was his seasonal début but Wilson still deemed it prudent to avoid pitting him against Distel again, opting instead to field Carnival Boy, a colt unextended in five-hurdle races so far. Robin O'Chantry had won four in a row before capsizing at Windsor, while The Diver, who separated Distel and Brains Trust at Nottingham, also took his chance.

These viable alternatives in the field of eight, all of them newcomers to the championship and six owned by ladies, failed to dissuade the bookmakers, who were only interested in Distel, a 5/4 on favourite. What could possibly upset him? Rain was forecast but his Nottingham victory was gained in a quagmire. He was a

THE CHAMPION HURDLE

notoriously 'one jockey horse' according to the *Sporting Life*. Yet deprived of his regular partner Mickey Gordon's services at Nottingham, he still won handily enough for Bobby O'Ryan. 'Mickey Gordon had flu and as I was at Nottingham riding one for Charlie Rogers, a friend of Arnott's, I got the mount. Distel was a funny bastard – you had to make him afraid of you or he'd rear up as straight as a gun-barrel as soon as you got up on him. At home there were days when you could hardly get him out of the yard, and on the racecourse the biggest problem you had was to get him to jump off. I was told to give him a sharp tap between the ears, frighten him, otherwise he'd go nowhere. I never took my eyes off the starter that day and when the gate went up I gave Distel two cracks between the lugs and off we went.' Bobby O'Ryan's last six rides had all been winners and his golden streak was never in danger as Distel strode majestically up the hill to win by four lengths. 'I was always going to win. Odette was supposed to make the pace but she tried to run out passing the stables and I never saw her again.'

Turning for home, Distel and The Diver were upsides, but O'Ryan was merely cruising on the little Irish bay, who skipped over the last and was hardly out of a canter. 'All quality, gallant little Distel,' said Meyrick Good, judging him superior to Insurance. O'Ryan later extended his record to eight straight wins by taking the National Hunt Handicap Chase on Miss Paget's Dunshaughlin, and one of the owner's greatest Festival days was completed by Loyal King's victory in the Grand Annual, with Dan Moore riding.

The racing press had no sooner elevated Distel to stardom than they were paying homage to one greater than he. As Distel's story ended in sadness, National Spirit emerged to provide the Champion Hurdle with its first legendary character.

5

The Two Peter Pans

If ever a horse became the living embodiment of his name it was National Spirit. Just as well it was changed from the original — Avago. He competed in six championships and at his peak, between the spring of 1946 and February 1950, he was beaten only four times in twenty races over timber. In the process he educated the public in the art of hurdling.

Hurdle racing certainly gained the idol for which it had been yearning, though National Spirit scarcely looked the part. His withers were so low he was difficult to saddle, he was a washy chestnut and invariably wore protective bandages and a hood. The latter was no rogue's badge, however, for National Spirit had courage and character in abundance. He loved nothing better than 'dropping' his rider at exercise by whipping round without warning, and then standing stock-still, daring him to remount. Only Bill Magee, the elderly Irish stable lad who 'did' him, was exempted. Instead, he was subject to National Spirit's impersonation of a runaway train. 'There's National Spirit taking Bill Magee out for exercise,' Epsom folk used to observe as the champion's distinctive white blaze made a beeline for the Downs.

National Spirit did not restrict his exuberance to the training grounds. In his races he was something to behold, a big, rangy 17 hands animal possessing a mighty jump. Many's the time these prodigious leaps gained him yards, although on one occasion at Plumpton when he took off outside the wing even a jockey of Frenchie Nicholson's calibre failed to stay in the irons.

National Spirit belonged to Len Abelson, a Birmingham businessman, who bought his dam, Cocktail, from the Aga Khan after she proved a dismal failure in each of her four races. However, she was by Coronach, whose great-grandsire Marco was a noted influence in jumping pedigrees. Abelson took Cocktail home and, to

47

THE CHAMPION HURDLE

a covering by St Leger winner Scottish Union, she gave birth to a chestnut foal in 1941. Unlike Distel's dam Laitron, who prospered with age and resale, poor Cocktail's subsequent career in the paddocks was disastrous. Abelson sold her and she was barren for the next three years. National Spirit was her solitary winner.

At the age of four, National Spirit was sent to Vic Smyth never having worn a pair of shoes. Smyth took a half share in the gelding and changed his name to something more memorable. One look at his new charge's powerful frame was sufficient to convince Smyth that chasing would be National Spirit's métier. Two preparatory hurdle races and many schooling fences later, National Spirit faced his first proper test at Nottingham in February of his fifth year and promptly ran out! A week later he surpassed that by falling heavily at the first fence. 'It was coincidence more than anything,' said Ron Smyth, his rider on both occasions, 'but he tipped up properly at Windsor and it seemed pointless to persevere.' By the summer, he had secured three of his nineteen hurdle victories, and such was his promise that his owners received an attractive offer from America.

Smyth now directed the horse at the Flat and he proved no mug at that game either. 'This slashing fine chestnut was improving rapidly last back-end,' commented Phil Bull in *Best Horses of 1946*, referring to National Spirit's two successes in long distance handicaps at Doncaster and Thirsk. He eventually won 13 races on the Flat, including at least one decent prize per season during his heyday. In 1947 he won the King George VI Stakes at Liverpool and the Cosmopolitan Cup at Lingfield (ridden by Gordon Richards) despite a slipping saddle, and the following year he again won the King George and beat the subsequent Cesarewitch and Yorkshire Cup winner in the Melbourne Stakes at Newmarket.

Within three weeks of that Thirsk victory National Spirit won a handicap hurdle and began to ascend the ladder of fame and fortune. When Cheltenham came round he had won five on the trot, including a five-length success under 12st 5lb in Doncaster's Princess Elizabeth Handicap Hurdle. A measure of his remarkable improvement was the fact that in the weights for the Liverpool Hurdle he was set to concede Brains Trust 2lb, albeit some 11lb behind Distel.

Miss Paget's star no longer seemed enamoured with racing. After winning at Leopardstown by six lengths, he ran mulishly in the Imperial Cup and was pulled up. The Imperial Cup could be used

THE CHAMPION HURDLE

as a prep race because an incredibly hard winter destroyed any hope of racing on the appointed day of 6 March. Fifty-two days and twenty-eight fixtures came and went without racing, which did not resume until 15 March at Taunton. The long-awaited thaw acted slowly and both Gold Cup and Champion Hurdle were reallocated to Saturday 12 April, the final occasion the two events would share the same card.

Thanks to this delay National Spirit was able to win the King George and he was not the only Champion Hurdle contender who took the opportunity of keeping in trim on the level. Triona, fifth in the Imperial Cup, won at the Esher track on Grand National day, while General Factotum, a dual winner before running unplaced in the Liverpool Hurdle, came third at Kempton. Mention of Flat racing brings one to Le Paillon, a very rare bird indeed, because six months later he would win the Prix de l'Arc de Triomphe. All that glory and more (he also won the French Champion Hurdle – the Grand Course des Haies d'Auteuil – in June) was in the future. A five-year-old trained by Willie Head, he would be ridden by Head's young son Alec. A sequence of wins that had stretched to seven ended at Auteuil on 23 March when he could only finish fourth after leading over the last. Even so, he was made a 2/1 favourite to win France her first Champion Hurdle.

An afternoon redolent of high summer was a welcome relief in view of the Arctic winter just passed and a huge crowd headed for Prestbury Park. They soon witnessed drama as Coloured Schoolboy gave Fred Rimell an excruciating fall in the Gold Cup. Thus, 30 minutes before the championship, National Spirit (number 13 on the card) was left without a jockey. Ron Smyth was booked to ride Lord Bicester's Freddy Fox and Fred Rickaby, who had also won on National Spirit, was partnering Gay Scot. All the principal hurdle-race jockeys were committed elsewhere. That is except the 35-year-old 'veteran' of Chenango's triumph, Danny Morgan, who was barely weeks away from relinquishing his licence and setting up as a trainer.

As the race developed it became very much a case of old fox showing the young cub a thing or two. Alec Head elected to pursue a conspicuously extravagant course on the wide outside, whereas Morgan clung to the inside rail, saving lengths in the process. Distel continued his wretched behaviour and refused point blank to jump the flight alongside the water, and swinging into the straight the race

THE CHAMPION HURDLE

clearly lay between National Spirit and the favourite but the latter had shot his bolt before crossing the last. Le Paillon only succumbed by a length and, given the extra ground he covered, must be regarded one of the race's unluckiest losers.

If the merit of National Spirit's first Champion Hurdle could be questioned, that of 1948 was beyond dispute, slicing over five seconds off the old race record with the first sub-four-minute time of 3.54.8. Distel did not enter the lists against him for the new year brought tragedy to a second Paget champion. As a result of his increasingly erratic behaviour, Miss Paget had Distel thoroughly examined during the summer by Professor Brayley Reynolds, who reported the horse to be suffering from heart disease brought on by muscle overstrain. In January the condition worsened and Distel was destroyed. A very upset owner was moved to state in the *Sporting Life*: 'This should exonerate the horse from the peculiar lapses in some of his races towards the end of his career.'

Nor had everything been going National Spirit's way. His image had been dented by two defeats, albeit in concession of 30lb and a stone, which on the book gave him precious little to spare over Ivor Anthony's DUKW who, as a five-year-old, received 4lb in the championship. On the debit side DUKW (named after the amphibious landing craft – his dam was called Aquatic) was prone to the odd jumping lapse which National Spirit's breathtaking gallop might possibly induce.

Sunshine quickly cleared the course of early morning fog but the rising temperature failed to disturb National Spirit. 'What a gentleman he looked in the paddock,' said the *Life*, 'as cool and sober as if he was being taken for an exercise walk.' Smyth reckoned he had never been better.

Urgay led until falling on the descent towards the home turn, whereupon Ron Smyth and the 6/4 favourite, once more railing like a greyhound, dared anyone to catch them. Despite clipping the last two obstacles to momentarily raise the hopes of his nearest pursuers, DUKW and Encoroli, National Spirit drew away on the hill to win comfortably by two lengths. 'A real champion in every way,' trumpeted the *Life*.

Vic Smyth had now saddled his fourth winner of the Champion Hurdle in six runnings and nephew Ron had ridden his third (each a different horse), a feat which would be equalled by only one other jockey.

THE CHAMPION HURDLE

National Spirit's reign as king of the hurdling fraternity seemed assured for the next few years. He was as sound as a bell and, if anything, improving rather than deteriorating. He would undoubtedly become the first triple champion. Few noticed, let alone recognised as a potential thorn in his side, the plain-looking Irish outsider plugging on gamely up the hill to finish fifth. Yet it was he who would become the first triple champion, not the dashing chestnut. His name was Hatton's Grace and he was soon to pass into the care of a 31-year-old son of County Cork, Michael Vincent O'Brien.

When Hatton's Grace arrived at Churchtown in the summer of 1948, Vincent O'Brien was already something of a miracle worker. Within a year of inheriting his father's yard that housed just a single inmate (Oversway, to become his first winner, at Limerick Junction on 20 May 1943), he landed the Irish autumn double of 1944 with Drybob and Good Days while still having only seven horses in his care. At odds of 800/1, O'Brien's £2 each way double should have netted £2,000 but the payout was halved as Drybob dead-heated. Punting was a necessary evil if the embryonic O'Brien training operation was to stay on the road. Yet he had never ducked a bet when it mattered. For instance, desperately short of funds three years earlier when the war had curtailed a nice sideline exporting greyhounds to race in England, he scraped together £4 to back a grey mare called White Squirrel that he was preparing on behalf of his father Dan to run in a 27-runner Clonmel bumper. With young MV in the plate she won at odds of 10/1. 'That bet would probably have to take front place in terms of importance because that was when I most needed the money.'

Were the man's genius and perfectionism not so well known, one might subsequently have been tempted to believe in black magic. Hatton's Grace, for instance, was eight in the summer of 1948 and seemed unlikely to have much improvement left in him. Bearing in mind he was later christened 'the ugly duckling of the parade ring' his story may encompass a trace of Hans Christian Andersen after all.

'But he was a great little horse, only a pony and full of courage,' according to O'Brien, who professed to no particular magic potion. 'Contrary to rumour, we never had a replica of Cheltenham laid out at home. Neither do we have scouts out combing Ireland for potential Cheltenham stars. The secret of my success? Possibly

THE CHAMPION HURDLE

patience, logic and ambition.' Upon his eventual retirement from the sport in 1994, O'Brien used a different five-word explanation in response to the same inevitable question: 'A capacity to take pains.' Whatever O'Brien was touched with – and genius remains by far the best bet – it triggered 23 winners through 12 consecutive NH Festivals before he began concentrating on the Flat in 1959.

If O'Brien possessed a 'secret' it was best explained by his wife Jacqueline: 'Vincent always planned and worked for the big occasion – small races did not interest him – and in planning a programme for a horse, he worked backwards from the main event. Attention to detail . . . great common sense . . . extremely good powers of observation . . . limitless patience with his horses and the ability to concentrate fiercely on them and their training to the exclusion of everything else . . . no hesitation in trying new ideas – he flew Hatton's Grace and Cottage Rake to Cheltenham in 1949 when no one put horses on aeroplanes and he was still a small country trainer – and the willingness to listen, because, as he always said: "You must listen to even the silliest fellow because he may say something interesting or useful." And he was definitely not at all the quiet, self-effacing person people were accustomed to seeing on the racecourse. Staff stayed for many years but he was very demanding of them, and at home he was known as "The Fuhrer"!'

Hatton's Grace was bred by the Victor Stud of County Tipperary and was initially sold at Goffs for 18 guineas. He was no oil painting, being rather narrow with very little neck, but he had 'good limbs, good depth of heart', in his trainer's words. Plain, perhaps, but tough. As an unbroken four-year-old he attracted the attention of that fine judge, Major Noel Furlong, the owner-trainer of Reynoldstown, who baulked at the asking price of £2,000. Eventually, Hatton's Grace became the property of Harry and Moya Keogh, also the owners of the future Gold Cup winner Knock Hard, and had won two bumpers and three hurdles from 23 starts when he arrived at Churchtown. Three races later he won the Champion Hurdle!

Two outings at Naas prepared the way, the second of which, the Rathcoole Handicap Hurdle (often a dress rehearsal for Irish Champion Hurdle contenders), he won at 7/4. On both occasions the jockey was Aubrey Brabazon, he of the silk-smooth hands and lifestyle. When a newspaper headline once blared 'Brabazon caught napping' after he had unwisely dropped his hands on an odds-on

THE CHAMPION HURDLE

favourite, O'Brien opined, 'If so, it was the only sleep poor Aubrey got all week.' As the Festival neared, however, Hatton's Grace contracted a mild dose of flu and was stopped in his work. On Champion Hurdle day there was no knowing how fit he was and the Irish partnership proved easy to back at 100/7.

Aside from uncharacteristically falling at Plumpton, National Spirit, one year younger than Hatton's Grace, had done nothing wrong and started a hot 5/4 favourite for his third title. As Ron Smyth had retired he required a new rider, the job going to champion jockey Bryan Marshall, a noted tactician. He seldom made errors of judgement, but one of the few allegedly occurred in the 1949 Champion Hurdle.

On paper National Spirit's task did not appear any stiffer than the previous two years. The front-running northerner Shining Gold disliked the heavy ground and the Imperial Cup winner Anglesey was reputedly short of a gallop. Vatelys had been a decent animal in France a season or two back but had only just resumed after a long lay-off. A blustery, cold wind dried the course although it still rode heavy in places.

Shining Gold duly blazed the trail for most of the race, but once Hatton's Grace went to the front three out 'nothing had the slightest chance with him', wrote the *Bloodstock Breeders' Review*, 'and he sprinted away to win by six lengths'. The *Irish Field* was less charitable: 'This was a dumbfounding result to serious students of racing, for Hatton's Grace had never before shown form up to this standard.'

National Spirit finished fourth, beaten by around four and a half lengths and, as would happen again when their idol Mill House was humbled by Arkle, the English searched high and low for an explanation. Of countless theories, that pinning the blame on Marshall found most favour. Instead of allowing National Spirit to bound along in domineering fashion, Marshall held him up for a late challenge but only succeeded in meeting interference when Captain Fox made a mistake directly in front of him. Once National Spirit reversed the placings with the championship runner-up Vatelys on 7lb worse terms in the Cheltenham Hurdle a month later (converting a deficit of four lengths into a winning margin of three), the fat was well and truly thrown in the fire. He had definitely been robbed of his third title.

The rematch in 1950 thus contained all the ingredients of a

THE CHAMPION HURDLE

thriller. The going was perfect and the Cotswold mists cleared in time to reveal an epic confrontation. Hatton's Grace had gone from strength to strength, winning the Irish Lincoln with nine stone less than a month after taking the hurdling crown, followed by the Irish Cesarewitch (under 9st 2lb) over twice the distance in November. Two hurdle victories under 12st 7lb suggested that even at ten years of age the champion would be difficult to dethrone. National Spirit, meanwhile, had won all four of his races in the current campaign, and though not quite the speed merchant of old, still had a massive fan club.

Both champions were aided by a revision in the weights, which reduced their concession to four-year-olds by 4lb and halved that to five-year-olds to only 2lb. The latter generation mounted a worthy challenger in Harlech who, since being defeated by National Spirit in December, had notched a succession of wins. His stablemate DUKW had won all three of his races after breaking down and having to forego the 1949 championship.

Doubts concerning National Spirit's well-being had been circulating ever since he was found cast in his box three days before the race. These were given credence when he arrived at the course on Tuesday morning for Smyth kept him continuously on the move to prevent his knee stiffening up.

Once in motion, National Spirit (Dennis Dillon) flowed along, exuding all his old élan, and still held the call at the final flight. Pressing him were Hatton's Grace, Speciality and Harlech, travelling particularly smoothly on the bridle. The big chestnut took the hurdle sloppily and Brabazon snatched a valuable advantage which Harlech, who found nothing off the bit, could not peg back. 'Hatton's Grace had an amazing heart, the way he used to tackle that hill,' says O'Brien.

But for his blunder, National Spirit would almost certainly have finished second. As it was he dropped away to be fourth, beaten nine lengths. However, perhaps he was far unluckier than this because the racecourse drums were soon beating to the rumour that his injured knee resulted from foul play, not an accident. In defeat he had thus displayed class and courage the equal of any victory.

Twelve months on, the sight of Hatton's Grace and National Spirit again upsides at the last hurdle suggested a case of *déjà vu*. Once more the 'two Peter Pans', as Peter O'Sullevan called them, carried their age wonderfully well and kept the youngsters in their

THE CHAMPION HURDLE

place. Although both champions had shown decent form neither started favourite, that honour going to the northern-trained Average, unbeaten since his arrival from Ireland. Brabazon honoured a retainer to ride Average, his replacement on Hatton's Grace being Tim Molony, once a classmate of O'Brien. (Years later Brabazon offered an alternative reason for not being aboard Hatton's Grace. He'd been taken off because Harry Keogh suspected him of 'not trying' on the champion in the Irish Cambridgeshire which was won by a horse trained by Brabazon's father.) The elder of the Molony brothers and dubbed the 'Rubber Man' by his fellow jockeys, because he somehow avoided serious injury, Tim had already collected two of his five jockeys' championships (he was never out of the top three from 1948 to 1957) and if not so brilliant as his brother Martin, lacked nothing in bravery or a limpet-like ability to stay in the saddle. Before the race, Molony walked the last part of the course with Sydney McGregor, one of O'Brien's patrons, who told him there was a ridge in the centre of the track where the ground was invariably faster. 'Jump the second last in the middle,' he was instructed. 'Don't go onto the rails, but come round and aim to the middle of the last.'

The champion's preparation followed its customary course: the Irish Cesarewitch (won with ten stone), the Shankhill Hurdle on Boxing Day (won with 12st 7lb) and the Scalp Hurdle on 17 February (this year only fourth).

For his part, National Spirit was being trained with but one aim in view – that elusive third title. To Smyth's dismay the heavens opened on the Monday morning and it did not stop raining until just before the race. The watery sun which broke through the clouds was powerless to alleviate the atrociously deep ground. Indeed, at the end of the day the course was so waterlogged that the stewards decided to abandon the rest of the meeting.

The prospect of history being made attracted a vast crowd and an hour before the first race traffic jams had reached four miles in length. Latecomers were still entering as the two French horses, Prince Hindou (fourth in the French Derby and undefeated over hurdles) and Pyrrhus, led the field past the stands, but after half a mile Dennis Dillon allowed National Spirit to stretch out and he began to steal lengths off the other two at every hurdle. Behind the leading trio there was a big gap back to Hatton's Grace, but at the bottom of the hill he began to retrieve the ground and close on

THE CHAMPION HURDLE

National Spirit. For one of the 'Peter Pans' an historic hat-trick awaited. 'Again it was at the last flight that tragedy intervened,' said the *Sporting Life*. 'Once again National Spirit was just in the lead and he went at it with determination to clinch his length advantage, made the most tremendous leap, slipped on landing and rolled over nearly two lengths beyond it.' So Hatton's Grace it was who strode up the hill to the crowd's acclaim and a place in jumping annals. 'I knew I had the race won long before the last,' said Molony. 'It was one of the few hurdles my chap ever stood off from – usually he nipped over them.' With the French horses occupying the minor places this constitutes the only occasion on which foreign animals have swept the board.

Hatton's Grace and National Spirit had dominated the championship for five years and established it once and for all as a truly great race. Although both returned in 1952 they would be eclipsed by an even brighter star and their story is best concluded here. Hatton's Grace came out the better, finishing fifth. Switched to fences, he won a little race at Leopardstown in January 1953, shortly after his thirteenth birthday, and was retired forthwith to O'Brien's new headquarters at Ballydoyle, where he led the youngsters in their work. 'The public loved him too,' said Brabazon. 'It was probably because he was such a miserable and scraggy-looking devil that they took him to their hearts.' His six Flat races, eleven hurdles and one chase had earned £12,658.

National Spirit ran the last of his 85 races two months later at Wye, finishing third. He won 19 hurdles worth £8,802 and 13 Flat races for £6,900. Like his great Irish rival, National Spirit was not yet done with. A race was founded in his honour at Fontwell, scene of five of his victories, and he paraded on the course prior to the inaugural running in 1965. Even a fire at his new home in Cobham could not kill off the old warhorse who had done so much to popularise the sport of hurdling and one morning at Epsom early risers enjoyed the unique privilege of seeing no less than George Duller riding National Spirit a canter up six-mile hill.

6

'Well done, you ould divil'

Ever since Chuchoteur and Lobau chased home Our Hope in 1938, French-bred horses had played a not insignificant role in the glamour and excitement of the Champion Hurdle. Increasingly, France became a convenient market place for English trainers on the lookout for cheap hurdling talent. 'It would be foolish to ignore the quality and merits of these imported horses which seem to be brought out to the greatest advantage by the skill and patience of our experienced trainers,' observed the *Bloodstock Breeders' Review*. They seldom needed to search very far. Young horses possessing reasonable but not top-class credentials were often sent hurdling, thoroughly schooled, as early as the February of their third year. Consequently, French jumpers matured faster than their English counterparts. Moreover, helped by a lower range of weights (top weight rarely exceeding 11st 11lb – compared to 12st 7lb in England – reducing to 9st 7lb) and the programming of countless races over shorter distances than two miles, French hurdle races were run at an exceptionally fast pace. Therefore, it came as no surprise that French horses farmed England's premier hurdle race for four-year-olds, the Triumph at Hurst Park (winning six of the first seven), yet no French-bred horse had succeeded in winning the Champion Hurdle. All that would now change.

Royston trainer Willie Stephenson was one of those who shopped in France. Despite being on the verge of winning the Derby with Arctic Prince, Stephenson maintained a mixed stable until the day he retired. In 1959 he would win the National with Oxo, thereby joining the select group to achieve the Derby–National double (Messrs Jewitt, Dawson, Blackwell and O'Brien are the others).

In the autumn of 1950 Stephenson entertained his wife to a short holiday in Paris but could not resist visiting Auteuil where he had a

THE CHAMPION HURDLE

possible purchase in mind. The animal did not come up to expectations. But another took his eye, a raw young horse belonging to M. Maurice Adele, running third in a hurdle race. 'I thought he should have won and fancied him. So after some parleying, I bought him for the equivalent of £750.' By such fortuitous circumstances Sir Ken became a naturalised Englishman.

Bred by M. Marcel Chenorio, Sir Ken was a bay by the French government stallion Laëken. He was lightly raced as he had been gelded relatively late in his second year but had finished second on the flat. Stephenson's judgement deserves high praise for in terms of conformation Sir Ken resembled a Hatton's Grace rather than a National Spirit. In truth, Sir Ken was never an imposing individual, even in later years. 'An unimpressive sort in conformation though he is well made and his coat is rough and dull,' wrote Tom Nickalls prior to the 1952 Champion Hurdle. *The Times* was more brutal: 'On looks and breeding he has remarkably little suggestion of the champion about him.' After his second title, Meyrick Good showed greater respect: 'He is more muscular and heavier of bone. A delightfully actioned gelding, with a wonderful hind stroke, he gets his hocks well under him and it is this power from behind that makes him such a great jumper.'

However, 'handsome is as handsome does', and Sir Ken set about proving it. Making his English début in the Lancashire Hurdle of April 1951, the 'unknown' was unwisely laid by some bookmakers at 50/1 but heavy betting forced the odds down to 7s. Sir Ken cantered home by five lengths. By the end of the season he had won four more and during the next two years he extended this unbeaten sequence over hurdles to 16 (plus one on the flat), until Impney lowered his colours at Uttoxeter on 24 October 1953. No hurdler, or chaser for that matter, can match the utter domination Sir Ken displayed throughout this period, as indicated by the fact that he started 13 of those races at odds-on. Altogether, Sir Ken's record over hurdles would read 20 wins from 28 races (two of which were defeats in his swansong season of 1957–58 when past his prime) worth £16,375, four from twelve over fences (£1,912) and one on the Flat of £138.

By the time he retired in February 1958 Sir Ken's induction into the pantheon of immortal hurdlers was complete. 'Sir Ken cannot be regarded as other than out of the ordinary,' said the *Sporting Life*'s much-respected R.C. Long. 'As good and probably better than

THE CHAMPION HURDLE

Trespasser,' averred Harry Brown with reference to the perennial yardstick of hurdling greatness. 'Sir Ken supreme,' suggested *The Times* simply and authoritatively in 1954. Willie Stephenson can with justification afford to be even more fulsome. 'Sir Ken possessed unlimited courage and no matter how tough the pace he could be relied upon to produce something better than his rivals at the finish. He was a great horse in every way, a great character – he always had to have a lead horse – who came back three times to win the Champion Hurdle after breaking down. We had a lot of anxiety with him before each championship and had to patch up his forelegs on each occasion. He was the hurdler of the century.'

In his pomp Sir Ken could indeed claim to be the complete hurdler. All his rider had to do was select the appropriate weapon from his armoury for the job in hand. That rider, on 19 successful occasions, was Tim Molony. 'Hatton's Grace was undoubtedly a superb performer but, personally, I will always consider Sir Ken the greatest of them all. He was marvellous. I have never ridden anything like him. He positively flew those hurdles. He stood off so far that you would feel your tummy going but he was away from them like lightning. He was a powerful fellow and a tremendous battler. If a horse was in front of him, he'd say, "I've got to have a go at that one and beat him".' Like many a creature of genius, Sir Ken was not without vices. 'Nobody knew what a moody old bugger he was,' recalls Molony. 'He'd tell you to go and stuff yourself in his own words.' He loathed equine companionship and one summer fought and killed the horse with whom he was turned out.

Stephenson initially owned Sir Ken in partnership with Fred Honour but the gelding ultimately raced in the pink and quartered colours of Manchester businessman Maurice Kingsley. Sir Ken's tally stood at eight (gained in contemptuous style by an aggregate of 36 lengths) when he visited his first Festival in 1952.

Sir Ken's 15 opponents contained a number of extremely high-class individuals, including the two 'Peter Pans'. The Irish version had won the Shankhill for the third time before disappointing in the Rathcoole. His English alter ego also possessed a win to his name but had principally been acting as target practice for aspiring champions like Dorothy Paget's Telegram II and Stanley Wootton's Noholme, both five-year-olds. The former bay 'looked the very epitome of class' according to the *Life*, and so he might. Another

THE CHAMPION HURDLE

French-bred animal, Telegram, ran fourth in Galcador's Derby. Trained now by Fulke Walwyn, he had won all his four hurdle races, the first by ten lengths, the second by five, and then inflicted on National Spirit his first defeat at Sandown when thwarting the veteran's attempt to land a third Oteley Hurdle. However, in the Champion Hurdle, Telegram would be a stone worse off in the weights. Noholme had beaten a fitter National Spirit and, despite putting up the better performance (smashing two hurdles out of the ground into the bargain), he could be backed at 100/7 whereas Telegram, the subject of a 'welter of money', was backed down to 9/1 third favourite. The quality field stimulated some hefty wagering, particularly on Sir Ken. Observed the *Bloodstock Breeders' Review*: '7/2 in thousands four times is a big bet these days and when taken about a hurdler it shows uncommon confidence to say the least of it.' Further indication of this champion's calibre can be gleaned from the price of National Spirit who started at 20s.

A pre-race gamble on Hatton's Grace, backed from 10/1 to 13/2, could be easily explained. A misty dawn bequeathed rain and the sort of dead ground to the champion's taste, though not the Paget hope who was soon in difficulties, blundering the third flight so disastrously that Dave Dick pulled up. The tempo noticeably increased once National Spirit took up the running passing the stands and he was shadowed by Average and Noholme with Molony, always alert to the possibility of the old champion using his hurdling technique to break away from the field, keeping Sir Ken in the first half dozen. The familiar chestnut figure led the charge down the hill. Royal Oak momentarily flattered to deceive. National Spirit saw him off. The task of heading him was left to Noholme. He attacked the last with a length in hand of Approval, in the centre, and Sir Ken on the stands side. Not for the last time Cheltenham's incline discovered whose appetite for battle was keenest. 'Sir Ken took the final climb in the fashion of a true glutton,' said the *Life*. 'The true merit of his win lay in the fact that every good horse had his chance but the favourite beat them all fair and square.' Quite possibly Miss Paget disagreed with that sentiment – even more so after Telegram had won the Tudor Rose Hurdle at Hurst Park and the Coronation Hurdle at Liverpool.

National Spirit and Hatton's Grace were, at last, missing when Sir Ken came out for his second Champion Hurdle. Considering he had won all his six races (one at 33/1) it was not surprising that he

THE CHAMPION HURDLE

started 5/2 on to beat his six rivals, the shortest price in the Championship's history. 'I was never in doubt about the result,' said Stephenson afterwards. 'I had a bet of £5,000 to £1,000 about him a long while ago.'

Yet Sir Ken's opposition was again far from mediocre. The O'Brien horse, Galatian, had won his last two and possessed the speed to win the previous year's Grosvenor Cup on the Flat at Liverpool, although in his trainer's opinion, 'he was not a natural jumper, not clever'. On his seasonal début he had been defeated by Teapot II (another French-bred, owned and trained by the Magniers), who subsequently confirmed his championship potential by winning the Rathcoole in concession of three stone. He, too, was no plodder on the flat, having finished third in the Irish Cambridgeshire. Another classy Flat performer was Flush Royal. Winner of the Prix de Ferrières from the future Derby winner My Love and placed in the French Derby, he was then bought by the Scottish bookmaker James McLean and had recently won the Cesarewitch with 8st 13lb.

Poor visibility was fast becoming a Festival trademark. In 1953 an icy fog blotted out all except the last two furlongs. It made no difference to Sir Ken. 'He jumped magnificently and at no stage of the race was out of a canter,' said Molony after his third consecutive Champion Hurdle success. A lengthy post mortem revealed that Sir Ken's pacemaker Assunto made a complete hash of his obligations. It took him half a mile of such exertion to get to the front that he immediately fell away exhausted, leaving Sir Ken to make the best of a bad job. This presented Molony with a dilemma since Sir Ken was hurdling so fast and low that it was extremely difficult to restrain him. Halfway down the hill the leader, Campari, began to wilt and Molony allowed the champion to go on. Once Galatian bungled the second last any prospect of a competitive finish evaporated. 'The wonder horse won easing up by two lengths,' said the *Sporting Life*. Willie Stephenson deflected comparisons with Brown Jack and Trespasser by saying merely, 'I think no one can dispute the fact that Sir Ken is the best hurdler we have had for many years.'

The fog provided the villain of the piece in more ways than one. Unlike Galatian, who was flown over with typical O'Brien foresight before the fog descended, poor Teapot endured a 12-hour wait at Collinstown airport to no avail, for he was eventually rerouted by

THE CHAMPION HURDLE

sea. He arrived at Cheltenham only three hours before the race after a journey lasting 23 hours. To finish a three-and-a-half-length third was no disgrace in the circumstances and when Magnier brought him out again on the Thursday to win the County Hurdle under 12st 7lb some began to wonder what might have happened in the championship had his pre-race traumas been avoided. Further support for these heretical views was provided by Teapot's next two races – an eight-length victory (conceding 41lb) at Phoenix Park and another outstanding display under top weight (conceding 31lb) to win the Liverpool Hurdle. Alternatively, what a compliment these performances paid Sir Ken.

Seven months after Cheltenham Sir Ken started his fourth English campaign in an insignificant £102 race at Uttoxeter. It was the first race of the day and he started 7/1 on. In one of racing's greatest shocks he was beaten two lengths into third place by the four-year-old Impney at weight-for-age of 5lb. Three weeks later Sir Ken proved the form all wrong by giving Impney 19lb and beating him seven lengths round Birmingham, a much more testing track. The younger horse's three subsequent victories went some way to explaining the Uttoxeter upset but Sir Ken's defences had been breached and Noholme beat him at Windsor, while on Boxing Day two lightweights did likewise at Kempton. However, all three defeats occurred on sharp tracks which no longer suited the ageing champion. 'He was getting a bit of an old man,' says Stephenson, recalling those disappointments, 'and his legs weren't so good either. At Uttoxeter he'd not been fit so I never lost confidence in him.' The crunch would come at Birmingham when Sir Ken attempted to win the Champion Trial Hurdle for the third time en route to the Festival. The track was more to his liking and the opposition included Noholme, Galatian and Limber Hill, a giant ex-point-to-pointer who would one day achieve great things over fences. Giving his rivals 7lb, Sir Ken still had plenty on his plate up the run-in but, showing tremendous determination, he whittled away Lively Lord's advantage and won by a length. Galatian was third, Noholme fifth. Prior to the race punters could obtain odds of 9/4 about Sir Ken for the championship. 'It's a one horse race for the Champion Hurdle now,' reported the *Sporting Life*, 'for he will be much better next time.' No one demurred, least of all the bookies, who despatched him 9/4 on favourite to complete the treble. 'Perhaps the threat from the weather will melt away in the same way as the opposition

THE CHAMPION HURDLE

to Sir Ken,' remarked *The Times*. 'To most of those who have been watching the racing during the winter no doubt has ever arisen about the champion's ability to defend his title successfully.' Recent weather had run the gamut from ice and snow to fog and floods. Sunday's frost disappeared sufficiently to allow the track to be used for exercise on the Monday though straw was laid either side of the jumps. They also ran safely enough at Worcester, but to Stephenson's consternation both his fancied runners were turned over. Which sort of hat-trick would Sir Ken complete?

In bright sunshine Sir Ken's new hare, Florestan, accomplished his brief better than Assunto, leading till passed by Impney at the top of the hill. Behind him ranged Galatian, Assynt and Sir Ken, making ground after being baulked at halfway. Turning into the straight, Impney was clear and defeat for the favourite was a distinct possibility. But Molony was deliberately holding on to Sir Ken. 'He was in a bad mood that day. I just sat on him, squeezing him enough to win.' He was still a length down at the last but Sir Ken's great ally – the Cheltenham hill – was about to deliver a body blow to his young adversary. 'Sir Ken came storming up,' reported *The Times*, 'his head stretched in resolute and splendid endeavour, and silence gave way to a roar of cheering as he mastered Impney 150 yards from home.'

Tim Molony steered Sir Ken through an ecstatic crowd of well-wishers to the winner's circle. 'Well done, you ould divil,' was all he could say as he gave his exhausted partner's left ear an affectionate tug on dismounting. No jockey can match his four consecutive Champion Hurdle victories. Stephenson's champion had vindicated himself. 'This last one was the most impressive of the three. They took him on and fancied to beat him with Impney, but he was a great horse.' As in 1953, one of the placed horses, this year Galatian, went on to frank the form by winning the Liverpool Hurdle under a welter weight.

Sir Ken might easily have won a fourth title. In fact, Stephenson placed a bet of £5,000 to £500 there and then to that effect. But lurking down in Sussex was someone with a different point of view. Ryan Price had also been shopping across the Channel and reckoned his Clair Soleil a certainty for the 1955 championship. Assisted by Fred Winter, the outstanding jockey of his generation and quite possibly the greatest of them all, Price wove his undoubted magic to win three of the next seven Champion Hurdles.

7

HRP and the Shropshire Lads

Any race boasting a pedigree as lengthy and blue-blooded as the Champion Hurdle will contain a fair number of legendary characters renowned more for the manner of their achievements than the nature of them. Captain Henry Ryan Price was just such a character. A curious amalgam of barrackroom toughness and officers' mess charm, he was often outspoken and arrogant and never far removed from controversy yet by his death on 16 August 1986 (his 74th birthday, stage management he would have applauded) after a major operation for a stomach ulcer, 'The Captain' had indisputably proved himself a trainer of rare talent and one of the truly great British horsemasters of all time. 'I fear the real knowledge has died with him because it was an instinct,' said his biographer Peter Bromley. 'People could see him doing things with horses and then do it themselves, but I don't think they ever knew why. He was a tyrant to work for, really, but though he was a very hard man and tough on others, underneath that hardness he was very generous. And as a trainer of racehorses, he was a genius.'

Price developed horse husbandry to an almost unbelievably high degree. Nothing was too much trouble for him if it contributed to the welfare of his horses – 'I'd feed them on gold dust if I thought it would do them any good' – who were always immaculately turned out and gleamed at 100 yards. His father was a lifelong friend of Fred Darling, a noted martinet and stickler for standards of turnout which would have done the Household Cavalry proud, and as a teenager Price was privileged to visit Darling's sumptuous Beckhampton headquarters on several occasions. Price was also to run his own yard, Soldiers Field, with a rod of iron. Once, in 1961, Price was faced with a lads' strike. Calling out the ringleader, he allowed him to say his piece – before laying him spark out courtesy of a huge haymaker. 'Who,' he enquired 'is your next spokesman?'

THE CHAMPION HURDLE

End of strike. Few staff left Soldiers Field, however, and running through a turbulent career, containing more than one brush with racing authority, was Price's profound understanding and deep love of horses, reflected in the field of crocks and pensioners he maintained at home till his dying day. 'These horses helped to make me famous and I will never forget them. I'd rather talk to them than most people I know. They are my friends.'

Under the tuition of his father George, a hard taskmaster ('Whatever you do in the world, even if it's only breaking stones, try to do it better than anyone else'), the young Price became a fearless rider in shows and point-to-points and to some he was the south's outstanding rider between the flags during the '30s. In the war he served with No. 6 Commando in Normandy (after 90 days he was one of only two officers left alive in his unit – 'I must have been saved for something!') and later was personally entrusted by Winston Churchill with Montgomery's safety. These experiences undoubtedly enabled him to bring the best out of men like Fred Winter, Josh Gifford and Paul Kelleway for example, all of whom became successful jockeys and trainers. When Price lost his licence after Rosyth's running in the 1964 Schweppes Gold Trophy, many of his staff volunteered to stay on unpaid such was the loyalty he engendered. Price survived this ordeal but with the inevitable cigarette, and trilby rakishly tilted, he could never quite convince everyone of his honesty. 'Ryan Price may not be crooked, I just don't know,' one racegoer was overheard to say, 'but my goodness he looks crooked.'

The most memorable of those working relationships involved Fred Winter. Price knew the Winter family from pre-war days and when Fred junior, an ex-paratrooper, was trying to re-establish a riding career already cruelly interrupted by a broken back, he put him up on a moderate horse of his called Smoke Piece at Taunton in November 1949. They were beaten a neck but a few days afterwards a Winter victory on Dick the Gee at Plumpton persuaded Price this was the jockey he wanted. Fred Winter brings to mind every facet of jockeyship – courage, good hands, judgement of pace, tactical acumen, enormous strength in a finish and, above all, an indomitable spirit which he shared with his guv'nor. 'We both had the same outlook, we both liked winning and we were both at the breakthrough point in our careers,' Winter later recalled. 'We helped each other along.' The partnership lasted 15 years and

THE CHAMPION HURDLE

provided over half Winter's 929 winners in a career in which he won four jockeys' championships and Price five trainers' titles, though surprisingly they were never champion in the same season. In all those years fraught with jumping's habitual ups and downs, these two proud and forthright individuals managed to fall out, briefly, on only two occasions. The first of these involved a race won not lost, and what a race it was – the 1955 Champion Hurdle. The horse was a talented, cantankerous character called Clair Soleil.

Clair Soleil was a dark brown – almost black – horse with a roguish eye bred by Francois Dupre, whose name is more usually linked with such as Relko or Bella Paola. Sent into training with Francois Mathet, Clair Soleil won twice on the Flat as a three-year-old before making a successful début over hurdles in the Prix d'Iena in November 1952. A good, clean jumper, he won again at Auteuil in February, after which news of his possible sale was relayed to Price by his French spies. Since the war Price repeatedly returned in search of bargains, mostly on behalf of wealthy patron Gerry Judd. Priorit, who cost £4,000 in 1948, was followed by the likes of Vermilion and Nuage Dore; later on came Cantab (£3,000), Beaver II (free) and Catapult (£6,000). Both Cantab and Beaver were destined to win the Triumph Hurdle. In 1953 this was Clair Soleil's objective and Price determined to buy him. When Baron Hatvany dropped out at the last moment, Gerry Judd was persuaded to put up the £5,000 and Price drove to Hurst Park on the morning before the race to see the horse schooled. Revealing more than a hint of what was to come, Clair Soleil flatly refused to go near a hurdle let alone jump one. Even so, the horse, still an entire, took the eye and Price confirmed the deal. News of the schooling fiasco was diplomatically withheld from Fred Winter!

Cantering to post, Winter was enormously impressed by Clair Soleil's action but then all hell broke loose. 'I was standing beside Tim Molony and Clair Soleil reached over and tried to grab him! Then through the race I was about fifth at the bend by the stands and some horse squeezed us and Clair Soleil turned round and grabbed him by the neck!' This was about as much as Winter could tolerate. He really set about Clair Soleil over the last mile, forcing him up to beat Molony, on the favourite, by a length.

Clair Soleil had unfurled his true colours all right; tremendous courage and ability but a vile temper. 'A desperate character really and an absolute sod of a horse when he was young,' says Winter.

THE CHAMPION HURDLE

'When he was 90 per cent fit he was a great horse and when he was 100 per cent fit he was a little bit mad. He literally used to go down and eat the ground sometimes.' He performed this trick once too often. When an exasperated Price strode across to kick him on the nose, Clair Soleil instantly sank his teeth into Price's boot and flung the trainer in the air. No record of the Captain's comments exists, and in any event would be unprintable, but suffice it to say Clair Soleil was promptly gelded. Not that castration cured all his anti-social tendencies. Price's travelling head lad, Snowy Davis, remembers how quiet he was in his box but how the atmosphere soon altered once he left it. 'We couldn't go near the others – he'd rear up and go for them. But he was very game, bags of guts and a class horse.' Over the next seven years his lad, Tommy Winters, lavished attention on his brilliant but wayward charge. 'I used to ride him out in a chifney at the back of the string. When he was tuned up for the Champion Hurdle he used to get a bit funny, a little nasty.'

An ambitious summer campaign on the Flat came to nought and a combination of problems caused Clair Soleil to miss the entire 1953–54 jumping season. Three outings on the Flat in late 1954 got Clair Soleil cherry ripe for a successful return to hurdling at Sandown where his principal victim was Impney. Then he won Manchester's Rose of Lancashire Hurdle by ten lengths from Assynt with Impney again third. 'He loved Manchester, especially when it was heavy,' says Tommy Winters. 'Three times I took him and three times he won. On this occasion I greeted him with a cut eye, six stitches in my face and minus a filling in my teeth! When we were leaving Euston station the train backed into the platform. It didn't bother Clair Soleil but left me battered and bruised.'

Fred Winter had also spent the 1953–54 season on the sidelines, having sustained a compound fracture of the left leg in a fall at the very first fence of his very first ride. Clair Soleil would be his fourth mount in the Champion Hurdle. To date neither he nor Price had gained as much as a place. Of Winter's remaining ten rides in the championship only Retour de Flamme (1960) and Catapult (his last in 1964) were not for Price, and the latter merely because the horse had been transferred to Tom Masson after the Rosyth affair.

The 1955 Champion Hurdle took some winning, with an unprecedented field of 21, including Sir Ken and the heavily backed O'Brien seven-year-old Stroller. Indeed, remarked the *Bloodstock*

THE CHAMPION HURDLE

Breeders' Review, 'the race was one of the few events of its kind which had been the subject of ante-post betting because, although there are a number of good-class hurdle events, handicaps and otherwise, there is nothing on this branch of the sport to decide which are the outstanding hurdlers of the season'. Nevertheless, many of these 'good-class' events were providing a series of stepping stones towards the Champion Hurdle. December's Victory Hurdle and January's Rose of Lancashire Hurdle (both at Manchester), February's Princess Royal (Doncaster), Oteley (Sandown) and Champion Trial (Birmingham) preceded the championship, whilst the Imperial Cup, Triumph Hurdle and Aintree's Lancashire, Coronation and Liverpool Hurdles offered early clues for the following season. None, however, rivalled the financial supremacy of the Champion Hurdle which since Hatton's Grace's third victory had been worth well in excess of £3,000 to the winner, on the last four occasions, in fact, richer than the Gold Cup.

Sir Ken's season had been restricted to three races, only the first of which brought success. Noholme (receiving 7lb) beat him at Birmingham and in the Victory he could only finish fourth, some 15 lengths behind Stroller. In spite of this, the Royston horse retained his position as ante-post favourite for the championship at 4/1.

Stroller had enjoyed a wonderful 12 months. He won a division of the Gloucestershire Hurdle and finished third in the County Hurdle at the Festival before winning the Coronation Hurdle. He returned to Liverpool to win the November Handicap Hurdle and then added the Victory. Fate then conspired against him. He was laid up for a month with an infected heel and before O'Brien could get a much-needed prep race into him the weather deteriorated. In the championship he met a fitter Sir Ken on terms 11lb worse than Manchester.

A two-hour snowfall on the morning of the race postponed matters for 24 hours and altered the going to the heavy conditions Clair Soleil relished. Accordingly, he started a warm favourite at 5/2 with Stroller at 7/2. Sir Ken (11/2) had completed his preparations on the sands at Shoeburyness but Stephenson was not altogether happy with his legs and as a precautionary measure had him bandaged in front.

The Queen and Queen Mother were in the stands to watch a thrilling race between Clair Soleil and Stroller. 'Both horses ran

THE CHAMPION HURDLE

with the utmost courage,' declared the *Bloodstock Breeders' Review*, 'and raised the crowd to a pitch of enthusiasm only displayed on rare occasions.' One particular spectator 'roused' to the verge of apoplexy was Ryan Price, anxious to discover why his jockey had disobeyed orders and not delayed his challenge. 'I had to go on when I did,' explained Winter, taking his life in his hands. 'Anyway, I won the —— race, didn't I!'

As far as the press was concerned Winter's performance was the difference between victory and defeat. 'Winter's riding decisive in close finish' stated *The Times'* headline of a race run at a furious pace considering the soft ground. Prince Charlemagne was the individual responsible. As he tired, some three-quarters of a mile out, Winter and Clair Soleil were left in the lead. Up to this point the favourite had not been especially co-operative but finding himself in front he cheered up enormously and began to stride out more purposefully.

To a master jockey like Winter there was no question of sticking to orders. Shadowed by Stroller, Cruachan and Sir Ken, it would have been suicidal to retrain Clair Soleil, and lose the initiative, now the horse was running. Although Stroller blundered the third and second-last hurdles, allowing Winter to steal the rail into the straight, he had gained a slight lead after landing over the final flight. Under the whip for all of three furlongs, Clair Soleil now responded to a classic Winter finish. Head bowed and shoulders hunched as if in prayer, the impulsion and will to win Winter transmitted to Clair Soleil suggested some brand of extraterrestrial power, for he almost lifted him past Stroller to win by a head. 'I thought I was beaten but this rivalry seemed to produce a fresh spark of life in Clair Soleil.' Sir Ken, unable to quicken up his favourite hill, was fourth.

Due to one thing and another Clair Soleil's perfect record over English hurdles of four from four had taken two years to accumulate and once he pulled a ligament in his off hind during the build-up to the 1956 championship there seemed little likelihood of his appearances becoming any more frequent. Confined to the sands of the Sussex coast he was hardly half straight when March came round again and could not be expected to play a significant part in proceedings. In fact, the Champion Hurdle constituted his only race of the season.

Well beaten by Charlie Hall's Ingoe in the Victory, Stroller reversed the form in the Rose of Lancashire to earn favouritism at 2/1. There was only one really outstanding hurdler on view at the Festival

THE CHAMPION HURDLE

according to the cynics and that was Sir Ken – and he was jumping fences. The old champion won the Cotswold all right and in 1957 became the first Champion Hurdler to run in the Gold Cup, though he only reached the fifteenth. There was never much hope of Sir Ken reproducing his hurdling prowess (he fell in four of his last five chases and was pulled up in the other) and he was retired in February 1958 after failing to win the lowly Westgate Hurdle at Warwick. He spent his last years with Rodney Ward, master of the Puckeridge Hounds, with whom he dropped dead one day in 1964, aged 17.

Stroller stole the show on looks, few racegoers affording Charlie Hall's second runner, Doorknocker, more than a cursory glance. 'A big, rather clumsy-looking horse,' said Vincent Orchard, 'he would have been more at home in a field of chasers.'

With no early pace of any consequence, the runners were tightly bunched at the top of the hill and as they bore left Stroller was badly baulked. This may have affected his confidence because the favourite slipped on landing over the next flight and came down. To underline how cruel fate had been, Stroller won the Spa Hurdle two days later. Down the hill and towards the last, the glory seemed destined for Quita Que, on whom Mr J.R. 'Bunny' Cox had ridden a beautiful race along the rails. The only horse at this stage who appeared to have no chance was Doorknocker, but as all round him tired he 'continued to bash along with increasing gusto'. Unbeknown to the riders in the stand, Harry Sprague, and few were his superior over timber, was following his instructions to the letter by not asking anything of his partner until inside the last half mile. The unconsidered duo battered the last but still outstayed Quita Que up the hill.

Chastened scribes hurried to make amends. Doorknocker has not yet filled out, they wrote, trying to make the best of a bad job, and when he develops more muscle in his quarters and lets down he should make the chaser his owner Clifford Nicholson intended him to be. The chestnut son of Cacador was bred in Ireland and bought as a yearling by Paddy Sleator. After winning first time out over hurdles as a four-year-old he knocked himself so badly that he was unable to run for two years. Before joining the majority of Nicholson's horses in the care of Charlie Hall at Tadcaster he won a bumper, but prior to the Festival his seasonal haul numbered just three novice hurdles. This was the North's first Champion Hurdle and it assisted Hall to his sole trainers' title.

THE CHAMPION HURDLE

The background stories to the next two Champion Hurdles encourage belief in fairy tales. Each race went to a horse family owned and trained in Shropshire – the first from Arthur Jones's stable of four near Oswestry, and the second from Stan Wright's Leintwardine yard housing all of six.

Arthur Jones very nearly missed Merry Deal. He was attending the 1953 Doncaster Sales during his first season as a trainer when Merry Deal, then an unbroken three-year-old, was knocked down at 135 guineas. 'I went to buy another that was due in the ring but I liked this bay walking round so I told a friend to dash after the purchaser and offer him a ten-guinea profit.' Thus did Jones acquire the winner of 17 hurdles and two chases worth over £13,598. 'He also possessed wonderful breeding, by a Derby winner in Straight Deal out of a mare called Merryland by the French Derby winner Mieuxce.' This was Miss Paget's bloodstock and Merry Deal had already passed through the sales ring once, as a two-year-old at Ballsbridge, where he fetched 40 guineas.

Jones returned to Oswestry highly delighted. 'He was a damned nice horse, about 16.1 hands, sometimes looking a bit spare but he could stand a lot of work. He was very difficult to break and would keep rearing over backwards until I got plain fed up and just sat on him! He was a nice character really. He had a trait of standing stock-still as if staring out to sea, not registering a thing.' However, Merry Deal gave scant indication that a Champion Hurdler lurked at Pentre David. He made his début in March 1954 and by the start of the 1956–57 season he had won only five of his thrity-one races. Three outings carrying low weights before Christmas scarcely hinted at an imminent breakthrough. His mark of 10st 2lb in the Victory Hurdle seemed a fair reflection of his abilities but he proceeded to win comfortably. 'He was just beginning to come to himself and had been very angular till then but the form was not very good and certainly not up to the Champion Hurdle.' When Merry Deal lost his next race that indeed looked the case. 'It was a disappointing run but I watched him at home that night and he was eating more straw than anything else. I immediately switched him to peat moss bedding. It improved him enormously. Three days later he did the most tremendous gallop and then won the Princess Royal by four lengths.'

Partnering Merry Deal to victory in these two £1,000-plus events was a young Warwickshire boy called Grenville Underwood

THE CHAMPION HURDLE

whom Jones had noticed one day at Hereford. 'He was strong, saw no danger and won a race he shouldn't have. He was very dedicated and was always accompanied by his mother who personally supervised all his meals so that he kept his strength up.'

The general consensus of opinion insisted the race lay between Clair Soleil and Rosati, trained by Fulke Walwyn and ridden by Johnny Gilbert, a brilliant hurdle race jockey whose attention to detail extended to walking the course before racing and marking the best going with lollipop sticks. The actual outcome depended on the ground, maintained the press; if good, Rosati wins; if soft, Clair Soleil triumphs as he had when they clashed in the Rose of Lancashire. Having shown signs of total recovery from his leg injury, and aided by a week's heavy rain, the former champion was made 7/4 favourite.

With the thermometer nudging 70° F a record crowd discarded overcoats to watch a sensational race. Merry Deal was reluctant to go to post (though knowing his foibles Jones was unruffled) but the two favourites were the most devilish of all. Rosati fired the first salvo by lashing out with his hind legs and landing a blow to the midriff of Clair Soleil who, one writer tactfully phrased it, 'immediately took justifiable affront and from then on seemed to be more interested in fighting than racing, pawing the ground in rage'. Only robust treatment from Winter got the favourite to start and even under way he paid more attention to Rosati's neck than either of the first two hurdles.

Quita Que repeated his tactics of the previous year and with less than half a mile to go held sway ahead of Rosati, Clair Soleil, Merry Deal and Tout Ou Rien, a French-trained five-year-old with eight victories to his name. The Frenchman briefly threatened but dropped away before the last and the two pugilists had understandably drained every drop of their nervous energy, which left Merry Deal with a relatively simple task to overhaul Quita Que. The longest-priced winner of the Champion Hurdle thus far (28/1) was only Underwood's second at Cheltenham and the 25th of his career.

Merry Deal continued on the crest of a wave until Retour de Flamme beat him in the 1958 Oteley Hurdle. However, in this magnificent run of four further victories, thinks Arthur Jones, lay the seeds of his downfall. 'He had an accident out at grass when a piece of branch – about as thick as your thumb – penetrated near

THE CHAMPION HURDLE

the eye and as a result he came in earlier than usual, late June not August. Therefore he had a very long season and was feeling its effects by March.'

Despite having defeated a number of his rivals, Tokoroa and Retour de Flamme were nonetheless preferred to him in the betting. In fact, seven of the eighteen runners went off at odds between 5/1 and 9/1, so it was anyone's race if the bookies were to be believed. Last year's Gloucestershire Hurdle winner, the hard-pulling Tokoroa, trained by Fred Rimell and ridden by Dave Dick, was favourite at 5/1 yet Merry Deal had twice given him a beating. Syd Warren's handsome Retour de Flamme (partnered by Jimmy Lindley) was half a point longer. At his best, as in the Oteley, very useful, but on bad days, viz the Triumph Hurdle, an infuriating beast. On balance, though, he seemed to have the edge of Fare Time, representing the Price–Winter combination.

The 20/1 outsider Bandalore, ridden by George Slack and trained by Stan Wright for his wife Dorothy, set off at a blistering gallop, which precipitated a pile-up at the first flight involving Chamanna, Owen's Image and, crucially, Fare Time. Bandalore dragged the remainder along until, as planned, Slack gave him a breather descending the hill, whereupon he was joined by Tokoroa, King, Merry Deal and Retour de Flamme, who was not jumping cleanly. Approaching the last, Tokoroa led Bandalore by a length but Slack was merely biding his time. Halfway up the hill he edged Bandalore past the favourite and went two lengths clear. Thanks to the fierce gallop (and it must be said a few yards being taken off the distance) a new race record of 3 minutes 56 seconds had been set. Furthermore, Bandalore had led very nearly all the way.

Bandalore's victory provided the championship's second successive upset. He had not run since finishing fourth in the Victory as his intended prep race had been lost to snow and Merry Deal had twice beaten him. In five years Wright had trained 37 winners from his yard on the Shropshire–Herefordshire border. Bandalore's preparation was unique to say the least because Wright's farm had no gallops in the accepted sense. His string got fit by lengthy roadwork and long, steady trots through the wooded hillsides.

Bandalore had been bred locally by Mrs A. Warman, for whom he won a Chepstow hurdle over Easter 1955. His sire Tambourin won the Grand Prix de la Ville de Vichy but had made little impact

THE CHAMPION HURDLE

as a stallion, and the dam, Smart Woman, was of no account. Bandalore was her first foal. Wright paid £500 for him and later on bought the dam, carrying Bandalore's own brother and with a foal at foot, for £200. He had recovered this outlay when Bandalore won the November Handicap Hurdle but the following season Bandalore failed to score in seven attempts.

The first-flight exit of Fare Time was a bitter disappointment to Ryan Price. Though he did not rate Fare Time in the same class as Clair Soleil, because he was not a fluent jumper, Price knew him to be a tough and resolute stayer. Mind you, when it came to temperament all at Findon agreed he was an absolute gentleman in comparison to Clair Soleil. However, Fare Time's legs constantly taxed Price's genius for achieving the improbable since the threat of the horse breaking down was never too distant.

Fare Time was sold as a foal for 180 guineas and resold as a yearling for 490 guineas to Mrs R.A. Thrale, acting on behalf of Gerry Judd. His sire Thoroughfare won a single small contest during the war but his dam Septime had won twice and finished second in the Park Hill Stakes, while her family was a noted producer of winners on the flat. Fare Time, a bay with a white face, never looked like continuing that record. His ten efforts yielded only a one-and-a-half-mile maiden plate at Wolverhampton. Hurdling allowed him to capitalise on his bottomless stamina. He won four in his first season and twice in 1957–58, including the Berkshire Hurdle, before that Cheltenham disaster.

The first five home in the 1958 Champion Hurdle stood between Fare Time and a second title for Judd, Price and Winter, and contrary to the norm they confronted each other before Cheltenham. In the big sponsored hurdle race at Kempton over Christmas, Tokoroa (third), Merry Deal (fifth) and Fare Time (second) were all beaten by a lightweight, though at the weights Tokoroa emerged clearly best. A month later Tokoroa and Fare Time were joined by Bandalore, Retour de Flamme and King in Windsor's Blacknest Handicap. At levels Tokoroa confirmed the interpretation of the Kempton race, beating Fare Time by one and a half lengths and, overcoming Retour de Flamme a second time at Birmingham, came to the championship as a 7/2 favourite. Fare Time, meanwhile, made a hard job of winning the Oteley.

Of the three previous champions only Merry Deal (100/9) and Bandalore (22/1) took part. They, and Clair Soleil, had suffered a

THE CHAMPION HURDLE

disrupted season. Merry Deal had trod awkwardly on some gravel at Kempton and developed a poisoned foot. Clair Soleil returned from a tilt at fences (actually winning the first) to win the Victory by six lengths only to contract jaundice. 'There was no time for the guv'nor to get him ready for the Champion,' says Tommy Winters, 'but he livened up enough for us to give him a couple of gallops, so we aimed him at the three-mile race instead.'

Fred Winter's Festival began in cracking style when Flame Gun landed the Cotswold Chase from the heavily backed Irish horse Cashel View. The Emerald Isle was also massively represented in the Champion Hurdle through Havasnack, Prudent King and the stablemates, Ivy Green and Friendly Boy. The last-named won the County Hurdle with a low weight 12 months before but had latterly run unsuccessfully with huge weights in four Irish handicaps. Nonetheless, money talked and he was best backed of the invaders at 4/1.

For the first time the race used the new course which, because the final uphill stretch commenced earlier, placed more of a premium on stamina. Straight Lad's fall at the fourth left Tokoroa ahead of King, Fare Time, Merry Deal and Prudent King. Yet again the downhill flight brought drama. Tokoroa lost his hind legs on landing and came down, injuring his back and stifle. In addition, he cannoned into Merry Deal, who eventually ended up facing in the wrong direction with his jockey thrown right up his neck. Fred Winter, instantly assessing the situation, grabbed his favourite inside berth into the straight, ready to withstand the challenges of Prudent King and the mare Ivy Green. The former weakened, but a version of the inimitable Winter finish, high on thou-shalt-not-pass, was necessary to keep the mare at bay. All four Irish horses finished in the leading six, the gallant Merry Deal making up masses of leeway to split them in fifth.

It was a memorable day, and meeting, for Winter. He completed a treble when Top Twenty won the Grand Annual and he rode two more winners on the Thursday, one of which was the mercurial Clair Soleil who made every yard of the Spa Hurdle. It was his thirteenth and final victory over hurdles and after running four times unplaced in 1959–60 he was retired to Ian Muir's Fawley Stud, near Wantage. 'He always used to come here for his summer holidays with Vermilion,' chuckles Muir, recalling the havoc they invariably caused. 'Vermilion was another tartar and the pair used to fight for

THE CHAMPION HURDLE

hours, the sweat running off them. But Clair Soleil was a kind old horse in retirement, falling in love with one particular mare here and acting as her protector. At one point Gerry Judd wanted him put down but Ryan wouldn't wear it and told me to charge Clair Soleil to him personally until the day the old horse died. He lived well into his twenties until one afternoon I found him lying dead in the paddock.' It comes as no surprise to learn that Ryan Price was visibly upset when told the news.

The greatest obstacles in Fare Time's path towards a second championship seemed to be Irish, Albergo and Another Flash, or ex-Irish, namely Saffron Tartan, once with Vincent O'Brien but now residing with Don Butchers at Epsom. However, as Albergo was English bred, and classically bred at that, perhaps this constituted a fair swap.

A good-looking horse by Dante, Albergo hailed from Lord Astor's famous Popingaol line which nurtured Classic winners in the 1920s and '30s and the doughty stayer Trelawny in the '60s. However, Albergo ran dismally in Crepello's Derby and after straining a tendon in the Gordon Stakes, he was bought by Mrs Clem Magnier for 400 guineas. His career began to flourish early in 1959 when he came to England and won the Gloucestershire, Grey Talk and Coronation Hurdles. He won his Cheltenham race in a time five seconds faster than Fare Time's Champion Hurdle.

In Albergo's last appearance before the championship he scrambled home by a short head after comprehensively demolishing the final flight. The horse he defeated was not subjected to a hard race and was backed to turn the tables. His name was Another Flash.

A bay six-year-old, the same as Albergo, Another Flash was bred in Mullingar but, unlike his Irish rival, his pedigree was rather plebeian. Although his sire, Roi d'Egypte, was a full brother to Gold Cup winner Medoc II and had won the Cathcart, he stood at the lordly sum of £7 while his dam Cissie Gay had changed hands on numerous occasions, once for nothing. Still, she was a half sister to an Irish National winner and had produced the useful chaser Flashaway. In time she emphasised her worth by throwing two more above-average jumpers in Flash Bulb and Super Flash.

Eventually, Another Flash became the property of John Byrne who sent him into training with Paddy Sleator. Standing barely 16 hands, and 'a bit like a cob to look at', according to his rider Bobby

THE CHAMPION HURDLE

Beasley, Another Flash seemed to lack the scope for a hurdler but he 'possessed a tremendous natural spring', winning all four of his races during the 1958–59 season besides collecting the Irish Cesarewitch. Carrying the greater Irish confidence, he was made 11/4 favourite.

Another Flash's elevation was facilitated by the late defection of Fare Time, who struck into himself at exercise six days before the race. He had endorsed his claim to be the best of the English by hammering Saffron Tartan and Retour de Flamme in the Oteley. When second and third exactly reproduced that form in the Birmingham Trial, Saffron Tartan became the main domestic hope at 3/1. Since winning a division of the Gloucestershire Hurdle in 1957 and being ante-post favourite for the 1959 Gold Cup until coughing forced him out of the race, Saffron Tartan had been hobdayed. His reversion to hurdles was considered only a temporary measure.

Festivalgoers were treated to a revamped Cheltenham as £125,000 had been spent on rebuilding the Tattersalls' grandstand and enlarging the members', while another £10,000 had gone on hardcore for those car parks and approaches annually transformed into paddy fields by the English spring. The new stands proved most welcome in view of a bitterly cold east wind which was rapidly drying out the ground.

Tokoroa and Bandalore locked horns from the start, Another Flash lying handy mid-division and Saffron Tartan bringing up the rear. Tokoroa's fall at the same flight as the previous year gave Albergo the initiative, but rounding the turn he was joined in line abreast by Saffron Tartan, Lord O' Montrose and Another Flash. However, Beasley had plenty up his sleeve and merely had to shake the favourite up for him to come right away from Albergo and Saffron Tartan to win (despite swerving left on the hill) in a new record time of three minutes 55 seconds. 'He won so decisively,' said *The Times*, 'that he marked himself as outstanding among present day hurdlers.'

One man unlikely to have shown the new champion such respect was Ryan Price because on his Oteley Hurdle form with Saffron Tartan, Fare Time would have troubled Another Flash. If Price was to dethrone Another Flash it would have to be with a different candidate. Injury ruled Fare Time out of the 1961 championship.

Price was convinced he had the necessary ammunition in the

THE CHAMPION HURDLE

shape of Eborneezer, a six-year-old entire bred by his owner, Dr Burjar Pajgar. As was to be expected from a horse sired by an Ascot Gold Cup winner (Ocean Swell) out of a mare by a second one (Precipitation), Eborneezer did not run at two but he won twice as a three-year-old over distances beyond one and a half miles. During the 1959 Ebor something was kicked up into his eye causing him to become very short-sighted (and ultimately go blind) and he was equipped with a hood when he comfortably won the Queen's Prize at Kempton over Easter 1960. Disability or not, 'Eb' was everyone's favourite at Findon. 'A nice-natured horse,' remembers Snowy Davis, 'though a terribly bad traveller who never stopped kicking.' To Fred Winter he was a typical Flat-racer, 'fairly tall and narrow yet a very good jumper, a bloody sight better than Fare Time'.

The ease of that Queen's Prize success was undoubtedly attributable to a couple of winning runs over hurdles but Eborneezer had not run over timber for 11 months when he competed for the 1961 Oteley. Nevertheless, conceding the second 5lb, he quickened close to home to win by a length. Findon's dreams of a third Champion Hurdle were dampened after Eborneezer failed at Birmingham and some consideration was given to the possibility of scratching him until Winter assured Price that the horse's defeat was due to a muddling pace.

The Irish challenge was three-handed, opinions differing as to which of Another Flash, Albergo or Moss Bank would come out on top. Owing to an exceptionally wet autumn the champion's début was delayed until 21 January. Giving weight all round, he understandably tired in the closing stages, finishing fourth to Vulsea and seven lengths behind Moss Bank but with Albergo well beaten. Some explanation of Albergo's poor performance lay in his endeavours since the previous Champion Hurdle. Two days later he took the County Hurdle under 12st 5lb, then finished second in the Imperial Cup with 12st 6lb, won the Liverpool Hurdle carrying 12st 7lb and won a hurdle race in France before running second in the French Champion Hurdle. If that was not sufficiently enervating, he also appeared seven times unsuccessfully on the Flat and the Champion Hurdle would be his eighth outing of the current season. Captain Magee's handicapping of the three Irish horses favoured Another Flash but this opinion took a knock when the champion was beaten in a rough contest at Baldoyle. Rumours of the champion's

THE CHAMPION HURDLE

health subsequently flew thick and fast and were sadly confirmed by an announcement on 1 March that a leg injury made it impossible for him to defend his title.

In a weak championship Moss Bank was made favourite. The fast ground was thought likely to expose Eborneezer's alleged lack of speed and even old Merry Deal, now 11 and competing in his fifth Champion Hurdle, had his supporters in the wake of his magnificent six-length triumph in the Victory Hurdle. Sentiment probably played some part in Merry Deal's cause for he was lucky to be alive. He had fallen awkwardly at Liverpool and the course vet wanted to put him down. 'He couldn't put his leg to the ground,' says Jones. 'It was twisted in all sorts of different shapes and the radial nerve had also been damaged. Sir Charles Strong treated him with faradism, which may have cured all sorts of other problems at the same time. Two months later he comes back, wins the Victory and might well have won the Champion as well if his saddle had not slipped forward at the third flight so that he had to pull up.'

Merry Deal was not the only sufferer in an eventful race. Albergo, looking dangerous, crashed two out, bringing down three others. The gallop was not severe and Winter, having no intention of wasting Eborneezer's trump card, kept his mount in the van and kicked on at the first opportunity. 'All I saw of Albergo was his neck as he came alongside me at the second last and after he fell I was alone.' Doug Page, Albergo's jockey, was adamant he would have won and rued the stiffness of Cheltenham's hurdles. 'He landed in the middle of it – it would have given way in Ireland.' Moss Bank, who was slightly impeded by all this chaos, chased Eborneezer home. Two days later Winter rode Saffron Tartan to victory in the Gold Cup, thereby becoming the eighth jockey to achieve the double at the same Festival after Rees (1929), Cullinan (1930), Leader (1932), Stott (1933), Wilson (1935), Brabazon (1949 and 1950) and Molony (1953), and the last until Messrs Williamson (1995) and McCoy (1997) in the millennium's final decade.

Eborneezer's involvement in the Champion Hurdle was not repeated. After running second in the French Champion Hurdle and twice unplaced on the flat, he was rested with a view to contesting the 1962 championship but in February was retired to the Ardenrun Stud, Lingfield, at a fee of 148 sovereigns. The first Champion Hurdler to stand in England, he eventually moved to the Chesterton

THE CHAMPION HURDLE

Stud where he changed his spots and became a right so-and-so to cover, expressing an aversion to clipped mares in particular.

Nor would a more familiar face contest another championship. However, although Merry Deal might be too old for the Champion Hurdle, the Festival could not pass without his participation and as he stormed up the hill to win the 1962 Spa Hurdle as a 12-year-old, the cheers reverberated round Prestbury Park. He still wasn't done with. That season he won twice more and in 1964 won two chases. Not until he was pulled up in his 105th race, a hunter chase at Bangor on 16 April 1966, aged 16, did Merry Deal finally call it a day. 'He went point-to-pointing with a friend of mine after that,' says Jones, 'and would have won but he was a lot fitter than the jockey! He eventually died of colic.'

What a grand servant he had been to Arthur Jones, who has never spent ten guineas more wisely or to such good effect.

8

Pot Pourri

One name conspicuous by its absence from the lengthening list of winning trainers was that of Fulke Walwyn. Since taking out a licence in 1939 the closest he had come to landing the Champion Hurdle was the third place of Ephorus, his very first runner in the race in 1941. Though he had won four trainers' championships, a Gold Cup and countless other top races, the Champion Hurdle had constantly eluded him in spite of outstanding candidates like Distel (1947), Telegram (1952) and Rosati (1957).

Fulke Thomas Tyndall Walwyn was lucky to be alive. A soldier's son who emulated his father's prowess in the saddle and followed him into the army, he rode his first winner under Rules at the age of 19 and six years later won the 1936 Grand National on Reynoldstown when Frank Furlong, a brother officer from the 9th Lancers, could no longer make the weight. By this stage Walwyn had been obliged to resign from the regiment (he was later recalled to the colours during the Second World War, having earlier served in the improbable role of military policeman) following salacious newspaper coverage of a court hearing into a fracas in a Soho nightclub. Walwyn, very much an innocent party according to Clive Graham, who was one of the other revellers, wound up in Charing Cross Hospital. Nightspots and Walwyn did not mix. When a direct hit from a German bomb decimated the Café de Paris in March 1941 killing 84 people, Walwyn was one of the fortunate few to walk away unscathed. On the racecourse he had not been so lucky. Although twice leading amateur rider, Walwyn's professional career was dogged by a series of dreadful falls, in the last of which, at Ludlow, on 19 April 1939, he fractured his skull so badly he was unconscious for a week. He was fitted with a metal plate in his head and warned that further injury might prove fatal.

Left with little option other than to retire, Walwyn set up at

THE CHAMPION HURDLE

Delamere House in Lambourn and very nearly achieved a remarkable treble, having won on his first rides both as an amateur and a professional, when his second runner, Poor Duke, won at Buckfastleigh. However, war was only eight days away and Walwyn's training career did not take off until he moved across Lambourn to Ted Gwilt's former yard at Saxon House in 1944. Winners began to flow freely, especially after he was asked to take Dorothy Paget's horses in 1946. In their first season together Walwyn won the trainers' title with 60 winners, half of which wore the Paget colours. In an eight-year association he won 365 races for her. Twice he landed a four-timer at Cheltenham (the only trainer to do so), in November 1945 and October 1949, yet, irritatingly, that Champion Hurdle success would not materialise. Then, along came Anzio.

Anzio was a grey or roan by Herbert Blagrave's imported French horse Vic Day out of Lido Lady, the dam of five other winners. Purchased for 500 guineas at Goffs by Sir Thomas Ainsworth, he won his first three races as a three-year-old in Ireland before running disappointingly in the Queen's Vase. Anzio was subsequently transferred to Walwyn for a career over hurdles which began inauspiciously at Newbury in October 1960 when he was tailed off, but he was a warm order at Birmingham in February, breaking his duck by ten lengths. A powerhouse Winter finish on Cantab denied Anzio victory in the Triumph though compensation arrived with a smooth success in the Lancashire Hurdle.

Walwyn was convinced Anzio's low, skimming action was more suited to top of the ground conditions. Certainly his only defeat during the 1961–62 season came in heavy ground at Cheltenham. Conversely, with the ground in his favour, not even 12st 7lb could stop him bolting home at Newbury the week before the Festival. If the fine weather held, Anzio possessed as good a chance of the title as any previous Walwyn contender.

Had the Price battalions not constantly been in opposition, Fred Winter would have ridden Anzio. Given the choice of Fare Time or Cantab he decided to partner the younger horse, another French-bred entire bought for £3,000 on behalf of Miss Enid Chanelle. He had lost only two races and on Triumph form little separated him and Anzio. Considering his injury problems, Fare Time did well to win one of his races but he failed to cope with Snuff Box in the Oteley. Unfortunately, Snuff Box was cast in his box on the

THE CHAMPION HURDLE

morning of the Champion Hurdle and could not run, leaving the way clear for a triumphant return by Another Flash, apparently restored to all his former glory.

Housed for the season with Arthur Thomas at Warwick, Another Flash had won all his five starts. Neither Thomas nor Sleator would hear of defeat; it was merely a case of Another Flash (11/10 favourite) doing the honours. Like many a well-laid plan that is not how things turned out.

The Price horses led through the early stages which were as uneventful as the finale was exciting. Quelle Chance showed ahead at the penultimate hurdle from Fidus Achates, Cantab and Another Flash. Straining eyes, however, could identify Anzio, full of running, trapped on the inside rail with a wall of horses to his right. Anzio's new jockey, that quiet, polished horseman Willie Robinson, had no option but to sit tight and pray for an opening.

Landing over the last his pleas were answered. Quelle Chance drifted slightly to the right and Robinson, gratefully accepting the gap, shot Anzio up the fence to forge clear and win by three lengths.

Anzio was the youngest champion since Sir Ken and quite possibly heralded a new era in the sport as his illustrious predecessor had done, but any likelihood that he might become the first since Sir Ken to win two titles was destroyed by deep ground throughout 1962–63. Another Flash was a second notable absentee, confined to his box for the best part of a year by a vicious bout of enteritis that nearly killed him. In fact the decade unwound to an increasingly familiar ring – an open race with large fields (averaging 20), a different champion every year, several of them relatively unfancied and one at the race's longest odds of 50/1 (the eight championships between 1961–68 constitute the longest sequence of losing favourites). The Champion Hurdle also had to withstand a challenge to its financial status from the influx of sponsorship. The value of both the Gillette (£5,667) and Schweppes (£7,825), for instance, exceeded that of the Champion Hurdle (£5,585) in 1963. Despite all this, arguably the best horse ever to contest the race started 15/8 favourite in 1966. Flyingbolt could not match the specialist hurdling speed of Salmon Spray, arguably the best hurdler of the period. Yet, like Free Fare, who in some ways he resembled, Salmon Spray did not get the roll of the dice at Cheltenham.

In the circumstances it is perhaps highly appropriate that the

THE CHAMPION HURDLE

1963 race should have gone to a one-eyed gift horse owned and trained by a man enjoying his first excursion out of Ireland. In all honesty this was a field of poor quality. Nor did an incredibly harsh winter help matters. Newbury's 8 March meeting — four days before the Festival — was the first for 75 days, easily a post-war record.

Form was thus hard to interpret. The Gillette, run at Newcastle in December on ground as testing as Cheltenham was going to be, seemed to offer the most informative clues as seven championship contenders had turned out. Old Mull looked to have the race in his pocket until dropping to a walk 50 yards from the post and being caught by the lightweight Stirling, trained by an up-and-coming Yorkshireman named Peter Easterby. Behind this pair came Greektown, Pawnbroker, Quelle Chance, Height O' Fashion and Catapult, all of whom renewed rivalry at Cheltenham. At levels, Old Mull was fancied to have the beating of these but he had yet to win on the soft. The fly in this ointment might be Ryan Price's French buy Catapult II, who had been going well until tiring three out. The season before, his stablemate Beaver II had just touched him off in the Triumph and Price reckoned he was potentially the best hurdler he had trained. Significantly, Catapult was backed to win £12,000 at 40/1 and 33/1 the day before the Champion Hurdle, causing his odds to shrink dramatically.

Apart from Stirling, the best soft-ground performer had been White Park Bay, a classy handicapper on the Flat who had adapted well to hurdling and, moreover, needed only a light preparation. Winner of both his starts this winter he ended up favourite at 5/2.

On the Festival's first day the Irish had expected to win six of the seven races but were obliged to settle for one success — Arkle's in the Broadway. Their four runners in the Champion Hurdle had met already, in the Scalp Hurdle, victory in the soft going to Winning Fair with Farrney Fox seven lengths back in third. Ross Sea in fourth and the mare Height O' Fashion nowhere. Farrney Fox, another decent Flat-racer, was making his seasonal début, whereas Winning Fair had won at Limerick. On his next start the latter ran courageously to finish fourth under 12st 2lb in desperately heavy ground at Naas. Irish money said Farrney Fox (10/1) could reverse placings with the one-eyed Winning Fair (100/9), who would be ridden by the amateur Mr Alan Lillingston.

The huge gamble on White Park Bay quickly came unstuck when

THE CHAMPION HURDLE

Farrney Fox kicked him on the stifle down at the gate. The favourite was always struggling thereafter and finished lame. Catapult set a good gallop until weakening at the second last, as he had done in the Triumph and Gillette (he was later found to have a heart defect), whereupon the northern outsider Pawnbroker and Winning Fair took up the running. Lillingston had obeyed to the letter his instructions to hold up Winning Fair. 'We jumped off last and had a beautiful run up the inside to the bottom of the hill where I was stopped, very rightly, by David Nicholson. I shouldered my way out to the right – the horse's blind side – but sat as quiet as a mouse because I did not want to pick him up too soon.'

Winning Fair hurdled the last unchallenged and won by three lengths from Farrney Fox, who came through to shade Quelle Chance by a neck. The scenes in the winner's enclosure were unprecedented. Winning Fair's owner-trainer George Spencer was borne aloft on the shoulders of his supporters. The roisterous Irish welcome had arrived! Back home, outside Thurles in County Tipperary, his stable housed just three other animals. A pretty near-black gelding bred by Paddy Finn at Ballinahowall, the eight-year-old Winning Fair was given to Spencer and had lost his right eye after running into an apple tree. The unfortunate beast was virtually unridable as a yearling when put into training with John Oxx but the sight of his respected neighbour Willie O'Grady at work with his string encouraged Spencer to try his own luck with Winning Fair. Now, the unbelievable had happened and Spencer's head was yet to descend from the clouds. After all, to reach Cheltenham he had endured his first ride in an aeroplane. 'Wouldn't he be good enough for the Derby if he had two eyes?' he quipped.

Winning Fair was certainly not 'good enough' to win most Champion Hurdles. 'He was a very rugged horse, very competent but not brilliant,' recalls Lillingston, whose victory was only the second by an amateur ('No professional could have ridden a better race,' said the *Sporting Life*). He had ridden his first winner at Tralee in 1948 while still a 13 year-old Eton schoolboy, and later on, at the advanced age of 44, won a team gold at the European three-day event championship. George Spencer (whose jockey son Jamie became one of the rising stars of the new millennium) had not been very keen to run Winning Fair in the Champion. Lillingston continued: 'I got the ride only because my services were free! The whole operation was in the best sporting traditions because George

THE CHAMPION HURDLE

was a true and utter sportsman. When we returned to Ireland there was a parade in the village led by a pipe band and George sitting on the bonnet of the local taxi followed by me on the horse.'

After the unusual preparation of three steeplechases, Winning Fair trailed home 14th in defence of his title. Then, one day as Spencer was exercising him in the field beside his house, Winning Fair suffered a fatal heart attack.

Irish hopes in 1964 were pinned on Another Flash. Off the course with hock trouble for three months after winning at Windsor, he returned to carry top weight in the Schweppes Gold Trophy. In the circumstances he ran creditably to finish sixth in what became a *cause célèbre* of the highest magnitude. For the second year the race went to Ryan Price's Rosyth, but on this occasion the stewards felt his performance needed some explaining. Price's licence to train was withdrawn.

With a record field of 24 facing the tape, Another Flash started favourite for the third time and, at 6/1, the longest priced in the race's history. 'It is a good policy to row in with London Gazette and Sun Hat,' suggested the *Life*, 'who are well-bred Flat-racers and have shown grand form over hurdles in their first season.' Indeed, the former, trained by Harry Thomson Jones and ridden by Greville Starkey, had won two of his three races, while Sir Winston Churchill's Sun Hat, a half brother to High Hat, boasted an unbeaten record in four races. As a four-year-old, furthermore, he received 8lb from London Gazette and 10lb from the likes of Another Flash and Salmon Spray.

A second undefeated four-year-old on show was Fulke Walwyn's Kirriemuir whose perfect score stretched to six. 'He was not so classy or good looking as Anzio, who had a good turn of foot, but he was a very sweet, game horse,' recalled Walwyn. Anzio himself was unfit, 'a pity, because he would have won another on good ground'. Walwyn eventually tried him over fences and although 'he didn't like them very much' he won three times. 'He'd always had trouble with his breathing – when he got excited his throat tightened up. In the end he couldn't swallow and the vet had to operate, but after being kept alive on tubes for a few days he died.'

So Kirriemuir alone flew the flag for Saxon House. He was a 100/6 shot, the same odds as Magic Court, a reject from Noel Murless's blue-blooded yard, trained by the former jockey and vet Tommy Robson at Greystoke in the Lake District. After heavy snow

THE CHAMPION HURDLE

delayed the Festival two days, the Champion Hurdle was run for the first and only time on a Friday.

Sun Hat looked an assured winner until a series of mistakes down the hill knocked him out of contention. London Gazette, likewise, bungled the second-last, forfeiting his chance, and it was Magic Court who crossed the final hurdle fractionally ahead of Another Flash. However, no former champion had regained his title and although Magic Court veered left up the hill, causing the stewards to consult the newly installed camera patrol, he was already well clear and in no danger of disqualification. Kirriemuir ran on stoutly to be third. The four-year-olds had more than distinguished themselves for Sun Hat finished sixth yet, surprisingly, none of this age group subsequently contested the championship. For a Champion Hurdle largely denigrated by posterity it is worthy of note that all three placed horses won a championship which, if one adds Salmon Spray and Winning Fair, made a record total of five Champion Hurdlers in the field. Beasley felt Another Flash was unlucky not to be awarded the race. 'He deserved a second title because he was a lot better than the record books say. He was a lively character who'd see a bird you wouldn't of a morning. When Flash was retired, he kept jumping out of the paddock and had to be sent point-to-pointing. That shows what kind of horse he was.'

Magic Court belonged to Scotsman James McGhie, who did not even hold an account with Weatherbys, so that Robson was politely asked at weighing out for the necessary cash enabling Magic Court to participate. 'We had the Champion Hurdle in mind for two years,' said McGhie. 'We always knew he had the ability. I backed him at 50s – the biggest bet I've had.' The northern connection was strengthened by Ulsterman Pat McCarron, one half of the partnership which made Freddie an equine Scottish legend.

Magic Court was Robson's first winner at Cheltenham. He bought the horse as a three-year-old at the Houghton Sales of 1961 and this was Magic Court's fourth success of the season. Only 11 days earlier he had carried 11st 9lb to victory in the Princess Royal. He also won three of his eight races during the 1963 Flat season so could hardly be accused of spending the previous 12 months in idleness. A robust 16.1 hands brown gelding by Supreme Court out of the Blue Peter mare Blue Prelude, he was the latest in a long line of well-bred cast-offs the astute Robson had bought cheaply out of fashionable stables. Magic Court was a bit of a lad who craved

THE CHAMPION HURDLE

tranquillity and lots of understanding. In his last race for Murless he unceremoniously dislodged Lester Piggott and he was disqualified on two of the first three occasions he 'won' a hurdle race. 'He wouldn't go 50 yards on the gallops without pulling himself up so we had to geld him.' In addition, Magic Court suffered from muscle trouble and attendant stiffness which imposed heavy demands on Robson's veterinary skill. Injections of a vitamin composite plus two or three pints of milk in his evening mash began to do the trick while exercising around the hills and lakes, a welcome change from Newmarket's bustling expanses, completed the rehabilitation. With Tiny, the pony, to keep him happy, and the barest acquaintance with jumping between his races, Magic Court was a contented horse at last and emphasised the fact on the racecourse.

After going under by three-quarters of a length to Grey of Falloden in the Cesarewitch, Magic Court reeled off four straight wins over hurdles en route to a defence of his title. His Oteley victory was especially noteworthy as he had done only one piece of work in nine weeks (he'd been turned out for five) and got into all sorts of difficulty in the Sandown straight. Despite being baulked twice he got up in the last 100 yards to beat London Gazette (receiving a stone) by half a length with Kirriemuir (receiving 12lb) four lengths back in third. No horse was within six points of him in the ante-post market for the Champion Hurdle.

Second favourite was Salmon Spray. Turnell's horse had done little wrong, his solitary reverse occurring over fences, and he came fresh from a four-length victory in National Spirit's race. Wilhelmina Henrietta, too, had been especially prepared for the Champion Hurdle, her last race before embarking on a stud career. She had a preliminary run on the Flat in the autumn and then ran second in the Osborne Hurdle at Windsor. Her only other outing was the Bass Worthington at Sandown where, giving lumps of weight all round, she won comfortably. In 1964 the mare finished like a train on ground faster than she preferred; in 1965 the gods had even worse luck in store.

There can be no doubt which competitor would have been the most popular winner. Her Majesty Queen Elizabeth the Queen Mother had never won a race at the Festival but clearly possessed a live contender in the French-bred Worcran. Wearing the blue and buff for the first time at Birmingham, Worcran, hurdling superbly, defeated Fulke Walwyn's Exhibit A in a time 13 seconds faster than

THE CHAMPION HURDLE

that clocked by Anzio and four seconds faster than Magic Court in the day's other two races over the distance. Walwyn was trebly represented. Exhibit A had won seven hurdle races back home in America. He had been in England only six weeks when finishing fourth to Magic Court in the Oteley. The unquestioned Saxon House third string was Kirriemuir, whose odds of 50/1 accurately reflected his fall from grace. In six runs he had recorded just a Wincanton victory on his last appearance.

The race began sensationally. George Todd, trainer of the quietly fancied Nosey, instructed his jockey to track Salmon Spray as he was 'the best jumper in the race'. The chestnut repaid the compliment by standing off too far at the second flight, landed on top of it and fell, bringing down Nosey! As he had at Birmingham, Exhibit A set a spanking gallop and was still in front jumping the last. Walwyn's second championship was in the record books. But not with Exhibit A. He hit the final hurdle hard and Kirriemuir passed him on the inside and Spartan General on the outside. Worcran and Magic Court (who found the early pace a trifle too hot) now began to gain ground hand over fist but neither could quite reach the two leaders. Kirriemuir held off Spartan General by a length.

Notwithstanding the fact that Kirriemuir is the longest-priced winner of the Champion Hurdle, the 1965 race was unsatisfactory in other ways. Salmon Spray had departed early, both Spartan General and third-placed Worcran were crucially squeezed for room by Exhibit A when beginning their challenges and, worst of all, game little Wilhelmina Henrietta collapsed and died before the final flight. She had broken the pulmonary artery, the post-mortem showing she was soaked in blood from her throat to her lungs.

Kirriemuir was owned by Mrs Doreen Beddington, an aunt of Mrs Fred Winter. 'I was so excited during the race I didn't know what to think.' Walwyn acquired him on her behalf from Peter Payne-Gallwey after he had won a Chepstow Flat race as a three-year-old. By the sprinter Tangle, he was a 'little rabbit of a thing, very sweet and game', according to his trainer. Mrs Beddington only speculated a small sum on her horse but Walwyn was somewhat more fortunate. On the day he backed Exhibit A and was still cursing his decision some days later when a cheque arrived from his bookmaker. He had taken odds of 33/1 about Kirriemuir at Christmas and forgotten all about it!

Walwyn never saddled another winner of the championship,

although Dramatist might well have obliged had he not been running in the era of Night Nurse, Monksfield and Sea Pigeon. Nevertheless, he continued to plunder the sport's premier steeplechases with the stamp of horse with which his name will forever be associated – Mill House, The Dikler, Diamond Edge et al – until his retirement in 1990, by which time he had trained the winners of 2,188 races, including a record 40 at the Festival. Walwyn died on 18 February 1991, aged 80, rightly lauded as one of National Hunt racing's true greats. Bill Smith, the regular rider of Dramatist in his ten years as Walwyn's first jockey, put matters in a nutshell: 'I never rode for anyone who equalled his training ability. But the extraordinary thing about him was that he couldn't tell you what he was doing or why. Some people follow a plan but not Fulke, he followed his instinct. He could train horses to the day and the hour. He really was a genius. When someone dies they always say how great he was. But it was said about Fulke before he died.' Nor did Walwyn ever lose his yen for a party. 'We'd have dinner together before the Grand National,' continues Smith, 'and he'd always say he was going to bed, but every time he'd end up bopping away in the nightclub under the Adelphi. And I can tell you that when he was in top gear it needed a bloody good man to lay up with him!'

Salmon Spray desperately needed a change of luck if he was to win a Champion Hurdle. In 1965 he had been stopped in his work a fortnight before the race and hated the prevailing cold weather. 'He was a bit thin-skinned,' according to his rider John Haine, 'and was always 7lb better on a nice bright day.' He emphasised his 1965 misfortune by beating Magic Court in the Liverpool Hurdle with Haine sitting motionless. 'He was a real brave little horse. Not that big, good-looking, a very quiet character. He was a grand jumper and would gain four or five lengths at every hurdle – that's what kept him there.'

Salmon Spray ran in the colours of Mrs Eileen Rogerson, for whose husband, John, Bob Turnell had trained Pas Seul to win the Gold Cup. He bought Salmon Spray in Ireland for £2,400. 'Paddy Murphy kept telling me about this bay horse down at Nixie Halley's, so I finally went to see it and found this chestnut with a big white face! I was not greatly struck by him when I got home. He never gave you a thrill on the gallops but then he never did anything except on a racecourse. In fact I was very reluctant to run him because I thought he would be last.' Turnell had second

THE CHAMPION HURDLE

thoughts and entered Salmon Spray for Newbury's Challow Hurdle in January 1962. 'He ran well and never looked back afterwards. He was a lovely horse, the kindest little horse imaginable.' Yet it was touch and go whether he was born at all.

He was bred by Bill Corry at Ballysax, near Kilcullen, from his mare Fly Book who, when offered for sale as a three-year-old, was found to have a dicky heart and her owner told the vet, Bob Griffin, to shoot her. Instead Griffin showed her to Corry and the owner let her go for a 'luckpenny'. The heart gave no further trouble and before her death in 1962 she produced five winners from her six foals to race (all by Vulgan), who also included Larbawn, winner of two Whitbreads.

Like his mother, Salmon Spray had stared death in the face, for as he was being loaded as a foal he got loose and jumped four strands of barbed wire. Mercifully he was captured with not a mark on him. Sold privately as a yearling for £650, his resale at three fell through when he was 'spun' for his wind. Eventually Paddy Murphy took a chance and, after he had passed the vet, sold him to Halley.

Bob Turnell came from a farming family near Wellingborough and his entire life had revolved round horses and racing. Apprenticed at the age of 12 to Gil Bennett ('He was the hardest man to work for in racing that's ever been known'), six years elapsed before he rode a winner, Elcho, in a Buckfastleigh hurdle when he beat no less than Georges Pellerin. After war service with the Royal Armoured Corps, Turnell established two significant contacts. In 1949 he became first jockey to Ivor Anthony of Wroughton and learnt the trainer's art from a maestro. Secondly, he got to know the Rogersons, winning the Grand Sefton for them on War Risk.

Turnell was a formidable trainer of jockeys in addition to horses. Jeff King came from Sir Gordon Richards, John Haine from school; one as forceful as the other was stylish. Haine taught himself to ride on a pony given him by his father and rode 30 winners on the Flat, his streamlined technique modelled on Scobie Breasley (who by coincidence rode Salmon Spray to his single victory on the Flat) and he was particularly effective over hurdles. Then came Turnell's son Andy. 'Father was a hard taskmaster but if you asked any of the jockeys who learned from him they'll tell you he was a terrific horseman.'

Salmon Spray's progress towards a third Champion Hurdle again

THE CHAMPION HURDLE

included a flirtation with fences. In Ascot's Black and White Chase he finished third, 17 lengths behind the winner, another white-faced chestnut. This was Flyingbolt, stablemate of Arkle and, at one point later on, rated to within 2lb of the greatest chaser ever seen. Not that he shared Arkle's amiable disposition. 'He was a real savage of a horse,' observed Pat Taaffe, 'though he got more sensible as he got older. A small child could walk into Arkle's box in absolute safety. No child, no man ever willingly stepped into Flyingbolt's . . . at least, not twice! He'd kick the eye out of your head! Even the guv'nor wouldn't go in without a stick.'

He was also a decent hurdler, winning two novices and the highly competitive Scalp Hurdle (in a canter from Height O' Fashion) prior to lifting a division of the Gloucestershire Hurdle by four lengths. Fences then became his game and by March 1966 he had won nine chases in a row. Aside from a pipe opener over hurdles in the autumn, in which he finished fourth, Flyingbolt had not tasted defeat in over 29 months. His Festival target was the Two-Mile Champion Chase but he was also entered for the Champion Hurdle and rumour insisted his participation (and even Arkle's at one time) was pretty certain if Tuesday's racing went according to plan. It did: Flyingbolt sauntered in by 15 lengths from Turnell's Flash Bulb, whose efforts to assist Salmon Spray by tiring Flyingbolt fell decidedly flat. Money poured on the Irishman for the Champion Hurdle and he was laid to lose thousands at 7/4, 2/1 and 15/8. As it happened he was very nearly withdrawn in error. When Mrs Dreaper rang Weatherbys to scratch him from the Gold Cup, in which he had been on standby in case some accident befell Arkle, the buzz of a carpet sweeper was coming down the line and the secretary misheard the name of the race. Fortunately, Mrs Dreaper requested confirmation and spotted the mistake.

Salmon Spray had won two of his hurdle races since the Black and White but Robber Baron narrowly beat him at Cheltenham in January and Johns-wort (and clinging mud) proved three lengths too good for him at a difference of 10lb in the National Spirit. Haine believed he was already beginning to lose 'a bit of his old dash'. He feared Sempervivum, second in the Schweppes, whom Jeff King rode for Fulke Walwyn. Little Kirriemuir, winner of his Wincanton prep race, was back to defend his crown, though Magic Court (who ended his career in hunter chases) was an absentee, while public sympathy again rode with the Queen Mother's candidate, on this

THE CHAMPION HURDLE

occasion Makaldar, a gutsy winner from Kirriemuir of the Mackeson Handicap Hurdle over course and distance in November.

Makaldar was unable to cheer Her Majesty, the race developing into the anticipated duel between Flyingbolt and Salmon Spray. Pat Taaffe kept his mount on the outer to avoid interference, moving up to dispute the lead at halfway. Then, just as he wanted to kick on down the hill, Flyingbolt made his one mistake, uprooting the fourth last and losing all his impetus. His ego bruised, Flyingbolt fought back and by the penultimate flight had regained the lead from Kirriemuir.

The champion fell, and to his right Taaffe saw the menacing sight of Salmon Spray's white face and knew the game was up. A mighty roar rebounded from Cleeve Hill as the crowd realised the 'unbeatable' Irishman was indeed beaten. Salmon Spray flew the last with a one-and-a-half-length advantage which he doubled in the run-in. Sempervivum finished fast to deprive a tiring Flyingbolt of second place.

It had, after all, proved third time lucky for Salmon Spray, a championship-winning feat hitherto unaccomplished. 'He made a couple of mistakes,' said Haine, 'but it didn't cost him ground. The only time I was worried was when we became boxed in approaching the second last – I had to sit and suffer until an opening came.' This was Salmon Spray's twelfth hurdle race victory and, in fact, the last of any kind. Injury restricted him to one outing the following season and although he ran seventh in 1968 his attentions were mostly directed towards chasing. Unhappily, in May 1970, while still in training, he split his gut and had to be destroyed. Flyingbolt's period of glory was also drawing to a close. After winning the Irish National he was laid low by brucellosis, a blood disorder which nearly killed him. He won only once more, and that some three years later. Though the likes of Brown Jack, Le Paillon, Aurelius or Sea Pigeon might dispute his claim to be the best horse to have contested a Champion Hurdle because of their exploits on the Flat, Flyingbolt's right to be regarded the greatest jumper seems undeniable.

The TWW Hurdle at Cheltenham, in which Salmon Spray made his solitary appearance of the 1966–67 season, went to Makaldar. A lop-eared chestnut, he had been spotted in an Auteuil hurdle by Cazalet's French 'scout' Colonel Bobinski. Although he ran poorly in the 1966 championship, the combination of Cheltenham's

THE CHAMPION HURDLE

demanding finish and the promise of his favourite soft ground made him a leading ante-post choice. However, he failed to reach the Festival with reputation untarnished. At Sandown in December he could not concede 10lb to a rejuvenated Beaver II. The former Price hurdler, who came as a 'present' in one of Price's French deals because he was a rig and promptly beat the Findon first string Catapult in the 1962 Triumph, now resided with Ken Cundell. By a miracle of training, Cundell brought the little eight-year-old back after two years of nagging leg trouble to firstly win the Rank Challenge Cup and then defeat Makaldar. Ten days after this taxing encounter, perhaps too soon in retrospect, Makaldar was again beaten, in Kempton's NH Centenary Cup Hurdle, won by Saucy Kit. Given a long rest, Makaldar resumed at Newbury on 3 March and, on soft ground, pulverised the opposition in the Eastleigh Hurdle despite his 12st 7lb. Saucy Kit had been under a cloud since Kempton and was denied another outing.

His trainer was Miles Henry Easterby, universally known as Peter, who learnt the tools of his trade assisting his uncle, Walter, and honed them during a three-year stint with Frank Hartigan. A thorough grounding in the crafts of horsemanship was completed by service with the Royal Veterinary Corps and race-riding in point-to-points. Taking out a licence to train in 1950, Easterby quickly revealed the driving personality that would lead to fame and fortune. In order to attend the 1951 Newmarket Sales, he cycled five miles for a lift in Billy Dutton's horsebox, accomplishing the return journey courtesy of a furniture van, corporation bus and his trusty bike. Easterby had purchased three yearlings for 280 guineas and, though renowned as a man of few words, sold them within 24 hours of his return to Great Habton. He made his name on the Flat and in 1965 won the Lincoln with Old Tom and Royal Ascot's King's Stand with Goldhill, two of the fifty-five successes which made him the North's leading trainer that season. 'I've had more Flat than jumping winners. I think of myself as a Flat trainer. I just happen to have had a jumping star or two.'

Saucy Kit was a product of the Sassoon Studs in Ireland and, trained by Mickey Rogers, he managed to lose his maiden as a three-year-old in 1964, insufficient, however, to save him from the sales. Bidding for his brother-in-law David Dick, Easterby got him for 700 guineas. Dick trained the horse to win three hurdle races before he cracked a navicular bone during the 1965 Flat season. Somehow

THE CHAMPION HURDLE

Easterby coaxed Saucy Kit back into the firing line and a year later he ran out the 25/1 winner of Beverley's George Habbershaw Trophy for his new owner, Lloyds underwriter Kenneth Alder, who originally took a shine to him when attending the Curragh to watch stablemate Santa Claus win the Irish Derby. Alder had to pay three times that 1964 valuation to get his horse. A badly bruised foot and the incessant rain made Saucy Kit's participation in the championship doubtful right up to the last minute. Then, out came the sun and the bruise and, his own gallops waterlogged, Easterby gave Saucy Kit some sharp exercise round a local golf course. With a strong wind working in his favour (though not Makaldar's), he represented a sound each-way investment at 100/6. 'I didn't have a penny on him,' bemoaned Alder. 'I tried to strike a bet of £1,000 to £25 last week but could not get on!'

Despite the change in the weather, Makaldar started favourite at 11/4, followed by Beaver and Johns-wort at 10s, with Aurelius, an especially fascinating customer from Ken Cundell's yard, at 18/1. Several horses have competed in the Champion Hurdle after running in an English Classic on the Flat but to Aurelius falls the unique distinction of actually winning one, namely the 1961 St Leger. A big white-faced bay, Aurelius displayed signs of eccentricity even before he retired to stud. After failing to get any of his mares in foal he returned to the track and, gelded, had won three hurdle races the previous season, including one at Ascot where he had won the King Edward VII and Hardwicke Stakes in his prime. His victory in a 1968 steeplechase completed an Ascot treble unlikely of repetition.

The rapid amelioration of the going quite possibly affected the outcome of the race, preventing the success for the Queen Mother that was the fervent wish of every impartial racegoer. Worcran was put in to make the pace for Makaldar but experienced difficulty threading his way through the large field. By the time he reached the front passing the stands, Sempervivum had already crashed out of the contest at the first, breaking Tom Jennings' collarbone. Worcran's tenure was brief. Along the top of the hill Kirriemuir and Johns-wort vied for the lead chased by Makaldar, Rackham and Saucy Kit.

At the second last any number of horses held a winning chance, and with rival factions roaring on their respective favourites the din soared to fever pitch when Makaldar could be see making progress

THE CHAMPION HURDLE

on the inside. Saucy Kit and the curiously named Irish gelding Talgo Abbess raced nip and tuck towards the last with the mercurial Aurelius, who had extricated himself from the pack, jumping the hurdle in third place ahead of Makaldar.

Roy Edwards drove Saucy Kit over the last for all he was worth and the Yorkshire horse landed running. Makaldar and Aurelius collared Talgo Abbess but, after going a length up on the royal horse, Aurelius hung left and bored into Makaldar, causing him to be jerked up abruptly. At the post Saucy Kit had four lengths to spare over Aurelius, whose disqualification was inevitable. But for the attentions of Aurelius, Makaldar would have finished closer to the winner but certainly would not have embarrassed him. 'I was messed about and had trouble at the top of the hill,' reported jockey David Mould. Sadly, the race came one day too late – had the championship been held on the Tuesday, as has so often been the case, Makaldar would have got the soft ground he loved.

For Roy Edwards everything went strictly according to plan. 'I definitely thought he'd win. We did some work in the morning and the going was 100 per cent perfect for him. He was a super jumper and had a good turn of foot. I never thought of any other horses; I knew of them, but never feared any of them.'

In 1968 there would be a horse to give Roy Edwards, and every other jockey, due reason for fear.

9

The Ultimate Champion

'The hurdlers were the star turn at Cheltenham,' declared *Stud & Stable's* report of the 1968 Festival, a comment understandable on two counts. Firstly, in view of the void left in the chasing world by the retirement of Arkle and, secondly, after a considerable interregnum, by the emergence of a young hurdler who 'stamped himself in most people's minds as the best that we have seen since Sir Ken'.

The recipient of this lavish praise was Persian War, at the age of five already the winner of ten hurdles worth £22,765, making him the leading money winner of all time over timber, and destined to emulate Hatton's Grace and Sir Ken as a triple champion. 'He was the ultimate champion. He proved he could do it on any going and he ran and won as a true champion should, forcing the pace the whole way,' maintains Colin Davies, who trained him to those Champion Hurdles. 'Had he been spared by his owner he would have been even better. When we put the tongue strap on Persian War, a few people said it was a pity we didn't put it on the owner!'

The owner in question was Henry Alper, chairman of Chadwick Stone & Co., a well-known firm of insurance loss assessors and valuers, who came closer to forging the kind of horse-owner relationship associated with Sceptre and Robert Sievier than anyone in living memory. Alper's knowledge of racing, however, was much less than Sievier's but they shared the same roller-coaster of argument, sensation, triumph and disaster. In his seven-year career over hurdles, for instance, Persian War had no fewer than six trainers and was beset by a plethora of physical disabilities yet still managed to win 18 races including virtually every top event in the calendar. By any standards Persian War easily fulfils the claims of Colin Davies but within the context of the aforementioned circumstances he becomes a champion of monumental stature. Even

THE CHAMPION HURDLE

Arkle's record would have suffered had he been subjected to the pressures placed on Persian War, for if ever there was an instance of the heart ruling the head — and make no mistake, Alper's love for his horse, which verged on fanaticism, was the root of the problem — it was this one.

Although some might argue that television has a lot to answer for, the medium has benefited National Hunt racing to a considerable degree by introducing its thrills and spectacle to the fireside viewer. One such viewer on 30 December 1966 was Henry Alper. The race under scrutiny was a humble novices' hurdle at Newbury which turned into a procession when a big, not particularly handsome, bay animal detached itself from the pack and sped down the straight to win by six lengths. Cupid's arrow struck Alper with a vengeance. He was smitten. There and then he determined to buy the object of his desire and instructed his trainer, Brian Swift, to approach Tom Masson, who trained the gelding for Donald Leyland-Naylor. 'Son, you can buy anything from me except my mother,' said Masson, 'but you will have to dig deep for Persian War.' Due to illness, Leyland-Naylor found it increasingly difficult to go racing and inquiries had been tentatively extended in the direction of the Queen Mother as a possible purchaser. However, Alper did 'dig deep' and got his heart's desire for £9,000, the highest price paid for a hurdler up to that time, but a bargain all the same.

Persian War was a stoutly bred product of Astor bloodlines, being by Persian Gulf out of the Chanteur mare Warning, a coarse, big-boned individual with a plain head. The best Warning could do on the track was a third place, but of her six foals five were good winners and they included Sartorius (fourth in the Gold Cup) and Escort (fourth in the Derby). Persian War, a small and weak-legged foal, proved her seventh and last. In looks he resembled his mother more than the elegant, beautifully made Persian Gulf and once put into training with Dick Hern it seemed he also inherited her lack of ability. In keeping with Astor policy this cost Persian War his manhood. He contrived to win a couple of long-distance races as a three-year-old but if he possessed any future as a racehorse it would be over hurdles. Accordingly, he was sent up to the Newmarket Sales in September 1966 where the Lewes trainer Tom Masson, who had previously worked wonders with another Astor reject in Shatter, bought him for 3,600 guineas.

THE CHAMPION HURDLE

Persian War made his début over hurdles at Ascot in October. He did not jump too cleverly, recouping a lot of ground towards the finish to grab second place. Nevertheless, he got the message, winning both his next two races by 15 lengths. Masson immediately backed him to win the Champion Hurdle four months hence. Persian War was denied the opportunity of becoming the first four-year-old to win the title in peacetime since Brown Tony because his next race was the Kintbury Novices' Hurdle at Newbury.

Sporting the claret and blue colours of Alper's other love, West Ham FC, Persian War continued to sweep almost all before him from his new home at Brian Swift's Saddlecombe Farm Stables near Epsom. Swift had been assistant to Staff Ingham, one of whose pupils was Jimmy Uttley, the son of a Lancashire dairy farmer who later schooled Persian War on the Sussex Downs for Tom Masson. He was to be Persian War's new jockey. 'When Brian went on his own he was a Flat trainer but he had one or two jumpers, so I started riding his jumpers and it went on from there. Brian went to look at Persian War and Tom Masson advised him not to buy the horse! He was half a cripple, the first impression of riding him would put you off. He was a very poor-actioned horse – but the engine worked!'

Uttley and Persian War collected four races in the 1966–67 season, including both the prestigious juvenile hurdles, namely the Victor Ludorum at Haydock and the Daily Express Triumph at Cheltenham. The one setback occurred between these two when he clattered a hurdle at Kempton, striking the ground with his head, and returned minus two teeth and with a severely gashed tongue.

Persian War picked up where he left off, galloping his rivals into the ground to win by 25 lengths at Newbury in late October. The following Saturday his connections were reminded how racing's gods dislike being taken for granted. On a foul day at Cheltenham, Persian War slipped on take-off, hit the top bar with his head and screwed sideways to slither along the ground. Jimmy Uttley was mortified. 'I thought he was dead. He slid for all of 20 yards and there was a strange stillness as he lay there, completely motionless.'

The imperturbable Persian War soon recovered only to find himself, not for the last time, in the middle of a right old to-do. A foot-and-mouth epidemic had halted racing and Alper decided it would be a good idea for his horse to compete at Cagnes-sur-Mer. Swift was none too keen and after differences of opinion as to whose

THE CHAMPION HURDLE

stable in France Persian War should be sent to, owner and trainer parted company.

While at Chantilly, Persian War contracted a severe internal chill and was in a sorry state when he arrived at the Chepstow yard of the man selected to be his new trainer. Having flown planes from the decks of aircraft carriers, driven racing cars and successfully negotiated the Grand National fences, Colin Davies possessed the phlegmatic spirit necessary to keep Alper's restless feet firmly anchored to the ground. Slowly, and gently, brought back to his peak, Persian War carried top weight into a place in two handicaps prior to his first target, the Schweppes, in which he had been allotted 11st 13lb.

Among his 32 opponents was Ryan Price's Major Rose, who received 5lb. The Captain had netted four of the first five Schweppes, not without the odd bit of controversy, and had no doubts Major Rose would provide another. The six-year-old had cost him £250. 'I really don't know what I bought him for – he had very little bone really. He couldn't jump very well, he'd get from one side to the other, but he wasn't a natural.' In actual fact, Price regarded Major Rose as a Flat horse. He had won a Newbury Autumn Cup and eventually added a Chester Cup and Cesarewitch. Yet he was no mean hurdler, opening his account with three wins in 1966–67 and taking the scalp of Saucy Kit (albeit in receipt of two stone). Major Rose had not run over hurdles since, but such was the charisma of his trainer that he started second favourite to Persian War. Locking horns at the last, victory went to Persian War by half a length. No horse has carried more weight to victory than the five-year-old Persian War.

The going at Cheltenham was firm and as Persian War's best form had all been on soft he did not start favourite for the Champion Hurdle, that privilege being accorded Tom Jones's lightly raced Chorus II, winner of the Ackerman Skeaping Hurdle at Sandown. Major Rose missed the race, as did Kirriemuir, who retired to the hunting fields of Leicestershire and, ultimately, Ireland.

At no stage were the Alper colours not in the driving seat. Straight Point led until his stable companion loomed up on his outside with a mile to run. On the descent Saucy Kit nearly reached Persian War's quarters but made a dreadful hash of the second last, throwing Roy Edwards into the air. 'He jumped the hurdle too well

THE CHAMPION HURDLE

and landed on his belly. I'm sure he'd have won.' Coming to the last, Chorus delivered the final challenge yet, doggedly though he persevered, he could not reduce Persian War's four-length superiority. Firm ground or no, Persian War sprinted home with Uttley patting his head. The inspirational decision of Colin Davies to give him a course of five-furlong sprinting had undoubtedly sharpened his speed.

'Here beyond argument was a truly great performance,' wrote John Lawrence (now Lord Oaksey) in *Horse and Hound*, 'a new name to conjure with and a name which, barring accidents, will be in the headlines for many years to come.' One which would not was Saucy Kit. He ran once more before retiring to the Blakeley Stud, near Shrewsbury, managed by none other than his faithful partner Roy Edwards. 'He was a super horse and loved grey mares. He was covering a grey one day in 1980 when he rolled off dead. And she got in foal!'

John Lawrence's comments were prophetic in more ways than he could have imagined. Persian War and his owner were seldom out of the headlines throughout the next three seasons. Alper decided to win the French Champion Hurdle with his star, an admirable sentiment though foolishly brave considering the factors involved – the longer distance, the blistering heat of high summer, the furious pace. The expedition ended in honourable failure as Persian War finished third, after leading over 15 of the 16 obstacles.

Nonetheless, Persian War subsequently became the first hurdler to earn the Horse of the Year title and make a celebrity appearance at the Horse of the Year Show. The new season began ominously. He slipped and badly lamed himself at Worcester. It transpired that he had fractured his femur and chipped a piece of bone off its end. Confined to his box for a month he was unable to race until 1 February.

If any single moment elevated Persian War to superstar status it was the Lonsdale Hurdle at Kempton. Davies believed him to be no more than 75 per cent fit, he had 12st 7lb to carry and the tight track had never been his cup of tea. No matter; he came hurtling up the straight to win by three lengths and be met by a rapturous reception. John Lawrence, typically, best translated everyone's thoughts into words: 'Suddenly, unpredictably, like a child who opens a dull-looking parcel and finds a glittering, dreamed-of toy, the National Hunt world found a brand-new hero to worship last

THE CHAMPION HURDLE

week. This, all things considered, was the finest performance put up by a hurdler since Sir Ken – and probably the finest by any jumper since Arkle.'

Denied the opportunity of fêting Persian War in the Schweppes by the onset of frost, the racing public made do with increasing its knowledge of Persian War the character. A great 'doer' who happily put away 20lb of corn a day, and an endless stream of carrots besides, Persian War was the mildest of creatures in his box. This serenity was carried over to the training grounds where he rarely exerted himself, although like Sir Ken he often gave his companions (either a donkey or Alper's Bobby Moore) a hard time in the summer paddocks. His most amusing idiosyncrasy on holiday at Chepstow was to walk across to the head lad's cottage every morning and kick on the door until rewarded with a handful of carrots. Boredom was his greatest enemy. One summer he calmly barged open the gate of his paddock, strolled directly to his own box and stood there, obviously asking to be admitted.

Persian War's last race before a second Champion Hurdle was to be Wincanton's Kingswell Hurdle on 27 February. A week beforehand he pricked his off-hind and, showing some allergy to either the tetanus or penicillin jabs he received as treatment, ran a temperature of 103° F on the eve of the race. Although he appeared recovered the following afternoon and took his chance, he was never in the hunt. Disaster became débâcle in view of the fact that large sections of the public had been unaware of the champion's recent ailments. Should Persian War have run? Did the situation merit a press release? Once more controversy raged around Henry Alper's head.

But Persian War was an indefatigable character and he quickly threw off any ill effects. March opened to torrents of rain and the Cheltenham going was indescribably heavy, so holding that the Gloucestershire Hurdle, run over the championship course, was run in a time 28 seconds above average.

The biggest danger to Persian War was thought to be Ireland's L'Escargot, a confirmed mudlark, who had trotted up in the Scalp Hurdle, and he was backed down from 7s to 11/2 second favourite. Persian War hardened from 2/1 to 6/4 despite no favourite having won for eight years.

The pacemaking chore fell to Bobby Moore. Acquitting himself nobly over the first five flights, he gave way to Supermaster at the

THE CHAMPION HURDLE

sixth. By now the field was well strung out and only L'Escargot, Drumikill, Into View, Sempervivum and Persian War were going to play a part in the outcome. The northerner Drumikill, who had won his last three races all on soft, took command at the next and was still there approaching the last, fractionally ahead of Persian War. The remainder were now toiling. 'I thought Drumikill was really going to make things tough for a moment between the last two obstacles,' Uttley later recalled, 'but Persian War must have had his measure when that horse took the hurdle by its roots. My fellow put in a super jump and I knew then we were home and dried.' The drama proved too heady for Alper who collapsed to the ground totally drained. Persian War's four-length success reportedly landed him £25,000 in bets. The time of four minutes 41.8 seconds remains the slowest in Champion Hurdle history. Less than three weeks later Persian War staked further claim to immortality by winning the Welsh Champion Hurdle on contrasting rock-hard ground in concession of weight to all his rivals. 'He did it in three strides. It really was a marvellous performance,' said Davies.

Intense elation was followed, in customary Persian War fashion, by darkest despair. After falling in his warm-up race for another tilt at the French Champion Hurdle, Alper unwisely ran him on the Flat in September on exceptionally hard ground. Persian War, far from fit, suffered an over-reach and was found to have thrown a splint on his near-fore and jarred the joint on his off-fore. He was lame for a month, and *hors de combat* for three.

When he resumed, in Sandown's Gold Bond Hurdle, he was confronted by yet another problem, this time in his wind. In spite of this handicap, he ran creditably behind the Queen Mother's four-year-old Escalus. The latter won again at Ascot but on Boxing Day was put firmly in his place by a second promising juvenile in Fred Rimell's Coral Diver. Although no oil painting, being very leggy and lacking depth, Coral Diver was a neat jumper and this victory constituted his sixth in eight starts.

The team of owner Bryan Jenks, trainer Fred Rimell and jockey Terry Biddlecombe were doubly blessed. Normandy, a four-year-old entire, had lost only one of eight races. He, too, was a brilliant jumper and Rimell elected to challenge the champion in the newly instituted Irish Sweeps Hurdle at Fairyhouse on 27 December. Persian War ran with a tongue strap to alleviate the soft palate trouble which was causing him to make a gurgling noise under

THE CHAMPION HURDLE

pressure. Starting clear favourite, he had to concede his old foe Major Rose 11lb and Normandy 12lb. The race was full of incident. Persian War 'gurgled' after one and a half miles and lost his position and was given time to recover his breath before Uttley attempted to force his way between the two leaders at the final flight. One of them was Normandy on whom Biddlecombe had no intention of enlarging the gap for Persian War to pass. Under an inspired ride, Normandy won by a neck from Orient War with a weary Persian War (struck on the head by Biddlecombe's whip into the bargain) one and a half lengths back in third. Although the stewards allegedly examined the patrol film they decided not to take action.

Persian War competed in three more races before the championship without success. At Haydock he ran minus the tongue strap and finished out of a place for the first time (bar a fall) in his career; in the Lonsdale (equipped with the tongue strap again) he ran far better to be beaten only one and a half lengths in concession of 31lb and, finally, in Nottingham's City Trial Hurdle, Orient War pipped him a short head in receipt of 12lb. Davies, for one, was far from discouraged. 'That was a very good workout; we are much more hopeful now.' The race that mattered was still to come and, after a sparkling gallop on the Sunday, confidence in the champion's camp knew no bounds. 'Persian War has been wrong all season but he has come right back to his best at last.' He had not won a race for 11 months but as the race drew nearer more and more people decided there was nothing else of his quality in the field. The books went 8/1 bar the favourite at 5/4.

As in 1968 the Alper colours led throughout. Bobby Moore tugged his stablemate to the fifth, whereupon Uttley sent the favourite on. The Imperial Cup winner Solomon II pressed him hard down the hill, while Escalus and Coral Diver also had a cut. Over the last Persian War was still two lengths to the good and only Major Rose, making relentless progress up the rails, posed any threat. The champion was more than a match for anything thrown at him and, striding up the hill in the manner of Sir Ken, he comfortably resisted Major Rose by one and a half lengths. 'I could hear my pursuers slapping and banging,' said Uttley, 'and halfway to the winning post Persian War started to look around at the cheering crowds. The old boy gave me a great ride and what a wonderful job the guv'nor did with him.' The season's tribulations finally took their toll on Davies who, sickening from yellow

THE CHAMPION HURDLE

jaundice, had to be helped to his car and driven home straight after racing.

Persian War had joined the immortals. He achieved his hat-trick on extremes of ground (firm, heavy, good to yielding) and in the most testing of personal circumstances. 'He was the best hurdler I've ever seen,' averred Colin Davies right up until his death in October 1996. 'Each year I watch for a better one but so far there has been nothing to touch him.'

Whether Persian War was the best Champion Hurdle winner is a matter for the form pundits and number crunchers (Timeform rate him 3lb behind Night Nurse and one behind Monksfield and Istabraq), but greatness cannot be measured by talk – however learned – of pounds and lengths alone. In a Champions' Champion Hurdle poll conducted by the *Racing Post* in 1996, Persian War was priced up by Ladbrokes as 7/1 fifth best in the field of 14 – yet he came out on top, followed in order by Night Nurse (5/2 favourite), Bula (4/1), Sea Pigeon (9/2), Monksfield (4/1), See You Then, Dawn Run, Alderbrook, Lanzarote, Comedy of Errors, Royal Gait, Gaye Brief, Morley Street and Salmon Spray. Just as fascinating were the canvassed opinions of various winning trainers and jockeys. Neither John Francome (Sea Pigeon), Jonjo O'Neill (Sea Pigeon/Dawn Run) nor Steve Smith Eccles (See You Then) fell victim to understandable bias in favour of their own victorious partners. No, they voted for Persian War. So did Peter Scudamore. Likewise trainers Toby Balding (Morley Street), Kim Bailey (Alderbrook) and – most significantly of all – so did Peter Easterby, the man who prepared Night Nurse and Sea Pigeon. 'It's very hard to compare horses from different generations, and if I put one of mine on top I would be accused of being biased,' he explained. 'But I think Persian War is the best of this lot anyway! He was a helluva horse, but I also rate Sea Pigeon as one of the best. He wouldn't be far behind him and he might even beat Persian War if his run was timed right. Night Nurse would stretch them and they would all know they had been in a race, and Monksfield was a tough bugger so he would have to finish thereabouts.'

One horse who might conceivably 'touch Persian War' in the next Champion Hurdle was Fred Winter's unbeaten Bula. Persian War accepted this gauntlet from a different base. Henry Alper's relationship with his trainers was invariably as taut as piano wire – in June 1970 the Davies wire finally snapped.

10

Uplands versus Kinnersley

The Roman poet Ovid had in mind the thrill of an entirely different kind of chase when he wrote, 'A horse never runs so fast as when he has other horses to catch up and outpace.' Yet his perceptive view of love could equally describe the racing character of Bula who, ably assisted by Paul Kelleway's waiting tactics, regularly gave his opponents a head start only to cut them down with a dazzling flash of speed from the last hurdle. The Bula–Kelleway game plan was so effective that their Champion Hurdle victory of 1971 proved the twelfth in an unbeaten sequence of thirteen spread over two seasons.

If Persian War's style of running resembled the relentless power of a Sherman tank, Bula epitomised a Lamborghini with a tricky clutch. Once in gear, however, Bula could really motor. 'He could turn the engine on at the death,' said Kelleway, 'because he was only racing for 100 yards in the whole race.' Aside from this contrast, Bula and Persian War had much in common, for they were both magnificent champions. There would be no period of anticlimax at the demise of a triple champion on this occasion as there had after the defeat of Sir Ken. A golden era had begun which would encompass 14 championships and eclipse even the National Spirit–Hatton's Grace–Sir Ken years for duration and quality.

Bula also provided Fred Winter with his first Champion Hurdler as a trainer and was the first great horse to inhabit his Uplands stable in Upper Lambourn. His training career had exploded into action with two successive Grand National winners but, game as they were, neither Jay Trump nor Anglo were in Bula's class.

'Bula was an ideal National Hunt horse,' says Winter, 'but his lengthy sequence of victories absolutely amazed me because he never showed his true ability at home.' The only person, it seems, who recognised the seeds of greatness in him was former stable

THE CHAMPION HURDLE

jockey Bobby Beasley, his partner in some early workouts. 'There was a feel of power and possible acceleration – it was a feeling you get with some. The product of experience, I suppose.' Bula's lad, Vincent Brooks, deemed the 'luckiest lad in racing' since he also did Pendil, confirms his idiosyncratic nature. 'I used to ride him on his own most of the time because he was such a lunatic! He'd gallop off down the road with you for no apparent reason. He was such a stubborn so-and-so! He had a mind of his own. Bula was a Christian in his box, much better than Pendil, who had a bit of a mad streak about him. Bula would rather lick you than bite you.'

Bula entered Brooks' care in 1969. He had cost 1,350 guineas as an unbroken three-year-old when bought at Ballsbridge by Winter's old friend and adversary Martin Molony for Captain Bill Edwards-Heathcote. 'Most lads would not have looked at him twice,' remembers Brooks. 'He was big, ugly and fat, and after a week no one wanted him. Really he was more like a warhorse than a racehorse but I was one short and so was asked to do him.' Neither was Bula's pedigree much to enthuse over. He was the first foal of the affectionately named Pongo's Fancy, the winner of a bumper at Tuam and a hurdle at Mallow, whose own dam never ran. Bula's sire, Raincheck, ran unplaced in the 1951 Derby and won twice over hurdles before standing at stud in Ireland. A year after his purchase Bula was ready to make his début in a Lingfield novices' hurdle.

'He'd done nothing out of the ordinary at home,' says Winter, 'but at the top of the hill I turned to his owner and said, "Do you mind if he wins, because I think he will." He flew in without being touched.' Kelleway had been injured in the previous race and Winter asked his substitute, Stan Mellor, to teach the horse as best he could since he was not a good jumper. Bula responded by kicking the first three hurdles out of the ground, turned for home in third place and sprinted past the leader to win with breathtaking ease by six lengths. 'Fred told me he was a big, backward yoke, and he wanted to find out if he was worth taking home!' recalls Mellor. 'Jeff King was riding some hotpot and down at the start he asked me about Bula and I said not to bother about us as he was just having a first run. I have never forgotten the look Jeff gave me as we went by him at the last!' This devastating late burst set the pattern for most of Bula's races and in Paul Kelleway he possessed the ideal partner for exploiting such a weapon to the full.

THE CHAMPION HURDLE

Confident, brash (had he not spent nine years on and off with Ryan Price?) and something of a dab-hand with quirky horses (like his Gold Cup winner What a Myth), Kelleway fitted Bula like a glove. 'The Captain taught me to go for it. He always told me to make my own luck. I wasn't a fanny merchant. I never gave owners or trainers a tale. If a horse was a bastard I said so. I may not get the ride next time but we knew where we stood. What would I have become if I hadn't discovered horses? Getaway driver for the Kray twins most like.' Few jockeys would have the nerve to let Bula lob along at the rear of his field for as long as Kelleway but he had also spent time with Harry Wragg, the acknowledged master of the last-gasp challenge. 'When I took him down at Worcester on his second outing he was very warm and was white at the gate. I thought, this one's going to be a handful. So I let him switch off and he flew the last, winning by five lengths.'

Bula's novice season continued in this regal vein, with the rising star not seriously troubled for a single stride. He ran up a hat-trick at Wincanton and 24 hours before Persian War's third championship collected the Gloucestershire Hurdle by six lengths. His second campaign continued in the same swaggering manner though he occasionally had to show that besides talent he possessed buckets of courage. At Ascot he fought every inch of the way to beat Dondieu by a head and a few weeks later, in Sandown's Benson and Hedges Hurdle, he only got the upper hand over Moyne Road and Regit by two short heads. 'That was our closest call,' says Kelleway. 'He tore a boot off at the last and stopped dead.' After a more typical 15-length victory at Towcester, Bula was sent to Wincanton for his biggest test to date – a clash with Persian War.

It goes without saying that the triple champion's life had not been exactly uneventful since Cheltenham. Beaten into third place in the Welsh Champion Hurdle, he once more gave out gurgling noises and subsequently entered the Equine Research Centre at Newmarket where, in an effort to save his career, Robert Cook performed a revolutionary new operation necessitating 21 injections into the soft palate. If successful the injections harden the slackness and stop the tongue being 'swallowed'. Four teeth also required extraction. However, as a measure of what Persian War endured, only three could be dealt with – one took three hours to extract – on account of his losing so much blood. The champion weathered the storm with his customary fortitude only to find himself with a

THE CHAMPION HURDLE

new trainer. That Alper's dispute with Colin Davies was allegedly unconnected with Persian War scarcely mattered. In August he commenced training with Arthur Pitt at Epsom and proceeded to give ample evidence of rejuvenation. He won his first two races in October, finished fourth in the Fighting Fifth and travelled over to Fairyhouse to put the record straight in the Irish Sweeps Hurdle. Failing to concede 12lb to his old sparring partner Major Rose in the Oteley was no disgrace, but this was followed by a lethargic display in the Schweppes. The Kingwell brought Persian War as much luck in 1971 as it had in 1969. Receiving 4lb, Bula beat him ten lengths.

Persian War's hopes of hanging onto his crown lay in his love of the Cheltenham hill and the expectation of heavy ground which might take the sting out of Bula's famous finish. Persian War reportedly came fresh from a marvellous final gallop, unlike his notoriously lazy rival who had trailed behind Into View and Killiney in his last piece of work. When the latter proved an expensive failure in the Gloucestershire Hurdle, Fred Winter could be excused for feeling apprehensive.

He need not have worried. In the field of nine, the smallest since Sir Ken defeated six in 1953, the 15/8 favourite experienced no anxious moments whatsoever, storming up the stands rail to beat Persian War by four lengths. The old champion's pacemaker, Bowie's Brig, held sway until the second last, at which point Persian War disputed the lead with the Irishman Lockyersleigh, but hovering on the outside like some vulture at the end of Lent was Bula. He jumped the last in front from Persian War on the inner and Major Rose, who flattened the second last, challenging up the centre, but the two stalwarts had no answer to Bula's acceleration. Persian War won their private duel by a length, thereby confirming his superiority. Unless both horses were deteriorating at the same rate this showed Bula to be an exceptional champion. He put the issue beyond doubt in the Welsh Champion Hurdle by administering a third defeat to Persian War. He now boasted an unblemished record of 13 hurdle wins in a row.

For Persian War and Major Rose the fanfares ceased. Ryan Price's last representative in the championship ended up in a Welsh field, lame and unwanted, where, predictably, his former master came to the rescue. 'The farmer changed his mind and decided he didn't want to sell him to me. I had to go and get someone else to

THE CHAMPION HURDLE

buy him for me and had to pay £1,500! He had broken down so badly that he had to spend six months in his box before I could turn him out.'

Persian War was no more fortunate. He was on his travels again during the summer of 1971, moving to Dennis Rayson at Exning, from where he won his 18th and last race, the Latecomers' Hurdle worth £374 at Stratford in June 1972. It seems tragic when deities like Sir Ken and Persian War are allowed to plumb depths such as these. Even then Persian War's dignity was unsafe. After beating only one home in Cheltenham's Broadway Hurdle in January 1973, a career over fences was mooted which led to Alper and Rayson falling out. The horse was sent to Jack Gibson near Cheltenham but he hurt a leg and could not race again that season. The following year he was being optimistically prepared for a crack at the County Hurdle until a bruised leg finally brought about his retirement, just after his 11th birthday, no great age for most jumpers but for Persian War those 11 years must have seemed like 111. He spent ten happy years at the Genesis Green Stud where he had holidayed so often in the past and was put to sleep in September 1984, aged 21, when he began finding it difficult to get up and down. His heart lies buried beneath a headstone raised by his ever-loving owner.

The black cloud which frequently hung over Persian War now began to cast its shadow over Bula. His bubble had to burst eventually, although the pin's identity was totally unexpected. The villain of the piece was Happy Valley who, in receipt of three stone, beat Bula a neck on his seasonal début. He resumed winning ways in the Ackerman Skeaping Trophy (Persian War plodded round in the rear) but injured a leg and was incapacitated for three months. Fred Winter nursed Bula back into shape to win the Kingwell from the Irish Sweeps winner Kelanne, only to see him return with a bruised foot. Getting Bula to Cheltenham fit enough to defend his crown tested Winter's skill to the utmost, a fact from which Bula's eight-length victory should not be allowed to detract. Only Insurance (1932), and Istabraq (1998) have taken the championship by a wider margin.

Thanks to a massive injection of cash by Lloyds Bank, Bula's second title, at £15,648, was worth double the first. Eleven opposed him, notably Coral Diver, Kelanne, Canasta Lad (winner of the Cheltenham Trial) and the last two winners of the Daily Express Triumph Hurdle in Varma and Boxer. The latter hailed

THE CHAMPION HURDLE

from the stable of Ron Smyth who, better than most, knew the essential ingredients to make a Champion Hurdler. Boxer won his Triumph by an impressive five lengths and Smyth had actually toyed with the idea of pitting the four-year-old against Bula, Persian War and company in the 1971 championship.

With the ground soft, Bula was sent off an 11/8 favourite. Restrained at the rear of the field while Boxer and St Patrick's Blue cut out the running, Bula rapidly improved his position descending the hill towards the third last, always a tricky obstacle due to the gradient. Twelve months earlier Dondieu had thrown away his chance with an appalling mistake at this flight and Kelleway, sitting on his tail, now decided to pull the favourite out and follow Boxer instead. This manoeuvre was providential because Dondieu, possibly remembering last year, took off far too soon and broke his neck in a dreadful fall. In a trice the complexion of the race altered. Canasta Lad also toppled over, bringing down Garnishee and stopping Coral Diver in his tracks. It was only by about one horse's width that Bula slipped through unscathed on the inside but from then on the arrogance with which he trampled all over the opponents was awe-inspiring. Jumping up to Boxer at the second last, Kelleway held a 'double handful' and when he released Bula round the bend, the final ascent to the winning post constituted nothing less than a triumphal procession.

It seemed inconceivable that a race-fit Bula could be defeated by the current crop of hurdlers, yet the unfortunate Canasta Lad showed how costly a fall he had taken by beating Bula three-quarters of a length in the Welsh Champion Hurdle in receipt of 6lb. Bula twice comprehensively took his revenge on that horse the following season. However, back in third place on the second occasion, the Cheltenham Trial, was a strapping six-year-old trained by Fred Rimell named Comedy of Errors who, along with Bula's own stablemate Lanzarote (already considered his superior by some at Uplands), would make the champion's task of landing the treble enormously difficult.

For nigh on three seasons Comedy of Errors and Lanzarote vied for supremacy, their destinies seemingly intertwined by some invisible thread. Eight times these ambassadors of two mighty stables clashed, the spoils equally divided. These battles were waged in a chivalrous spirit which actually extended to both parties travelling over to Ireland together for the 1974 Sweeps Hurdle, staying in the

THE CHAMPION HURDLE

same hotel and permitting the two horses to work together on the morning of the race.

The affinity between Comedy of Errors and Lanzarote on the racecourse, which seldom exceeded a length or two, was repeated in their distaste for the hurdling championship's very arena. Comedy of Errors lost half his ten races at Cheltenham. 'He had a tendency to jump to the right,' says Bill Smith, his partner of 1973, 'which didn't help at Cheltenham. It wasn't his greatest track.' More to Comedy's liking was Newcastle, where he won three consecutive Fighting Fifth Hurdles. Lanzarote's sole victory round Cheltenham (from four attempts) was his 1974 Champion Hurdle. Fred Winter emphasises: 'The fact he won it was proof of his ability because he was so much better right-handed, in a different class completely.' At Kempton, Lanzarote was unbeaten in eight runs; at Ascot he lost just two from seven (both as a novice) and at Wincanton, after being brought down on his first start as a novice, he landed a hat-trick of Kingwell Hurdles. Their career records over hurdles are also remarkably alike. Comedy won 23 of his 48 races worth £94,708; Lanzarote 20 of 33 for £50,126. Thereafter the bond is severed. Comedy competed in one steeplechase and, though finishing second, did not look at home. Lanzarote, conversely, had always schooled brilliantly over fences (a frequently adopted ploy to wake him up for hurdling), and after winning three chases in the early part of 1977 earned a place in the Gold Cup field. Landing safely over the ninth, he faltered and crumpled to the ground. Tragically, he had broken his near-hind and had to be destroyed. 'He was without doubt the best horse I've trained,' maintains Winter, some praise from a man with yardsticks such as Pendil, Bula, Crisp and Killiney at his disposal.

Comedy's one year seniority helped him reach the top of the tree first. He had shown enough speed to win four times on the Flat, including the Edinburgh Gold Cup when trained by Tom Corrie, and as a son of the sprinter Goldhill was not considered jumping material but his dam, Comedy Actress, who had won the Lanark Silver Bell, was a fine big mare, just the type to breed jumpers. 'The stud groom said that when he was foaled he was one of the biggest and best he had ever seen,' said his breeder Elizabeth Sykes. 'I think his sire gave him that turn of foot at the end of his races and as for not being a jumper – from the age of a few weeks he

THE CHAMPION HURDLE

was jumping over things for fun and as a yearling went straight over a big thorn hedge to join some fillies on the other side.'

Fred Rimell had waited a long time to train a Champion Hurdler. Tokoroa, Coral Diver and Normandy had class but in Comedy of Errors he unearthed a gem of rare quality. He found him for Ted Wheatley, millionaire boss of Allied Carpets, who wanted a racehorse as a present for one of his partners. Wheatley forked out £12,000 for Comedy and Rimell was so besotted with him that he persuaded Wheatley to retain a half share, therefore ensuring he stayed at Kinnersley. Comedy did not make his hurdles début until the turn of his fifth year and then had six races, winning four of them (always with the formbook comment 'easily') and coming second in the other two.

The long-striding gelding was still growing and a bit of a baby at the start of his second season. His wolf teeth, which normally appear at the age of four, had yet to come through. His young jockey, Bill Smith, had also been in the wars. No stranger to Kinnersley, Smith had originally gone to Rimell at the age of 15 with the notion of becoming apprenticed, but after a month's trial ('I was so windy and homesick') he returned to his Hayling Island home and worked for 18 months in the Southsea branch of Moss Bros. Point-to-points and amateur races led to a professional licence in 1969 while a spare ride for Rimell on Zarib in the 1972 Triumph ensured his return to Kinnersley in succession to Terry Biddlecombe. Everything in Bill Smith's garden seemed rosy; that is until 27 April when, five weeks after his win on Zarib, his mount Lotus Land threw him on the way to the start at Devon and Exeter and he collided with a concrete post. Smith broke his left knee and cracked a shinbone in five places, was in hospital for a month and on crutches for three. Six months elapsed before he could take up his appointment with Rimell.

His racecourse introduction to Comedy of Errors came in Newcastle's Fighting Fifth which they won by six lengths from Easby Abbey. A second six-length canter in the Berkshire Hurdle preceded a clash with Bula in the Cheltenham Trial. The champion's appetite had been whetted by two wins and he summarily dealt with both his old adversary Canasta Lad and this newcomer by one and a half lengths and ten. Smith was not unduly perturbed. Comedy's wolf teeth, surfacing at last, were causing him some inconvenience. He was confident of revenge in the Irish Sweeps, but although Bula was

THE CHAMPION HURDLE

beaten six lengths, the concession of 4lb to Captain Christy proved well beyond him. Nicknamed Ireland's 'Jekyll and Hyde' by the press, Captain Christy was also likened to the little girl with the curl — when he was good he was very, very good but when he was bad he was horrid. Two attempts were necessary before he was broken as a three-year-old and then success only arrived after he had been starved into submission. The first time his trainer Pat Taaffe clipped him it took three days! The tearaway Captain had one more race before the Festival, the Scalp Hurdle, which he won by 15 lengths.

The two English horses recrossed the Irish Sea to lick their wounds. Neither was pressed in their preparatory races for the championship and the scene was set for a battle royal. Only eight faced the starter (not containing thankfully the unraced 17-year-old Prestidigitateur, bizarrely entered by his owner) and for the third time Bula (6/5 on) was favourite, one of five to be so honoured, of whom Sir Ken and Istabraq thrice succeeded in landing the odds (Free Fare and Another Flash were the other two). The cognoscenti had no reservations. 'Brilliant Bula to be triple champ' headlined the *Sporting Life*, all but one of whose tipsters made him their selection. Such trumpeting failed to discourage Bill Smith even though he had experienced a lean spell of late. 'I'd had a quieter season than I'd have liked but on the day I was never more confident. Fred Rimell just told me to do my best and not to fuss if he wasn't good enough to win.'

Peter Easterby's Easby Abbey led from tape till crossing the last. In hot pursuit was Captain Christy (the oddly quoted 84/40 second favourite) but Bill Smith could be detected on their near side winding up Comedy of Errors for a telling thrust up the hill. The Kinnersley pairing sprinted away to beat Easby Abbey by one and a half lengths with the Captain a further two in arrears. 'We tried new tactics and held him up,' moaned the latter's jockey Bobby Beasley, 'if we'd let him make the running as he liked he would have won.' Bula trailed in fifth, 'the old sparkle was missing and he was soundly trounced', said the *Life*. By this success Fred Rimell emulated Gerry Wilson and Fred Winter as the rider and trainer of a Champion Hurdler.

Fred Winter's hope that his champion's downfall was primarily due to the firm ground was shattered in the Welsh Champion Hurdle. Comedy gave Bula 6lb and beat him four lengths. After 21

THE CHAMPION HURDLE

victories for 26 starts, worth £44,334, Bula's future would be fences. Over the following four seasons he won 13 of his 25 chases and finished third in the 1975 Gold Cup before a crashing fall in the 1977 Two-Mile Champion Chase broke a bone in his off-fore shoulder. Somehow he struggled into a trailer, was bandaged, given painkillers and taken back to Uplands. 'He had severed a radial nerve in the shoulder as well,' says Winter, 'so he was in no pain but he got weaker and weaker, lost muscle and couldn't get up.' After eight weeks Winter and his vet Frank Mahon reluctantly agreed the kindest course was to put the old champion to rest. Later that morning a grim-faced Winter rode alongside Vincent Brooks at exercise and quietly broke the news he had been dreading. 'I was devastated. He'd been a large part of my life for so long and though I kept hoping, I knew the chances were slim and I was glad his suffering was over. They would not let me go near his box. When I went to work the next day the sight of his empty box was a dreadful thing.' The Cheltenham executive rightly commemorated a great champion by renaming the Trial Hurdle in his honour.

Another dangerous thorn was removed from Comedy of Errors' side when the enigmatic Captain Christy followed Bula over fences, to be replaced as Comedy's principal sparring partner by Lord Howard de Walden's home-bred Lanzarote. The almost black gelding was by Milesian out of the discourteously named Slag. Her first foal was a little chestnut called Scoria whom Lord Howard sold for £500 to see him win the Cesarewitch and Northumberland Plate. Scoria's second foal, Lanzarote's full brother Rio Tinto, had shown winning form over hurdles so that when Lanzarote failed to distinguish himself on the Flat (his solitary win in 11 outings came in a one mile seven furlongs maiden at Edinburgh) his future was never in doubt. 'I'm terribly ignorant about jumping,' his lordship said at the time. 'Although I'm usually abroad in the winter I thought jumping might be fun. I had a number of horses who were not very good on the Flat and one of my trainers said, "Why not send them to Fred Winter – he knows more about it than I do." So I just rang up and asked if he'd room. He said, "For you we'll build a box."'

Lanzarote made a quiet entry to the winter game, running only twice during 1971–72. In point of fact his trainer had worked wonders to get him this far as he was always dry in his coat and persistently afflicted by corns and back trouble. 'He looked like a

THE CHAMPION HURDLE

herring when he came to us but always had that charm, he wanted to do his best.' On his second appearance he made the successful acquaintance of Kempton Park in the hands of Paul Kelleway ('A big shell of a horse with the right idea but very weak') though it was agreed that Winter's young jockey John Francome would be his partner thereafter. They did not make the happiest of starts to the season and the responsibility of riding Lanzarote was entrusted to Uplands' new stable jockey Richard Pitman, who had waited long and patiently for his promotion. Back in the early 1960s it had taken him four years and 60 attempts to ride his first winner and he once rode 86 consecutive losers. Lady Luck now began to shine her torch in his direction. 'Lanzarote was much scopier than Pendil and was very exciting right from the start. He had tremendous speed and I've never been so fast as the day he won the Welsh Champion Hurdle. As an individual he was very placid. In short, he was Mr Nice Guy with a lot of ability.'

Lanzarote and Pitman immediately embarked on a ten-race winning spree which included the Imperial Cup under a post-war record weight of 12st 4lb and culminated in the 1974 Champion Hurdle. Significantly, Lanzarote gave Mon Plaisir 19lb and beat him a length at Sandown. Four days later the self-same Mon Plaisir finished less than four lengths behind Comedy of Errors in the Champion Hurdle. During 1973–74 Lanzarote literally swept aside all opposition, winning his five pre-Cheltenham races by a staggering aggregate of 54 lengths. However, such was the reigning champion's reputation that Lanzarote's price of 7/4 was still some three points longer than Comedy of Errors'. The champion had won a second Fighting Fifth and the Cheltenham Trial before collecting the Irish Sweeps with one of his most exhilarating displays. 'They tried to box him in,' recalls Smith, 'but he was built like a chaser and had such tremendous speed it didn't matter what they tried. He won pulling a cart by eight lengths.' Another canter round Nottingham brought him to the Festival cherry-ripe. The select field of seven has only been equalled post-war by Sir Ken's second championship, the two principals so dominating the remainder (one of whom was Lanzarote's pacemaker Calzado) that the betting went 25/1 bar the two. A tactical race seemed in prospect. Accordingly, Winter and Pitman had hatched a plan aimed at unseating the champion.

'The truth was that Lanzarote was not quite as good as Comedy,' says Pitman. 'We reasoned that the only way to beat him was to

THE CHAMPION HURDLE

get him at full stretch, test his stamina and show up his tendency to jump to the right – which would make him lose ground at left-handed Cheltenham. We put in a pacemaker and also figured that Fulke Walwyn's Brantridge Farmer would go on. But after one hurdle it was obvious that neither of them had the pace we needed. I had to put my head on the line and take it up much earlier than planned.'

Pitman set Lanzarote alight at the top of the hill and quickly stole a four-length advantage. With the champion off the bridle the Uplands plot seemed to be working, but just for a moment, as Comedy drew almost level at the second last, it looked as if he might hold on to his crown. Then, almost as swiftly, the illusion faded. Lanzarote inexorably regained the upper hand and, touching down slightly ahead over the final flight, he surged to the post a decisive three-length winner.

Winter was full of praise for his third Champion Hurdler in four years, confessing how worried he had been about the corns on Lanzarote's near-fore, which consequently had to be plated with a 'three-quarters' shoe. His feet were so dodgy that he was made to walk round the paddock on the grass rather than the tarmac. The Rimells had not been especially pleased with Bill Smith's riding. 'Fred thought he gave him too much leeway,' explained Mercy Rimell. 'Fred always believed that when you went past the water jump you wanted to be within striking distance of what you thought was your danger, and he was too far behind. Pitman stole a march on him, got first run down the hill and had really won his race at the second last. We never got within striking distance. I think he played into Lanzarote's hands. Comedy had got enormous speed but he didn't ride him to use it. That was the biggest disappointment we ever had.' However, Bill Smith remains convinced that Comedy of Errors was not himself that day. 'He was very sweaty at the start and even when we passed the water jump going down the back, I told Terry Biddlecombe on Brantridge Farmer that we were not going well. After three hurdles he couldn't go the pace and there was not one hurdler alive that could get him off the bit that soon. The horse who won the Sweeps would have trotted up.'

Smith had a point for with both horses at the height of their powers during the following season it was Comedy who prevailed in each of their three confrontations. In both the Cheltenham Trial, where Lanzarote hit the last, and the Sweeps, a length separated

THE CHAMPION HURDLE

them, but at a waterlogged Festival Lanzarote ran the worst race of his life to finish a bedraggled seventh as Comedy became the first Champion Hurdler to regain his title.

The Champion Hurdle capped a fine season for Comedy of Errors. Apart from an uncharacteristic fall on his début he boasted a faultless record in six races. By contrast, Lanzarote's season fell into two distinct halves. Before Cheltenham he won only twice and in addition to his losses against Comedy he was beaten by Tree Tangle at Sandown and ran appallingly in the Schweppes behind Tammuz. However, after the Festival Lanzarote gained his revenge on Tree Tangle and Tammuz in the Welsh Champion Hurdle and won the Sardan Long Distance Hurdle at Ascot. That Chepstow race confirmed the extent of his below-par displays in the Schweppes and Champion Hurdle because he now thrashed his Newbury and Cheltenham conquerors by over 15 lengths.

The Festival might so easily have been postponed and the fact that 13 of the scheduled 18 races were completed was a tribute to the ground staff. An ark seemed a more suitable conveyance than a horse in the circumstances and for safety reasons the flight of hurdles down the hill, normally the third last, was eliminated. The market went 10/1 bar the front two.

At first this replay of 1974's head-to-head duel followed the same storyline. Pitman slotted Lanzarote behind Calzado while Comedy of Errors was already being scrubbed along passing the stands. The plot then took a twist Pitman did not relish, for as Lanzarote took command running up the hill, Comedy was right on his tail. On the long, sweeping – now hurdle-less – descent, Lanzarote began to back-pedal. Comedy, partnered by Ken White, a quiet unsung hero of the weighing room who, appropriately enough for a Worcestershire lad, had become first jockey to the country's premier stable when Bill Smith switched to Fulke Walwyn, was moving up so smoothly that the bookies could start paying out. 'I knew they'd try the same tactics,' says White, 'but I had no qualms about the ground. I had to shut him off; I couldn't go too early and couldn't go too late. But he was at his peak in 1975, spot on. He had two gears – a good cruising pace to lay up, doing nothing, and an overdrive. He didn't come to life all at once, it took one hundred yards to get him wound up because he had such a big stride. When you got into overdrive you felt superior to everything else. When he was really A1 it was a fantastic feeling.

THE CHAMPION HURDLE

He was the greatest horse I rode. I was on him when he won his first hurdle at Nottingham and, what with Terry Biddlecombe and Bill Smith around, it was a pleasure to have the opportunity to get back on him just as he was coming to his peak.'

Tree Tangle led over the second-last but White could afford to swing wide rounding the bend. 'I was always conscious of him hanging to the right and tried to keep him covered up till the last so he wouldn't cross anything. I always tried to get him on the outside at the last.' Clear at the final obstacle, Comedy stormed up the stands rail in truly Homeric fashion, his 18th hurdle success enabling him to pass Arkle's National Hunt stakes earning record with a total of £79,509.

In his three seasons at the top only four horses (Bula, Canasta Lad, Captain Christy and Lanzarote) had beaten Comedy in any race other than his customary pipe-opener at Newbury. However, for both he and his alter ego Lanzarote, the sands of time were slipping away. A new generation of young bucks was waiting in the wings.

11

Six of the Best

In several respects Night Nurse was something of a bully, an intimidating, perpetually scowling, Churchillian type of individual who pounded his foes into helpless submission long before the winning post was reached, 'the machine of my career', according to his regular partner Paddy Broderick. On the other hand, forever wearing his heart on his sleeve, he was 'a tame lion, a kindly fighter', in the words of Jonjo O'Neill, who rode him later on, and became one of the most popular hurdlers since Trespasser and unquestionably one of the best. During the lifespan of Timeform's *Chasers and Hurdlers* annual, no hurdler has surpassed the 182 rating awarded Night Nurse in the 1976–77 season.

The late '70s and early '80s was a marvellous period for Peter Easterby. He collected three trainers' titles, over £500,0000 in winning prize-money and in Sea Pigeon was provided with a second champion, albeit as different from his stablemate as could be imagined. Whereas Night Nurse used the bludgeon on his opponents, Sea Pigeon preferred the stiletto to cold-bloodedly extinguish his victims with a short, sharp thrust on the flat.

O'Neill compared them thus: 'Night Nurse would take the obstacles in his stride not rising very high, just zipping over it at tremendous speed. He landed, switched on an extra engine which accelerated him away from the hurdle. Sea Pigeon was without doubt the fastest horse I rode. He was a tremendous speed merchant. It was just a matter of waiting on him. He was at his best when he was 85 or 90 per cent fit – better underdone than overcooked. When he was 100 per cent and really wound up he suffered from race nerves, sweated up, was too much on his toes and difficult to settle.'

Night Nurse and Sea Pigeon met six times but the latter only came out on top (twice) when Night Nurse's prowess as a hurdler

THE CHAMPION HURDLE

was declining. Easterby diplomatically refuses to pick between the pair. 'When Night Nurse was winning his championships, Sea Pigeon was behind. He wasn't good enough then, but he improved. Sea Pigeon was the more exciting horse because he used to come from behind. People love to see that.' Timeform place Sea Pigeon 7lb behind a peak-form Night Nurse, yet when Fred Winter and Fulke Walwyn, who between them have watched at close quarters all the great hurdlers for nigh on half a century, were asked in the summer of 1987 – quite independently – who was the most memorable Champion Hurdler in their experience, both unhesitatingly replied, 'Sea Pigeon.'

The Habton pair did not have the stage to themselves. Night Nurse had to unseat two formidable, if ageing, champions in Comedy of Errors and Lanzarote, and withstand fierce competition from assorted contemporaries besides Sea Pigeon. Chief among these perpetual bridesmaids, a veritable matron of honour one might say with due allowance for gender, was Bird's Nest, twice placed in a record-equalling six appearances between 1976 and 1981, a really quirky character whose innate ability would nevertheless have won him eight championships out of ten in any other era. Apart from Night Nurse only five Champion Hurdlers have exceeded his highest Timeform rating of 176, namely Lanzarote (177), Comedy of Errors (178), Persian War (179), Istabraq (180) and one of the six entires to win the Champion Hurdle, an Irish bay called Monksfield (180). Bred by mischance and neglected at the yearling sales because of his size and ungainly appearance, Monksfield made his detractors eat their words by dethroning Night Nurse and repelling Sea Pigeon. How Peter Easterby must have hated the sight of the little colt with the noble head and curious, round galloping action whom Night Nurse could only defeat once in five tries and Sea Pigeon once in six. These three mighty champions brought the curtain down on the glittering era initiated by Persian War in which the Champion Hurdlers illustrated their class and public appeal by securing 11 of the 14 National Hunt Horse of the Year awards.

When Monksfield's owner first clapped eyes on Night Nurse in action he thought him the best hurdler he had ever seen. Michael Mangan had every reason to be so impressed. Although Night Nurse could never string together as many consecutive victories as Sir Ken or Bula, no Champion Hurdler has gone through a championship campaign unbeaten in as many as eight races as he did in 1975–76.

THE CHAMPION HURDLE

Furthermore, in so doing he achieved a unique trawl of all four domestic championships by adding the Welsh, Scottish and Irish titles.

Like his two immediate predecessors, Night Nurse was bred with an eye to sprinting on the Flat. His sire Falcon won the New Stakes while his dam Florence Nightingale was by the Queen's useful miler Above Suspicion. Night Nurse was Florence Nightingale's fourth foal and all nine of her offspring to race have proved winners. He was the cheapest of the Cloghran Stud's seven yearlings to be sold at the 1972 Houghton Sales, fetching 1,300 guineas, and though well grown for a late May foal, Peter Easterby had great difficulty in finding an owner for him. 'He was a plain bugger then,' he confesses. Seven rejected him before Midlands businessman Edgar Rudkin was persuaded to sign a cheque and, says Easterby, 'I only sold him because the buyer was already over 90, almost blind and wore thick glasses!'

Easterby believed Night Nurse would make a decent hurdler but as Mr Rudkin did not wish to risk him over obstacles the horse was put up for sale after winning a Ripon maiden as a three-year-old. Fate then took a hand, for as Night Nurse was about to leave Great Habton, he was spun by a vet because of a suspected heart murmur. At this point Reg Spencer, a York estate agent who had admired Night Nurse from afar since that Ripon victory, offered Rudkin a small profit.

Once introduced to hurdles Night Nurse was in his element. He won five of his six starts before getting bogged down in the Daily Express Triumph. However, he was improving physically all the time and beginning to take some holding on the gallops (although he got lazier with age). At home he always wanted a lead, ducking and diving until he was allowed to drop behind, yet in a race he insisted on being out in front. 'Horses that go off in front and can relax doing it, that's all right,' explains Easterby, 'but the one that's tearing away won't win. Sea Pigeon was no good in front, hopeless! Always too keen. What made Night Nurse so special was he was a natural jumper, brilliant from the first time we ever schooled him. He was a very, very brave horse, hard and brave.'

Night Nurse soon issued a warning to the hurdling establishment that its days were numbered. He walloped Lanzarote by 17 lengths at Newbury and comfortably beat Comedy of Errors by two and a half lengths (with Sea Pigeon third) in the Fighting Fifth. However,

THE CHAMPION HURDLE

at terms better than weight for age this was all to be expected of any plausible Champion Hurdle contender. In the Sweeps, which Night Nurse won in record time, he again received 5lb more than weight for age from Comedy, who finished less than seven lengths behind in fourth after a bad run. Yet Night Nurse exuded such invincibility that neither champion was backed to beat him at levels in the championship itself. The fly in the ointment, and a virulent one, was that four-legged conundrum Bird's Nest, who had also defeated Comedy of Errors at Wolverhampton.

A rangy chestnut, Bird's Nest became the ablest hurdler to merit one of Timeform's famed 'squiggles'. Then, as soon as the cognoscenti wrote him off as fainthearted or unreliable, back Bird's Nest would come with another spectacular victory or two. 'He's genuine enough,' said trainer Bob Turnell in his defence, 'but he's no fool. If things don't suit him, he doesn't run well. He has a fairly serious heart murmur. The only time he swerves is when the old heart pinches him.' Turnell had handled one Champion Hurdler and had no doubt Bird's Nest was superior. At one time or another he lowered the colours of every class hurdler bar Monksfield. Unfortunately for Bird's Nest his clashes with Monksfield all came in the spring when he rarely produced his best form. 'His joints weren't very good,' explains jockey Andy Turnell, 'and I wonder whether he began to feel them a bit by the end of the season. Some said he didn't like Cheltenham but he won the Bula three times. He was such an exasperating horse, I couldn't work him out! He didn't always run to his best. He should have won a Champion Hurdle on his form in the trials. He was obviously quite clever and there was always a slight doubt about his resolution – one day he would run home straight as a gun and then another day, for no reason, you would find yourself heading for the bookies! But he was a tremendous horse on his day and had a lot of charisma.'

Sea Pigeon missed the championship. After a magnificent workout on Wetherby racecourse, in which he gave his companions 20 lengths' start and slaughtered them, he picked up a warble and developed a swollen shoulder. Gordon Richards, his trainer at the time, passionately believed Sea Pigeon could have beaten Night Nurse for speed on the prevailing firm ground. Perhaps he might, but the Pigeon would indeed have required wings because Night Nurse's performance was an awesome one, becoming the first winner since Victor Norman 40 years earlier to lead from pillar to post.

THE CHAMPION HURDLE

Paddy Broderick, who had not participated in a Champion Hurdle since his first ride on Pawnbroker in 1964, judged his gallop to perfection. For most of the way he kept Night Nurse two or three lengths ahead of the main bunch until asking him to quicken between the third and second last when Bird's Nest launched his challenge on the outside. The response was electrifying. Entering the straight Night Nurse had manufactured a four-length lead and, despite a shoddy jump at the final flight, never looked in danger of defeat, especially once Bird's Nest began to hang left up the hill. Flash Imp ran on from the back of the field to deprive Comedy of Errors (who would have preferred softer ground) of third place, with Lanzarote in fifth. 'I told Broderick to pile them up behind him and then kick on. What a grand horse. I reckon he's the best I've trained,' a jubilant Easterby told newsmen.

Broderick's victory was extremely popular. One of the great band of likeable, tough and underrated jump jockeys who are the backbone of the sport but seldom hit the headlines, he rode his first winner on his début, way back in June 1953. A native of County Westmeath, he quickly established a reputation for wonderful hands, an uncomplaining nature (however terrible the falls) and a genius for pitch and toss. He crossed the 'water' in 1961 and for eight years was linked with the North's legendary – in the truest sense of the word – trainer W.A. (Arthur) Stephenson (a cousin of Sir Ken's handler), for whom he won a Welsh Grand National on Rainbow Battle and a Mackeson Gold Cup on Pawnbroker. On three occasions Broderick was the leading northern jockey but it was not all plain sailing. A crashing fall from Stephenson's Dashing White Sergeant at Uttoxeter once rendered him unconscious for a fortnight. 'I remember waking up in Derby Hospital, telling them I was all right, and asking to go home. I shouldn't have done, but I did and I went home. It was right at the end of the season and I didn't ride again until midway through the next, and guess which horse W.A. put me on for my first ride back? Dashing White Sergeant. That was typical of Arthur. He wanted to test my nerve straightaway.'

When Night Nurse resumed in the autumn with a double which stretched his unbeaten sequence to ten, all sorts of records seemed endangered. Sensationally, after a 19-month period of absolute supremacy, Night Nurse lost two races in a row. In the Fighting Fifth he succumbed to Bird's Nest, who received only 4lb but

THE CHAMPION HURDLE

bolted in by no less than 15 lengths. Excuses were sought and there was talk of a back injury. The public did not have to wait long for the next instalment in the Night Nurse–Bird's Nest saga because they both contested Kempton's William Hill Christmas Hurdle. At levels, Night Nurse 'won' by a head but, in turn, Fulke Walwyn's Dramatist (receiving 3lb) pipped him by a neck.

With Night Nurse's ability to reproduce his best form on soft ground questionable, his indisputable right to a second Champion Hurdle became increasingly threatened by a wet spring. When a plan to send him to Ireland for the Erin Foods Champion Hurdle was abandoned at the last moment after the ground became heavy, it appeared his connections held similar reservations. That he once more led throughout the championship, at a Festival soaked by 24 hours of incessant rain and lashed by gale-force winds, was an extraordinary tribute to his valour, hurdling technique and class. Moreover, this was a Champion Hurdle of immense quality. The ten runners included Night Nurse's new stablemate Sea Pigeon, Bird's Nest and the Turnell second string Beacon Light, Dramatist and two fancied Irishmen, Master Monday and Monksfield. With the exception of Monksfield, all the principals were at their very peak. The notable absentees were Lanzarote, switched to fences, and Comedy of Errors, now a light of former years, who went for the three-mile Lloyd's Bank Hurdle instead. Sadly, he could only finish fifth (he came back lame) and after a bleak 1977–78 season he retired to Kinnersley as Mercy Rimell's hack.

'He looks like a show horse and his manners are marvellous,' she said. 'I came up in the showing world, and he would have won any middleweight hunter class. He was certainly the best horse we ever had at Kinnersley, even though for a hurdle-race horse he's massive at 17.1 hands. He was never the best jumper in the world because he was so big, but because he was so big he could get away with it. If he made an error it didn't make much difference to him, he was such a giant he could get away with kicking a few hurdles out of the ground. Speed was Comedy's great thing. He was a freak. His sire was a sprinter – he's the only good Goldhill jumper there's ever been – and his dam was of no consequence. Cheltenham wasn't really his track. Being by a sprinter you would have wondered whether he really got the trip up the hill, and I always wondered if he really came down the hill because of his massive size – you'd think he'd be much better off on a level, flat track. And, of course,

THE CHAMPION HURDLE

he tended to jump to the right, which again was no help at Cheltenham!'

Comedy and Mercy Rimell shared an idyllic dozen years together until the onset of arthritis demanded he be humanely put down on 26 May 1990 at the age of 23. Not that the dynamic duo led a quiet life. One day they rounded up a rogue bull that had escaped from a field and was running amok in the village; on another, Comedy stumbled and pitched his custodian to the ground, breaking her thumb. 'Obviously, he was my favourite. I know you shouldn't be sentimental in racing, but that's how it turned out with Comedy. He made a lot of people very happy.' Although inflation ensured Comedy of Errors would lose the earnings record for a hurdler, he remains the only champion to regain his title.

As Wednesday dawned to a grey, though temporarily rainless sky, Night Nurse was galloped to see how he could handle the gluepot conditions. 'I had to convince myself the horse was back to his old self,' said Broderick. 'Everyone knew he had been wrong. We thought he was on the mend but I needed to find out for myself.' His whispered prayers were answered. 'You could sense the horse was eager to race. He wanted to take hold of his bridle and he moved with ease through the ground.'

If Easterby and Broderick were satisfied Night Nurse could cope with the quagmire, the punters were not. The best price on offer before the storms had been 5/2 yet the champion was allowed to defend his title at an astonishing 15/2 (over 10/1 on the Tote), with three rivals preferred in the betting. Bird's Nest, winner of both his races since Christmas, was a hot favourite at 6/4; second best at 11/2 was Master Monday, winner of the Sweeps and Erin Foods. On form he certainly had the measure of Monksfield, who was beaten 12 and a half lengths (fourth) in the former and five and a half lengths (third) in the latter. But Monksfield was nothing if not durable – the Champion Hurdle constituted the 11th race of the season! Dramatist, winner of the Kingwell on his only appearance of the new year, was sent off at 6/1, while after Night Nurse came Sea Pigeon on 10s – another known to be unsuited by the heavy ground. 'Our only chance was to go wide all the way searching for the best going,' said a gloomy O'Neill.

Rain began to fall again as the runners paraded. Broderick chose to make the running close to the rails, where he hoped to find better ground, and towed the others along at a noticeably slower

THE CHAMPION HURDLE

gallop than that of 1976. In his slipstream lurked all the dangers, bar Sea Pigeon, in last place on the wide outside.

The first gauntlet thrown down was Beacon Light's at the third last but Night Nurse kicked it aside, to be confronted by Dramatist, Bird's Nest and, most ominous of all, Monksfield and Sea Pigeon, so that five horses were in line abreast coming to the flight at the bottom of the hill. Bird's Nest hit it and lost his place while Sea Pigeon and Monksfield (who had already forfeited ground when extricating himself from a pocket on the rails) collided twice as they struggled to accelerate away from the hurdle.

Consequently, the initiative passed back to Night Nurse. He had not made the semblance of a mistake so far, skimming over his hurdles superbly, regaining his stride instantly. Now he did so for the eighth time and, hugging the rail, he readied himself to finally send Dramatist and Monksfield packing.

The champion answered Broderick's demands for one last exhilarating leap and, with the Irishman's arm flailing, set off up the hill as if the hounds of hell were in pursuit. By contrast Monksfield bulldozed through the last having floundered on a bad patch of ground, a calamitous error at such a critical stage of the contest. Recovering his momentum, Monksfield drew on his reserves and attacked the long, sodden incline with all he could muster. At one point he reached the champion's quarters but the effort, that blunder, this ground, finally bottomed him and Night Nurse left him to win by two lengths.

Broderick had every reason to be even more content with this second victory. 'He gave my horse a hell of a ride,' said Reg Spencer. 'I walked the course with him and he assured me that we would win.' Easterby was equally euphoric: 'You must admit it, Night Nurse is a great champion.' Years later the trainer explained why he had been so confident: 'Paddy Broderick came up and rode Night Nurse work when we were getting him ready. We took the horse for a racecourse gallop and the ground was very soft. He worked superbly, so we knew he could go on it. At Cheltenham, he drifted out to 7/1 or more, so I backed him twice instead of once! We came out so late from Cheltenham, there were only three cars left in the car park!' For his part, Broderick immediately announced he would not ride over fences again since he did not wish to risk losing the mount on Night Nurse through injury. How ironic, given the events of the following Boxing Day.

THE CHAMPION HURDLE

Considering their exertions at Cheltenham, nobody could have reasonably expected Night Nurse and Monksfield to resume their rivalry barely a month later in Liverpool's Templegate Hurdle. Monksfield received 6lb and, using it to good effect, forced a deadheat after a thrilling tussle on the flat. Although the Templegate was half a mile longer than the Champion Hurdle, this result emphasised the increasingly live threat Monksfield posed for the 1978 championship. That is, until the little horse became ill. After running listlessly on the last day of October a swelling appeared low down on his off-hind fetlock and within days had engulfed his hock. The infection seemed impervious to drugs and every remedy (including a visit from the local quack) failed to effect a cure. Monksfield began to waste away until a course of folic acid tablets eventually did the trick.

Monksfield was born a tough little beggar. Up to the 1978 Champion Hurdle he had survived 52 races in four years, 30 of them over hurdles, a mark of durability unequalled by any other Champion Hurdler. Bearing in mind the illustrious Flat-race relatives on his dam's side, he fetched the surprisingly meagre sum of 740 guineas at Ballsbridge sales. His dam, Regina, belonged to one of the Aga Khan's best families, being the daughter of the Coronation Stakes winner Tambara and the granddaughter of Theresina, who won the Irish Oaks. However, Regina, a small filly with an attractive head, proved a useless racer and little better at stud. Consequently, her fourth owner, Peter Ryan, sent her to Coolmore's imported American stallion Gala Performance, who stood reasonably cheaply at £300. The marriage worked pretty well because the bay colt foal inherited his mother's good looks and his father's sturdiness. Unfortunately, the colt developed an appalling 'winding' motion in his faster paces, his forelegs going out and round in a vast circle. He was also a late foal (7 June) and the undersized yearling failed to stimulate any interest at Goffs. After being broken the following spring, another visit to the sales ring saw him fall to a bid from a young man with his left leg temporarily encased in plaster. Des McDonagh had been training barely 18 months at Billywood Stud, near Moynalty, on the border of County Meath and County Cavan, and did not anticipate buying anything but 'loved that head, that fabulous head, the instant I saw it'. He had trained three winners and the colt would be his only two-year-old. McDonagh could not afford to keep 'Smarty', as the fast-

THE CHAMPION HURDLE

learning colt was nicknamed, for long and by a stroke of luck was able to pass him on to Galway-born Dr Michael Mangan, on holiday from his job as a radiologist at a Newfoundland hospital, for £1,125. Mangan christened the colt Monksfield after his mother's old guesthouse.

Monkey started his racing career as if determined to erase the memory of his ignominious past. He won his only race as a juvenile, paying £129.56 for a 20p Tote stake — odds of 647/1. Nearly two years would pass before Monksfield again won on the Flat but he immediately showed his mettle over hurdles — 'Monkey adored it. He was like lightning,' says his trainer — by winning four times during his initial season, besides finishing second in the Daily Express Triumph after twice meeting interference.

McDonagh's thoughts began to focus on the Champion Hurdle. His horse required an enormous amount of work to get him even remotely fit. 'If you put together all the mileage he has done at home I'm quite convinced it would stretch from here to America and back again. He loves his work and enjoys his grub — especially Granny Smith apples — and his sleep. Most of all he loves his sleep and is the noisiest imaginable snorer.' Accordingly, Monkey demanded plenty of racing. He ran 13 times during his second winter campaign, improving with each, culminating in that epic duel at Liverpool.

Monksfield's leg infection kept him off the course for two months. By Christmas he was trotting again and on 21 January reappeared for a gentle breeze at Navan. McDonagh prepared him for a crack at the Erin Foods, not daring to contemplate any objective beyond that. Monksfield was a revelation. Disputing the lead at the last, he weakened in the final hundred yards and finished third. Cheltenham was just three weeks away but Monkey was recovering fast. Walking back to the racecourse stables after exercising on the Monday before the Champion Hurdle, who should overtake them but Night Nurse. 'Make the most of this,' McDonagh called across, 'because it's the last time you will pass Monksfield!'

The champion had not exactly enjoyed the happiest of years either. In five races he had registered only one victory. Worse still, he took a bone-shaking fall at the last flight of the Christmas Hurdle which terminated his 26-race association (18 of them victorious) with Broderick and, ultimately, the jockey's career. 'In 25 years of riding, Night Nurse was the best horse by far that I ever rode. He

THE CHAMPION HURDLE

was like a machine, nothing could go with him. Even when I rode him to win on his first outing over hurdles at Market Rasen I knew then that he would be really good. And yet he wouldn't have passed the vet because he had a slight heart murmur. One day at Newbury, Jeff King decided that he would try to beat us by taking him on, and not letting him lead. But it didn't make any difference. His horse went off very fast and I settled Night Nurse in behind him, and went on to win by eight lengths. He was a great horse at a time when there were a lot of brilliant hurdlers – Bird's Nest, Dramatist, Sea Pigeon and Monksfield – but he was the best of that time. He jumped so well he gained lengths at every hurdle and just sat in front – ping, ping all the way. And Peter Easterby was a fantastic trainer. He was cool, relaxed, he'd never panic. He never gave me orders. As he said himself, it was no use giving orders for Night Nurse as he did what he wanted in any case.' On Broderick's retirement O'Neill rode Night Nurse to a narrow success over Bird's Nest at Doncaster but to general surprise decided to partner Sea Pigeon at Cheltenham, leaving the mount on the champion to Colin Tinkler. In the event both jockeys were injured on the first day of the Festival, but though Tinkler's foot recovered sufficiently for him to limp aboard Night Nurse (3/1 favourite), O'Neill's concussion enforced a week's holiday. His place on Sea Pigeon went to fellow Irishman Frank Berry.

Sea Pigeon's season had been severely curtailed after a fall in the Colonial Cup in November. He returned to Habton looking like skin and bone, having eaten little for three days, and was very stiff and sore on his off-fore. Easterby's first reaction was that he might never race again. However, the Pigeon seemed to be maturing like a fine port. On his return to active service in the Oteley he beat Beacon Light and his renowned turn of foot might easily tip the scales in his favour at Cheltenham should the gallop prove too slow. Conversely, both Night Nurse and Monksfield wanted a good pace to test Sea Pigeon's stamina. A battle of wits seemed on the cards.

The 1978 Champion Hurdle, the first to be sponsored by Waterford Crystal Glass, carried a record prize of £21,332 – more than Sir Ken earned during his entire hurdling career. Passing the enclosures Night Nurse led Monksfield by four lengths, but as the gap was gradually whittled away Tinkler's confidence began to wane. By the foot of the hill he was already niggling at Night Nurse whereas Monksfield was cruising. 'My plan was to push and bustle

THE CHAMPION HURDLE

the leader along,' said Monksfield's rider Tommy Kinane. 'I wanted to torment him the whole way. I even gave Night Nurse a couple of kicks in the backside as we started up the hill!'

Beginning the descent Monksfield headed the champion for the first time and Kinane committed the little chestnut to a long run for home. He knew Monksfield would fight his way up the hill and, equally, knew he needed to extract the sting from fast-finishers like Sea Pigeon. To the dismay of his legion of supporters, Night Nurse was unable to rally and it was the tartan colours of his stable companion that represented the only danger to Monksfield approaching the last. Some thought Berry produced Sea Pigeon too early as the pair were almost level 50 yards from the flight, but Monksfield made no race-losing error on this occasion and Sea Pigeon was a spent force on the strength-sapping drag to the winning post. With his handsome head arched low, Monksfield powered home two lengths ahead of Sea Pigeon and eight in front of Night Nurse to a crescendo of Irish cheers. It was the first Irish victory for 15 years, McDonagh's first of any kind for ten months, and in the 44-year-old, gap-toothed Kinane ('My only good subject at school was fighting and I had plenty of practice') they had the oldest jockey ever to win hurdling's blue riband.

Before the 1979 Champion Hurdle came round Kinane had controversially lost the ride on Monksfield to the tall, soft-spoken Dessie Hughes, who had partnered the horse in that monumental race with Night Nurse at Liverpool when Kinane was carrying an injured shoulder. Hughes' slight build belied his toughness, a huge scar on his chest the visible legacy of the day he sustained a punctured lung. Besides their association with Monksfield, Kinane and Hughes share the further distinction of fathering successful Flat-race jockeys in Michael and Richard – the latter gaining early experience winning pony races decked out in the Monksfield colours.

Monksfield's second title marginally outshone the brilliance of the first, singularly apt since it celebrated the race's golden jubilee. The old guard predominated; Bird's Nest was competing in his fourth championship, Sea Pigeon, Beacon Light and Monksfield their third. The much-vaunted young Irish hurdler Golden Cygnet had met with a fatal accident in the Scottish Champion Hurdle (won by Sea Pigeon from Night Nurse, who subsequently went chasing), so the best of the younger brigade seemed Kybo, who was unbeaten

THE CHAMPION HURDLE

in three races, which included a victory over Bird's Nest in the Christmas Hurdle. Turnell's perennial delinquent had won the Bula and National Spirit Hurdles and been defeated one and a half lengths by Sea Pigeon in the Fighting Fifth. Now Easterby's undisputed standard-bearer, Sea Pigeon was not seen out again until the beginning of March when he ran second under 12st 7lb in a competitive handicap.

Over in Ireland, Monksfield's preparation involved the far more arduous ordeal of negotiating (unsuccessfully) a series of weight-carrying battles with the handicapper. After the fourth (the Erin Foods, in which he was a disappointing sixth of eight) he was found to be slightly anaemic. A prolonged freeze also hindered his training. McDonagh ventured to suggest, nonetheless, that 'Monksfield should always be able to beat Sea Pigeon by outstaying him'. Prophetic words.

Cheltenham week began to a blast of press speculation concerning the fitness of the two principals. Sea Pigeon, ante-post favourite at 7/2, had broken a blood vessel (later denied) and Monksfield was lame, it was reported. The champion soon scotched that story by galloping one and three-quarter miles upsides stablemate Stranfield in driving rain on the morning of the race. Two days of persistent rain once more contrived to make the going a vital factor. Though doubtless benefiting from O'Neill's presence, Sea Pigeon would detest the ground. When Stranfield won the opening race and Hughes the second, the omens looked propitious for Monksfield and he was backed down to 9/4 favourite.

Monksfield, Beacon Light, Kybo and Sea Pigeon were steered towards the outside of the track where the ground was not so poached and by the third last clearly had the measure of those, including Bird's Nest, who ploughed their way along the inner. Kybo misjudged the penultimate flight and tumbled to the floor, leaving Monksfield several lengths to the good. Sea Pigeon, however, was now eating up the ground. When would O'Neill show his hand? Perhaps he did so too soon, for he allowed the Pigeon to get his nose in front before the last, thereby gifting the indomitable Monksfield with something to fight against. Part of O'Neill wanted to sit behind a while longer but the words of owner Pat Muldoon, imploring him not to delay his challenge too long, kept drumming through his head. 'So I let my fellow stride on perhaps half a length into the lead and I was going so easily it was

THE CHAMPION HURDLE

just unbelievable.' Three paces off the hurdle O'Neill spotted his stride and launched Sea Pigeon into a race-winning leap. Alongside him Hughes likewise recognised the importance of this final jump. He had been working hard whilst O'Neill merely sat like the cat contemplating when to consume the cream.

Hughes administered three smacks. 'He just changed into another gear and stuck his head lower and lower. I've never ridden a horse to go so fast into a hurdle.' Now it was Monksfield who flew rather than the Pigeon. Thirty yards from glory Sea Pigeon began to falter, Monksfield drew level and, with the low carriage of his gallant head denoting the immense effort he was making, he forged ahead to win a classic contest by three-quarters of a length.

Seldom in the rich and varied annals of the Cheltenham Festival has there been such a pulsating finale. Sea Pigeon lost nothing in defeat. He refused to throw in the towel but Monksfield, in his jockey's words, 'behaved like a man of a horse. He took all I gave him and did not squirm from it.' Easterby was left to muse 'It's a pity pigeons can't swim', though years later he remained convinced Sea Pigeon ought to have won this particular championship and set up his hat-trick. 'If his owner hadn't come into the ring and told Jonjo, "Mind you don't come too late", he would have won. It was the last thing he said and it was enough to sway Jonjo, who ended up coming too early.'

The Sea Pigeon entourage had still not seen the last of Monksfield's backside. At Liverpool they met in the Colt Sigma Hurdle; Monksfield winning, Sea Pigeon falling. Five times they had clashed and five times the Pigeon had been bested. It really seemed as if Monksfield had the Indian sign over him. Perhaps more to the point, he was now rising ten, an age at which only Hatton's Grace had won a Champion Hurdle. No other horse had won a post-war championship above the age of eight. The Pigeon's ace in the hole remained the Flat-race speed, unveiled for the first time at Ascot in 1972 when he won the only race of his two-year-old career.

The well-grown, but immature, Sea Pigeon was not hurried, for his trainer, Jeremy Tree, had his eye on the Derby for this impeccably bred brown son of Sea Bird and the American mare Around the Roses, second in the Acorn Stakes – the first leg of the fillies' triple crown. Sea Pigeon's elder full brother Grebe won seven races in the USA while his half-brother, Bowl Game, proved himself America's premier grass horse over one and a half miles in

THE CHAMPION HURDLE

1979. Unfortunately, Sea Pigeon got very agitated during the Epsom preliminaries, failed to handle the infamous gradients and could only finish seventh to Morston. After two more disappointing displays, Sea Pigeon, like his two American brothers, was gelded in an effort to cure his highly strung temperament.

One man constantly on the alert for animals that failed to realise their promise on the Flat was Pat Muldoon, a wholesale wine importer in West Lothian. He was sufficiently intrigued to ask if Sea Pigeon was for sale but was told by Jeremy Tree that the horse looked rotten after being cut and any decision was best deferred. Sea Pigeon's convalescence took longer than expected. 'I happened to know the chap who was looking after him,' Muldoon said, 'and I asked him what he thought. He said Pigeon was basically a marvellous racehorse but at that stage was no more than a shadow of himself. If you had patience, he suggested, he would really become something.' Invited to make an offer, Muldoon mentioned £10,000 but the deal nearly fell through when Sea Pigeon failed the vet owing to a bruised foot (he suffered from brittle feet and was always difficult to shoe). Muldoon and his trainer Gordon Richards would not be denied and paid a second visit with more satisfactory results.

In five seasons over timber Sea Pigeon had won 15 races, including a Fighting Fifth and two Scottish Champion Hurdles. Nor had he been idle on the Flat, having won the Chester Cup and Vaux Breweries Gold Tankard twice apiece. Then, racing no fewer than ten times in the 1979 season, he won another four, notably the Ebor, under ten stone. Even so, Sea Pigeon had not been rigorously campaigned during the winter, just 28 races in those five seasons, and invariably enjoyed the mid-season break during the worst of the weather. Ten years of age or not, he was quite capable of unleashing that famed acceleration especially if the ground was fast, and winning the Champion Hurdle at the fourth attempt, something else no horse had previously achieved.

The Pigeon's quest encountered an irritating hitch. He bruised his near-fore just before he was due to compete in the Oteley. Easterby immersed the foot in salt water and applied poultices, all to no avail. Two weeks before the Champion Hurdle Sea Pigeon was still lame, his only exercise being on a horse walker. With ten days remaining the poison finally came out of the foot, enabling the trainer to give him three pieces of work. The last, upsides the smart

THE CHAMPION HURDLE

two-mile chaser King Weasel on Bill Elsey's private gallop at Malton which finished six furlongs against the collar, was particularly impressive.

Easterby knew the Pigeon to be short of a gallop and could only trust in providence. On the other hand, two decisions by the Cheltenham executive offered some consolation. Firstly, the Champion Hurdle course was shortened by 200 yards to two miles and there were eight flights instead of nine. This meant the hurdlers now followed the same route as the chasers in front of the grandstand, avoiding the long pull up the hill with its flight of hurdles at the top, which had hitherto constituted such a stern test. In short, the championship course would take less getting. Secondly, the Champion Hurdle would be run on Tuesday to ensure the best available ground. (Indeed, by Wednesday the soft ground had officially deteriorated to heavy.) Be that as it may, Sea Pigeon (13/2) was only third in the betting to Pollardstown (7/2) and Monksfield (6/5).

Monksfield's position owed more to his Festival record than any string of victories. Although McDonagh believed he had summered better than ever, Monksfield had won none of his four races and after finishing last at Navan in December was found to have a pulse rate of 126. He recovered to finish a brave second in the Erin Foods but McDonagh had not trained a winner for nine months and Hughes, too, had been under the cosh, breaking an arm and a leg in a fall before Christmas.

In a field of nine the most interesting challenger was the French Champion Hurdler Paiute and it was he who paved the way until making a mistake at the fourth. This left Monksfield in charge down the hill but Hughes failed to shake off Pollardstown, Bird's Nest, Connaught Ranger and, tracking this trio, the menacing figure of Sea Pigeon. Appearances were deceptive. O'Neill's mount had emitted the most disturbing gasps and pants running up the hill, his lungs fighting for oxygen which his interrupted training programme was unable to supply. O'Neill sat motionless, allowing him to get a second wind in his own time.

Swinging into the straight Monksfield put his cards on the table and outbid all except Sea Pigeon's. Photographs of the two protagonists at the last could easily be confused with either of the previous two years but as the hill beckoned, the outcome on this occasion was obviously going to differ. O'Neill's hands and heels

THE CHAMPION HURDLE

were enough to carve a seven-length gap by the post. The persevering Bird's Nest chased them home to achieve his own slice of history, albeit the less desirable tag of becoming the eighth horse to be placed twice in the championship without winning.

It was the end of the Cheltenham road for Monksfield. First or second in four consecutive Champion Hurdles was an enviable record. He won another race (his 17th) before retiring to the Anngrove Stud, County Laois, after a career totalling 76 races (49 over hurdles) in just six years. Sadly, Monksfield never managed to become the first Champion Hurdler to sire one before he had to be put down on 28 February 1989, at the age of 17, after shattering his near-hind leg while enjoying his customary morning roll. Hughes and O'Neill had contrasting reasons to remember Monkey. 'Monksfield was as tough as nails,' testified O'Neill. 'When I got there too soon on Sea Pigeon in 1979, he came back at me and beat me. No other horse would have done that. He was like a Jack Russell – once he got hold of you he wouldn't let go. That was the gamest race Sea Pigeon ever ran and my only bad luck was to come up against Monksfield. Even when I congratulated Dessie afterwards I couldn't believe I'd been beaten. I have nightmares about Monksfield at Cheltenham. He must be the gamest horse that's ever been in training.' His fellow Irishman eloquently put into words what most jumping fans thought about his former partner: 'People love a horse with a big heart and they don't come any bigger than Monksfield's. It's incredible how much a horse will give if he's willing. Monksfield gave me his last breath, his last ounce, every single bit he had left. He ran his heart out and offered it without complaint.'

O'Neill continued the winning sequence of Irish jockeys. Universally known by the Christian name Jonjo, a mark of public affection and esteem bestowed on few jockeys, his cherubic, twinkling-eyed exterior disguised a ferocious brand of determination. He cut his competitive teeth at the age of eight, borrowing a donkey called Neddy from the local milk cart to win £3 in the village carnival race. By the age of 11 he was hunting his pony Dolly with the Duhallows and four years later was riding on the Flat for local trainer Don Reid. In 1972 he joined Gordon Richards with three winners under his belt – one on the Flat, one over hurdles and one in a steeplechase. He overcame a bout of homesickness to become junior champion in 1972–73 and Sea

THE CHAMPION HURDLE

Pigeon's victory was one of 115 in 1979–80 which gave him his second senior title. Life had not always been so sweet. In January 1975 he broke his right leg in an ugly fall at Teesside and was sidelined for six months. Jonjo would need to bounce back once more, for in October 1980 he received the most fearful injury when his mount Simbad fell at Bangor. His right shin was snapped into 36 pieces by the scissors motion of another horse's flailing hind legs. The bone was plated together but O'Neill's eagerness to get back in the saddle before nature's work was complete landed him in a Swiss clinic for another operation. The Pigeon needed a new partner.

If Jonjo O'Neill resembled the pink-faced boy piping away angelically in the front row of the choir, John Francome represented the urchin who nips round the back of the organ for a crafty fag whenever the choirmaster is not looking. Stories abound of Francome's weighing room japes and his merciless tormenting of racecourse officialdom from the lowest to the highest, notably the occasions when he substituted yellow disinfectant squares from a urinal for real lemon drops before offering the sweets to a doorman preceived as a persistent cadger and he used a masculine part of his anatomy to stir a cup of tea intended for an especially pernickity clerk of the scales.

Aboard a horse their styles were no less at variance. O'Neill's all-action methods were never more evident, or profitable, than in a tight, drawn-out battle for the line whereas Francome, pony-club trained, winner of the 1970 Young Rider's Championship and a member of the winning British team at the Junior European Championships, was pure horseman, one who excelled in the fine art of presenting a horse at a fence – the best he ever saw according to his guv'nor Fred Winter. In time, Francome's finishing (which had lost him the ride on Lanzarote) became sufficiently adept as to be regarded in the same league as O'Neill's.

Francome and Sea Pigeon (fresh from a summer's activity that had seen his Flat race earnings rise to a record for a gelding of £96,985) opened their account with a confidently gained victory in the Holsten Diat Pils Hurdle at Sandown. Francome was unavailable for the Fighting Fifth, however, in which Sea Pigeon was beaten one and a half lengths by Bird's Nest, with Pollardstown a short head away in third, but got the race in the stewards' room as Bird's Nest had performed one of his walkabouts on the run-in. Easterby was now

THE CHAMPION HURDLE

content to let Sea Pigeon rest. All told he had run 15 races during 1980 and in view of the circumstances surrounding the last championship the trainer lost no sleep at the prospect of going straight for the Champion Hurdle without another run. This year there were no anxious moments. Some fresh faces had appeared in the ranks of the top hurdlers but none seemed within 7lb of him. The boards read 6/1 bar the champion at 7/4.

Tuesday dawned to spring-like blue skies, sunshine and a welcoming wind which began to dry the ground soaked by weekend rain, though it remained soft. Pollardstown's pacemaker Meladon set about his task with gusto and at the first hurdle Ivan King was a faller, luckily not hampering the favourite who was close behind him. Pollardstown replaced his stablemate at the fifth and by the second last had got most of his rivals in trouble. The exceptions were Daring Run, Starfen and Sea Pigeon still lobbing along on the bridle. 'Remembering how well Pollardstown stayed, I had decided beforehand to lie handy behind him during the first half of the race,' Francome later explained. 'I remember, too, that I had seen Sea Pigeon beaten by being in front too soon so I was determined to leave it to the last moment before asking him to win his race.'

The 'last moment' it certainly would be. At no time had Francome asked Sea Pigeon to move a muscle with any haste. Now, with barely 100 yards of Cheltenham's cloying uphill slog to be covered, he threw the switch and 2,000 volts appeared to pass through the Pigeon's sleek brown frame. He hurtled past Pollardstown and Daring Run as if they were on a treadmill. In 71 Champion Hurdles only 16 winners have not been leading or disputing the lead over the final flight. Yes, one of those 16, Brown Tony, only got his nose in front in the very last stride, but that was a frantic affair, not the impudently clinical execution of 1981. The winning margin of 1 and a half lengths over Pollardstown seemed irrelevant in the context of a display which to many experienced judges was the finest they had ever been privileged to see in a Champion Hurdle. 'Not many horses can struggle through such ground and then pull out what Sea Pigeon did at the end of a race. He is quite simply the best horse I have ever ridden,' said Francome. 'He was pure class. The feel he gave me when I let off the handbrake after the last was unbelievable — I can't think of another horse I rode that could quicken like him at the end of a top-class race. At the top of the hill I took a pull, so well was he

THE CHAMPION HURDLE

going and I kept restraining him so that we were third at the last. With most horses there would have been the worry of having to make up ground if you hit the last but he had so much in hand that day it wouldn't have mattered. I waited until halfway up the run-in before putting him into the lead, but I could easily have waited another 50 yards and still have won.'

Easterby's Festival was only just coming to the boil. Clayside won the Arkle Challenge Trophy and when he saddled Little Owl to win the Gold Cup, Easterby became the sixth trainer to achieve the coveted Cheltenham double in the wake of Walwyn, O'Brien, Briscoe and the Anthony brothers, Owen and Jack. He also occupied an élite perch all to himself for no other man has trained five winners of the Champion Hurdle. Although Easterby's supremacy began to wane after 1981, by the time he handed over the reins to his son Tim in 1996 he had sent out more than 2,500 winners and had become the only trainer to win 1,000 races over jumps and on the Flat. Even though he never scaled the pinnacle of achievements attained by his only serious rivals for the accolade of the finest ever dual-purpose trainer – Vincent O'Brien and Ryan Price – in securing a Flat championship and/or a Classic, on this score alone he deserves to be regarded as the most successful dual-purpose trainer of them all.

No one who witnessed Sea Pigeon's 37th and greatest victory could have guessed it would be his last. Hopes that he might win a third championship at the unprecedented age of 12 came to nought after he picked up some sort of virus or infection which affected his lungs and bronchial tubes. The prescribed long holiday following two lacklustre runs in the autumn failed to cure him and three weeks before the 1982 Champion Hurdle a substandard gallop in the hands of a fit-again O'Neill was enough to warrant his immediate retirement. His 21 victories over hurdles netted a National Hunt record of £130,394, which when added to his Flat-race winnings yielded a grand total of £227,480, a record for British-trained geldings until surpassed by Teleprompter, thanks to his Arlington Million purse of 1985.

For a while Sea Pigeon shared a paddock at Great Habton with Night Nurse, a nostalgic reminder to their trainer of the contribution all three made to a golden age in Champion Hurdle history, before 'Pidge' went to the Etchingham Stud, at Slingsby on the outskirts of Malton, where he was looked after by Polly Perkins.

THE CHAMPION HURDLE

Of the two old warriors, Night Nurse accepted the onset of retirement the more gracefully. He enjoyed the occasional day's hunting early on but increasingly assumed the guise of 'matron' to Great Habton's young stock. 'One week when I went down to see them,' reported Easterby, 'all the foals were lying down in a circle and in the middle was Night Nurse, standing up keeping a watchful eye over them – it would have made a great photo. He was a comical bugger! If he didn't want to do something, he wouldn't – and we had to put a head-collar on him when he was turned out, otherwise we couldn't catch him!' Eventually, as it must, Anno Domini finally caught up with Night Nurse in the first week of November 1998. 'He was in good health right up until this week,' Easterby informed the media after the 27-year-old's death. 'He was eating his head off and having his daily roll in his paddock. But then he got a bad stoppage and we had to have him put down. He had a great life, but we had a great life because of him. It's strange, but you don't miss them until they've gone and I'll always remember his honest head and floppy ears.'

Night Nurse was buried at Great Habton with a space left beside him for Sea Pigeon. At one stage it looked as if Pidge would predecease Night Nurse after he almost died in 1984 from an intestinal blockage which necessitated emergency surgery to remove two feet of intestine. Only the pluck of a true champion kept him alive. But survive he did for another 16 years, sharing his box at one time with a donkey called Arthur and a hen who marked her morning visit with an egg, and charging around his paddock when given half a chance. Christmas cards and mints continued to arrive, along with a little girl who had begged Jimmy Savile to 'fix it' for her, and the lady from Keighley who visited him every other month armed with thermal rugs, a supply of vitamins and any other elixirs for long life. Every now and then Polly Perkins would spruce him up for an outing to York and the Ebor parade, or maybe Malton's Open Day. 'When he goes off to engagements,' she said, 'he bounds up the ramp and then crashes about and rocks the lorry. You couldn't dream of leading him anywhere in public without having a chifney on him. He pushes and shoves you all over the place.'

In life Sea Pigeon and Night Nurse met for the last time at Malton's Open Day in September 1995, but, as Peter Easterby had promised, they were eventually reunited in death. Sea Pigeon was put down on 24 October 2000 after suffering from a disintegrating

THE CHAMPION HURDLE

pedal bone. He was 30-years-old. 'He was a horse of a lifetime,' said Easterby. 'He had ability, it was as simple as that. The big thing about him, and why he lasted so long, was his mental attitude. He got switched off in his mind. The most exciting part about him for the public was that they love a horse to come from behind, thinking "will he or won't he get there?" The two races that stick out in my memory are his second Champion Hurdle, when John Francome rode him, which was a masterpiece, and the Ebor, which he won under ten stone in soft ground when Jonjo dropped his hands near the line and nearly got caught, giving us all heart failure. I think Jonjo was the only one who thought he had won. We've had some great days and bad heads because of him – I think the champagne was flowing down the stands after the Ebor!'

Not altogether surprisingly that day on York's Knavesmire is likewise etched into O'Neill's memory. 'No doubt about it, it was a truly memorable day – it ranks right up with my Cheltenham triumphs. Winning the Ebor on him was fantastic because I was a jump jockey winning a Flat race. I dropped my hands on him and everyone thought he'd got beat. It was a bit closer than I thought it was! When they showed me the photo-finish print I almost died! When the judge announced his verdict the noise was deafening. He was the best I ever rode. He had lots of speed, plenty of toe – which could make you look fantastic or make you look stupid, because if you went too quick on him he'd turn it in. He possessed loads of character, like all good horses, and he was a beggar to ride out at home – he'd pull your arms out all day if you let him. One thing's for sure, we'll never see the likes of Night Nurse and Sea Pigeon and Monksfield together again.'

The two Great Habton stars lie buried in a plot marked with a plaque which states: 'Legends in their lifetime.' Enough said.

12

Three Lively Ladies

Deprived of Sea Pigeon, the 1982 Champion Hurdle resembled Othello without the Moor. Even Iago went missing for Anno Domini had also caught up with Bird's Nest. The continuing drama of the Champion Hurdle was being recast and, taken overall, the next three performances would see the leading roles dominated by ladies. The 1982 company now wore the distinct air of repertory and in the circumstances it was only to be expected that the Irish favourite would forget his lines, slip up and present the race to a 40/1 'spear-carrier'.

It's a curious coincidence that on the three previous occasions when long-priced horses lifted the championship some sort of disaster also befell a favoured animal. In 1957 the undignified brawl between Clair Soleil and Rosati removed two of Merry Deal's principal opponents when he won at 28/1; the following year Fare Time's exit at the first facilitated Bandalore's victory at 20/1; and in 1965 Salmon Spray crashed at the first when Kirriemuir became the longest-priced victor at 50/1. The favourite in 1982 was Daring Run.

Daring Run's recent form had been somewhat in and out, his market position resulting from an impressively gained six-length victory in the Leopardstown Champion Hurdle (formerly the Erin Foods). There were no English challengers but Ekbalco had made the journey for the Sweeps, finishing sixth. Trained by Roger Fisher and owned by Jordanian businessman Tawfik Fakhouri (from whose Telex number he derived his unusual name), Ekbalco's style of running closely resembled Sea Pigeon's, which helped to make him a public favourite. His speed was used to good effect when taking the 1981 Imperial Cup and Fighting Fifth and almost brought him success in the Schweppes, but desperately heavy ground and the concession of 13lb to Donegal Prince proved insurmountable. The

THE CHAMPION HURDLE

other major domestic contender was Broadsword, a five-year-old entire trained by David Nicholson. In nine races during his first season he lost only two and though the Daily Express Triumph was the second of them, he was widely regarded as the leader of his generation. He soon confirmed this status by chasing home Heighlin and Ekbalco in the Berkshire Hurdle and then defeating Heighlin and Pollardstown over two and a half miles at Cheltenham.

The death at Haydock of the season's outstanding English hurdler, Celtic Ryde, left Broadsword second in the Champion Hurdle betting at 100/30. On 40/1 was the Irishman For Auction, four lengths behind Ekbalco in the Schweppes (in receipt of 9lb) but about the same distance in front of him (receiving 16lb) when winning the Sweeps, his first victory for two years. Clearly, For Auction had a lot to find if he was to trouble Ekbalco at level weights but he seemed to be improving.

On the Monday evening a Gloucestershire monsoon struck Prestbury Park and at a 6.45 a.m. inspection water still lay on parts of the course. The ground was heavy, but loose on top, two sides of a coin that would bring contrasting fortunes to the Irish horses. Between the fifth and sixth flights Daring Run slipped up. Conversely, For Auction, who could not handle the holding ground, was able to go through these sloppier conditions. Prominent throughout, he delivered his challenge going to the second last, accompanied by Ekbalco and Broadsword.

Ekbalco's rider, David Goulding, glanced confidently across at his rivals on touching down fractionally ahead, but his mount could find nothing under pressure and, with Broadsword squeezed for room on the bend, For Auction had stolen half a length jumping the final flight. To raucous Irish cheers he galloped up the hill to win by seven handsome lengths from Broadsword, who finished strongly to deprive Ekbalco of second place. Only four horses had won the championship more convincingly – Blaris and Insurance pre-war; Bula and Comedy of Errors post-war – while Mr Colin Magnier was the third amateur rider to succeed. Irish joy knew no bounds. 'I've won fifty grand,' announced Dublin auctioneer Michael Heaslip, brother of owner Danno. 'I had £1,000 each way after the Schweppes at 40s. I originally had a half share in For Auction but sold for £2,000 – aren't I a desperate idiot!'

It was also a first Festival success for Michael Cunningham, usually considered by the English to be a Flat-race trainer thanks to

THE CHAMPION HURDLE

the exploits of Cairn Rouge, who won the 1980 Irish 1000 Guineas, Coronation Stakes and Champion Stakes. However, four years earlier, Cunningham engineered a masterly coup when Irish Gamble won the Schweppes by ten lengths after being backed down from 33s to 16/1. Cunningham started off in racing with Paddy Sleator and although intent on becoming a jockey he also received a superb grounding in the art of training ('If you didn't learn anything from that man you'd be very stupid'). After only 150 or so rides he switched to training in 1970 and had recently moved to Gormanstown, near Navan. Cunningham had a reputation for buying good horses cheaply. Cairn Rouge cost 3,000 guineas, For Auction 4,000. 'Ever since I bought this horse out of a field from local farmer Paul Finnegan I knew he was going to be a very good hurdler, but he is 17 hands and always needed time. Colin Magnier told me we would have won the Schweppes ten lengths if only For Auction could have got out of the heavy ground. I wasn't worried about today's ground – it was more loose – and I told his owner he had improved at least 18lb from Newbury. I've got some decent Flat horses and what For Auction was doing to them made me think that whoever beat him would be wearing wings.'

The passage of 12 months did little to enhance For Auction's stock because he failed to win, and in fact never won another hurdle race. Not that he performed too badly. Ekbalco beat him for pace in the Bula and a 28lb difference enabled Fredcoteri to beat him in the Sweeps. In the Wessel Industries Champion Hurdle (yet another new name for the Erin Foods) two jumping errors cost him any chance of beating Royal Vulcan and Daring Run. Last year's unfortunate Champion Hurdle favourite, who had subsequently won the Sun Templegate Hurdle from Pollardstown and Ekbalco, returned for a third crack at the title.

Broadsword and Ekbalco likewise renewed rivalry for the third time that season, the honours in the Bula and Christmas Hurdles having gone to the latter. However, Roger Fisher's horse had not raced since winning at Haydock in January. His intended outings in the Schweppes and Wolverhampton's Champion Hurdle Trial were both lost to the weather while he had not been entered for the Nottingham City Trial. His trainer was already regretting this decision since Ekbalco was a gross horse who needed plenty of preparation. The bookmakers were not about to suffer burnt fingers and installed him at 3/1 joint favourite with For Auction. At 9/2

THE CHAMPION HURDLE

came Royal Vulcan, bidding to extend his unbeaten record for the season to six. In the Gerry Fielden Hurdle (the old Berkshire) he beat Gaye Brief by two lengths.

One year older than Royal Vulcan, Gaye Brief was conceding him 7lb more than weight-for-age and was not asked to race again for two months. Patience had characterised Gaye Brief's entire career. He ran just five times during his novice season (winning four) and was not allowed to compete in the hurly-burly atmosphere of the 1982 Festival. He hurdled fluently and possessed a fine turn of foot. There was no point in hurrying his development.

Shrewdness such as this typified Kinnersley. Fred Rimell had died suddenly in 1981 – Gaye Brief was the last horse he bought – and the licence was now in the name of his widow, Mercy. Throughout his brilliantly successful career Fred Rimell made no bones about the debt he owed his wife. International showjumper at ten and point-to-point victress at fourteen, a formidable organiser and scrutineer of the formbook and blessed with a prodigious memory, Mercy Rimell was a daunting lady whose arrival in the training ranks, along with Mesdames Pitman and Dickinson, finally exploded the myth of male superiority in the profession. In her first season she finished seventh in the list; in her second she would become the first woman to train a winner of one of jumping's premier events.

Like so many of Fred Rimell's horses, Gaye Brief was bought in Ireland. He already trained Gaye Brief's elder brother Gaye Chance, a very talented and versatile hurdler who had won the Royal Doulton Hurdle at Haydock and the Sun Alliance Novices at the 1981 Festival, and would later add the Waterford Crystal Stayers Hurdle in 1984. Both were bred at the Orwell Stud (near Thurles) of Phil Sweeney from his remarkable mare Artiste Gaye. She was never broken, her dam ran little and the grandam not at all. The own brothers in Rimell's care (by the Dante Stakes winner Lucky Brief) raised her total of winning progeny to eight. The best of the first six was Royal Gaye with whom Rimell won the 1978 Royal Doulton from a field which included the first four in the Champion Hurdle. And the Artiste Gaye production line had not yet ground to a halt. Before her mother's death in 1985, Artist's Design made it nine while Gaye Memory and Gaye Le Moss subsequently won bumpers (all Rimell trained). All told, Artiste Gaye's progeny have won over 80 races of one description or another.

One final aspect of Gaye Brief's background is worthy of

THE CHAMPION HURDLE

comment for he ran in the distinctive red, black chevron jacket of Sheikh Ali Abu Khamsin who, unlike the majority of Arab owners, preferred the sport of National Hunt racing to the business of Flat racing. Since seeing his colours pass the post first at Worcester in March 1979, Sheikh Ali's progress had been as rapid as one would expect. By the time Gaye Brief (his first horse with the Rimells) went out for the 1983 Champion Hurdle his running total had reached the century mark and this magnificent victory was one of 32 which gave the Sheikh the second of his owners' titles with record prize-money of £142,937. In April 1982 the Sheikh retained Richard Linley as his jockey. A quietly effective stylist, who learned the ropes with Toby Balding and was champion amateur in 1975, Linley was never afraid to be self-critical. 'I hadn't ridden Gaye Brief before the Gerry Fielden and should have kicked on when I was going well at the third last.' The message was not lost.

After his mid-season lay-off Gaye Brief resumed winning ways in the Hereford race commemorating his trainer's late husband and the City Trial at Nottingham. Apart from Royal Vulcan he had yet to encounter a top hurdler and on the strength of this was permitted to start at 7/1.

On ground considerably faster than the previous March, Sula Bula and Broadsword set about ensuring the pace was a brisk one. Linley kept Gaye Brief in close contention and at the furthest point from the stands was nicely poised in third, slightly ahead of Daring Run, Fane Ranger and For Auction. The tempo showed no sign of slackening down the hill (the race time fell below four minutes for the first occasion since 1960) and over the second from home four horses – Fane Ranger, Sula Bula, Broadsword and Gaye Brief – were in the air together. Linley now excelled himself, gaining yards at this oh-so-vital obstacle, to sprint four lengths clear.

With the championship at their mercy, concentration of horse and jockey momentarily wandered. Gaye Brief hardly rose at the final flight, knocking a section out of the ground and landing flat-footed, but his supremacy was so vast that Linley only had to push him out to record a three-length victory over Boreen Prince with the defending champion For Auction a further seven adrift. Although still only seven-years-old, For Auction would enjoy no more days in the spotlight. A brief spell in France ended in disaster. 'He put a hind leg out through the stable door one night,' recalls Michael Cunningham, 'and though he came back to me and went

THE CHAMPION HURDLE

on to win over fences at Fairyhouse in January 1986 before running twice at Cheltenham, he broke the same leg on his next start back at Fairyhouse. When he was right, For Auction was one hell of a horse. But he was always difficult to train, plus he was a very finicky eater – it was a family trait – and would often go off his grub for weeks at a time.'

In Gaye Brief here was an outstanding young champion who looked fit to follow in the hoofprints of Sir Ken, Persian War and the other immortals. However, three weeks later he very nearly came unstuck in the Sun Templegate Hurdle (admittedly over a distance further than the championship) against an imposing five-year-old mare from Ireland who had, what's more, already won at the meeting 24 hours earlier. Gaye Brief gave her 6lb and won by a length. Given that mares would receive a 5lb allowance in all races from the commencement of the 1983–84 season, this gutsy, front-running daughter of Deep Run, trained by Paddy Mullins at Goresbridge in County Kilkenny, might prove to be a gigantic thorn in Gaye Brief's side. Of course she proved to be more than that, for her name was Dawn Run and in the space of two short years that name came to be spoken of in the same breath as Arkle, Golden Miller and Red Rum.

As with the distinguished females of most species, an unmistakable aura seems to surround an outstanding racemare. The winter game has relatively few racemares (under a quarter) in comparison to the Flat but in Dawn Run National Hunt racing discovered Juno, Diana and Venus rolled into one. She became the first mare to win the Champion Hurdle since 1939 and then the only horse of either sex to achieve the Champion Hurdle–Gold Cup double. Female participation in the two championships, never profuse, had been dwindling. African Sister was the first mare to actually contest a Champion Hurdle and none had reached a place since Ivy Green's second in 1959. A dozen tried their luck in the '60s but only the 500/1 shot River Belle (1979) had lined up in the 15 renewals prior to 1984. The Gold Cup painted a similar picture – three winning mares since 1924 and only one runner since the last success by Glencaraig Lady in 1972. In the past no Champion Hurdler was able to make the successful transition from one championship to the other, not even paragons like Sir Ken (1957), Bula (1975 and '76), Lanzarote (1977) and Night Nurse (1979, '81 and '82). The only Gold Cup winners to have earned a place in the

THE CHAMPION HURDLE

Champion Hurdle were Saffron Tartan (1961) and Captain Christy (1974).

Strict interpretation of the formbook insists that Dawn Run's unique feat resulted from, and depended upon, that 5lb sex allowance but only a brave man would have bet against her had the weights been equal, such was her combative nature. Her Cheltenham partner O'Neill reckoned she was a stone better than her Champion Hurdle winning form. 'She was inclined not to exert herself more than necessary but she loved a fight, and transmitted an exhilaration as the going got tougher. The bigger the challenge, the more she gave you.' These qualities combined to make Dawn Run a legend and, sadly, like many a hero or heroine, that legendary status was sealed by a premature death.

Foaled at the County Cork farm of Paddy Mangan (the breeder of Doorknocker), Dawn Run was a hard bay with dark points and a white star on her forehead. Her dam Twilight Slave was never broken and belonged to John Riordan, who paid 300 guineas for her as a yearling. Dawn Run would be her sixth winner over obstacles, the best of the others being Even Dawn, who won the Aldsworth Hurdle at the 1972 Festival besides 18 steeplechases. The grandam Early Light, a fair point-to-pointer, was a full sister to the Scottish National winner Brasher. Dawn Run's sire was the phenomenally successful and current champion National Hunt stallion, Deep Run. When visited by Twilight Slave in 1977 his fee was still only £200; by the year of Dawn Run's Gold Cup this had risen tenfold. Not that she could take all the credit. Hurdlers like Golden Cygnet, Daring Run, Ekbalco and chasers such as Half Free and Fifty Dollars More were also splendid advertisements for their sire. At his death in May 1987, aged 21, Deep Run had covered 2,100 mares resulting in 1,300 foals and over 600 races won.

Despite this attractive jumping pedigree, Dawn Run only made 5,800 guineas as a three-year-old at the Ballsbridge–Tattersalls November Sales in 1981. She was fortunate to get there. When only two months old she ran a high temperature, hovering at death's door for a week, and her first experience of a trailer induced such panic that a leg seemed sure to be broken. However, when she was led out of box 29 for the perusal of one prospective buyer the impact was instantaneous and spectacular. 'I said to myself, "Wow, here we go", I really and truly did.' By lunchtime Mrs Charmian Hill had bought herself a horse.

THE CHAMPION HURDLE

Sixty-two-year-old Mrs Hill was famous throughout Ireland as the 'Galloping Granny'. A fearless rider (her trainer reckoned 'it was as if the part of the brain that produces nerves and anxiety had been removed from her at birth') with wins to her name on the Flat, over hurdles and fences she was nevertheless, as Brough Scott so exquisitely put it, 'a lady so small and frail looking that you want to keep the grandchildren off her at teatime'. Her relationship with horses began aboard a 20-year-old, one-eyed pony called Bungie in pursuit of the Bree Hounds in County Wexford, and although competing in shows, she did not start riding in point-to-points until she was 40. Nonetheless, on her own horses Johnny, Sadlers Clerk and Boro Nickel, she eventually accumulated 18 victories. The next milestone was passed on 1 January 1973 when, in a Fairyhouse bumper, she became the first woman to ride against men under rules. She finished third that day but soon afterwards was successful on Yes Man at Killarney.

In November 1980 Yes Man and the 'Galloping Granny' were heading for another victory at Thurles. At the second-last hurdle Yes Man fell. It appeared a harmless parting of horse and rider until another runner landed on poor Yes Man, fatally injuring him, and Mrs Hill was crushed. Her own injuries were so serious – broken ribs and a broken neck – that she was flown to the National Rehabilitation Centre. To make matters worse, her kidneys stopped functioning. Despite losing 21lb from her tiny eight-stone frame, Mrs Hill was back in the saddle within a year, riding her new horse, Diamond Do, to victory in a bumper. 'I just bloody well made myself strong,' was the only explanation she could offer for such an unbelievable recovery.

Diamond Do subsequently hurt himself and Mrs Hill persuaded her son Oliver to join her in buying a replacement. They agreed on a maximum of £6,000. Mrs Hill ticked off likely candidates in the Ballsbridge catalogue, but in the event only had eyes for one. 'I feared she would fetch more than the £6,000 I had to spare. I started bidding and got to £5,800 and to my utter amazement the rival bidder stopped. He told me afterwards that he thought I was going on forever.'

The filly was brought home to the Hill residence on the outskirts of Waterford and broken. 'I never had less trouble with a young one but I was afraid she would not be competitive enough.' In the spring of 1982 Dawn Run was sent to Paddy Mullins. A farmer's

THE CHAMPION HURDLE

son, the reserved, almost shy Mullins took over his father's licence in 1953. Although he had won both legs of the Irish autumn double in addition to the Champion Stakes with Hurry Harriet, the stable was primarily a jumping one. By 1982 Mullins had won four Irish Nationals, for instance, and three races at the Cheltenham Festival. He had always done well with fillies and mares and sent out bonny Height O' Fashion to win a dozen races, including the Irish Cesarewitch, back in the early 1960s. Such was his knack that the year Height O' Fashion won the Cesarewitch she never had a saddle on her except in a race. 'I let the horse tell me what it is capable of. My aim is to do the best I can for them.' In Dawn Run, if truth be told, Mullins had inherited something more than just an ordinary filly. She was no meek and mild little thing. She could be as savage as an enraged witch when the mood seized her and one morning kicked the vet full in the chest when he tried to administer an injection, propelling him halfway across the yard. She looked more like a gelding or a colt, her ample derriere possessing the 'second leg' of extra muscle unusual for one of her sex. Dawn Run was, in the words of Mullins's son Tony, 'half masculine'.

Dawn Run made her début in a Clonmel bumper in May 1982, seemingly determined to make Charmian Hill eat her words. 'We went into the lead and when she was tackled by two others she stuck her ears back and ran on. She just hated being headed!' They slipped away to finish eighth but Dawn Run had revealed a glimpse of that inexhaustible pluck soon to become her trademark. Two races later she got her head in front at Tralee. It was an emotional victory for Mrs Hill since it would be her last – the previous day she had been informed by the Turf Club that they would not renew her licence.

The entire Mullins family, Paddy, wife Maureen and all five children, had ridden winners. A new jockey was therefore not hard to find. Tom Mullins won twice on the mare that summer although it was brother Tony who struck up the most famous rapport with her. Together they won five hurdle races during the 1982–83 season. However, Mrs Hill insisted on a more experienced jockey for Dawn Run's attack on Cheltenham's Sun Alliance Novices' Hurdle and engaged Ron Barry. Dawn Run led till collared by the winner Sabin du Loir. Afterwards Mrs Hill refused an offer of £50,000, a decision which began to look all the wiser in view of the mare's endeavours at Liverpool.

The subject of Dawn Run's jockey surfaced again after Ascot's

THE CHAMPION HURDLE

V.A.T. Watkins Hurdle in November. 'Dawn Run is a top-class mare, far better than anything I have ever had before,' said Mrs Hill, 'and I wanted an absolutely top-class jockey to ride her.' Tony Mullins never felt that he and Mrs Hill 'hit it off', though he knows not why. His father later aired his theory: 'She never gave a hint that she was in any way critical of anything I did with the horse except where Tony was concerned. She only took a dislike to Tony's connection with the horse because he was getting into the saddle that she thought was hers.' It was a surprised Jonjo O'Neill who received a phone call from Mullins, though a very grateful one. That horrific Bangor accident had kept him out of the sport he loved for 14 months, during which time he had undergone a bone graft in a Basle hospital. The new partnership prevailed by a short head in a driving finish with Amarach. The mare had not relished the firm ground yet still smashed the track record by four seconds. They lost their next race at Naas, giving away upwards of a stone to a smart field, before returning to England for the Christmas Hurdle where Gaye Brief would be in opposition.

The champion had won the Fighting Fifth on his reappearance, none too impressively as it happened, for he hit a couple of hurdles and would have been inconvenienced by Ekbalco had he not sustained a fatal fall. The sharp Kempton circuit and firm ground favoured Gaye Brief, but the stronger he pressed up the straight, the more Dawn Run found and she held on by a neck. It was afterwards revealed that Gaye Brief's training had been interrupted due to a small crack in a cannon bone incurred at Newcastle and he remained ante-post favourite for the Champion Hurdle.

Snow robbed Dawn Run of an outing in Haydock's Champion Hurdle Trial and she was rerouted to the Wessel Cable Champion Hurdle. Giving away lumps of weight to good horses, she won as she pleased by five lengths. The championship now assumed all the trappings of a match between Gaye Brief and Dawn Run — it was 20/1 bar the two in most lists — but a week before the shoot-out Gaye Brief was withdrawn owing to torn back ligaments. With the 5lb allowance increasing her advantage (she met the Wessel runner-up on 10lb better terms for instance), Dawn Run looked a cast-iron certainty and she dominated the betting in a manner not seen since the market went 9/1 bar Sir Ken in 1954. On this occasion the favourite started 5/4 on, with only the novice Desert Orchid (7/1) at odds shorter than 14/1 in a field of 14.

THE CHAMPION HURDLE

Dawn Run did not disappoint her public. Never out of the first two, O'Neill turned on the tap from the fifth hurdle. Desert Orchid immediately bequeathed Buck House the job of staying with her. However, he bashed the second-last, presenting Dawn Run with a two-length cushion entering the straight. O'Neill decided to run no risks and asked her to 'pop' the final obstacle but, as she had done at the last on several other occasions, the mare lost her concentration, struck the top and landed on all four feet. The only challenger remaining was the 66/1 outsider Cima. According to O'Neill, Dawn Run ground her teeth as soon as she heard him coming and, despite drifting right up the hill, eliciting three cracks down the shoulder from her rider, she had a bit to spare and won cosily by three-quarters of a length. The time, on good ground, was a new race record of three minutes 52.60 seconds.

The bedlam in the winner's enclosure was unimaginable even to veterans of previous Irish triumphs. A delirious throng of well-wishers breached the security cordon and Mrs Mill, dressed in clothes of her racing colours, was delicately hoisted aloft like a red and black flag. Inevitably, Dawn Run was voted Horse of the Year, the first of her sex to be so honoured. 'I did ask Paddy — a magic man who knew every grain of every oat she ate — what made her so special,' O'Neill recalled years later, 'and he just said she was always right on the right days. She never oozed with class like some horses, although she had a long old stride on her and you probably didn't know the ground you were covering. Above all she had guts. She was as tough as old boots. She needed humouring and, like most women, wanted to do things her own way and in her own time. You couldn't tell her what to do. She was a great challenge for any jockey to ride.'

The Dawn Run bandwagon continued to roll. She won the Sandeman at Aintree and two races in France, including the Grande Course de Haies d'Auteuil, thereby recording a hat-trick of Irish, English and French Champion Hurdles to amass record stakes for a single season of £149,957. 'The mare just keeps getting better and better,' said Mullins, 'and there is really no knowing just how good she really is. She has that will to win. When a horse goes past her, she fights back and simply won't give in. That's the one thing that makes her stand out above all the other horses I've ever trained.'

The new target was the Gold Cup. As the world knows that elusive goal was also achieved, on only her fifth outing over fences,

THE CHAMPION HURDLE

one gloriously memorable afternoon in 1986. Barely three months later she was dead, breaking her neck when attempting a repeat victory in the French Champion Hurdle. 'She was my life for four years,' said a heartbroken Mullins. O'Neill was not in the saddle that day at Auteuil as he had retired in April, but he has good cause to remember the month of June in 1986: he was diagnosed as having cancer of the lymphatic glands. In typical O'Neill fashion he licked the disease. 'The end is a sad old story,' he says. 'Thank God one of us is still here to tell it.' The 'Galloping Granny' survived her beloved mare by four years, dying on 11 January 1990 at the age of 70 after suffering a stroke on Christmas Day. Her morning visits to the Mullins yard to ride out had only finally been curtailed by another stroke two years earlier.

Dawn Run's meteoric career held the racing public spellbound to a degree unknown since the days of Arkle. Like him she mesmerised; like him she was worshipped; but unlike her immortal compatriot she took one chance too many. Dawn Run, in the words of the popular song, 'lived her life like a candle in the wind . . . the candle burned out long before the legend ever did'.

13

Lambourn Supreme

To overcome persistent leg problems and win three Champion Hurdles is enough in some people's eyes to merit See You Then being declared the greatest of them all. But because See You Then ran so infrequently, his detractors will inevitably harp on that fact as some kind of deficiency or failing on his part whenever comparisons – invidious, inadvisable but compelling all the same – are made with the other occupants of hurdling's hall of fame. See You Then's three titles only encompassed 6 hurdle races; Persian War competed in 15, Sir Ken 14, Hatton's Grace ten and Istabraq's subsequent hat-trick would also involve 14. In addition, both Persian War and Hatton's Grace ran on the Flat as reigning Champion Hurdlers.

Trainer Nicky Henderson is quick to acknowledge his champion's Achilles heel. 'I'd have loved to run him more and win more races with him – I'd have loved to run him in the Schweppes with 12 stone but he just wasn't made to take it. Basically, he had badly conformed front legs – he was back at the knee and with this condition you're going to get trouble.' This inherent disability ensured that See You Then was relatively unexposed to what top-class competition was available during a period when hurdling talent was pretty thin on the ground. 'Even so, he was a different class to anything else for three years and who's to say the horses around these days are worse than they were in Persian War or Sir Ken's day,' continued his eloquent trainer. 'You tend to think that Hatton's Grace and Sir Ken live on Mount Olympus. There's a magic about the names in history.' After See You Then appeared looking fitter and sharper than ever before in the spring of 1988, how ironic that he should lose the opportunity of humbling a far stronger field in the 1988 Champion Hurdle as a result of breaking down on his off-hind rather than those delicate forelegs. An historic

THE CHAMPION HURDLE

fourth victory would have put him out on his own and settled the carping once and for all.

See You Then's infrequent appearances meant he was never able to capture the public imagination in the way other champions had. In Henderson's words, 'He was always a mystery horse.' But he was a character and a half all the same, possibly the nastiest piece of work to win the Champion Hurdle since Clair Soleil. When See You Then first arrived in Henderson's yard his backside was plastered with mud and the staff soon discovered why – no one had ever got near enough to clean it off! 'He could easily have gone the wrong way,' says Henderson. 'I don't say he was unmanageable but looking after him is not the easiest job in the world.' The short straw fell to Glyn Foster, whose experiences as an apprentice with George Todd were to stand him in excellent stead. The Master of Manton invariably coaxed the best out of the old and temperamental alike. 'He wouldn't have them knocked about. If a horse has got ability, kindness makes them,' Foster explains. Large doses of tender loving care were needed to calm See You Then. 'He came with a bit of a reputation and I found he deserved it when mucking him out the next morning. The guv'nor came to ask if everything was all right and the horse flew across the box and had me in a corner! He was trying to kick me and his old head was coming round to try and bite me at the same time.' Nothing personal, of course. See You Then has also grabbed Frank Mahon, the vet, and, says Foster, 'He positively hates the guv'nor, never liked him from the moment he arrived. But it's only in the box, once outside he's fine. I wouldn't trust him 100 per cent and I'm always wary of him but I'm more awake than he is in the morning. I dread to think what he was like before he was gelded!'

See You Then was another example of the increasing trend among top-class hurdlers to own an aristocratic Flat race pedigree. Both his sire, dual classic winner Royal Palace, and his dam, the speedy Melodina, were trained by Noel Murless, as was the grandam Rose of Medina, who ran third in the Oaks. Indeed, See You Then's half sister Dubian was placed in the 1985 Oaks and won a Pattern race in Italy. He was sold for 17,000 guineas as a yearling to the Irish trainer Con Collins (who had won with his half brother Milverton), for whom he won five races (four on the Flat) before being purchased by the Marquis Cugliemi di Vulci, owner of the Stype Wood Stud, for a reported £60,000. His first outing in the

THE CHAMPION HURDLE

green and white checks resulted in another hurdle victory, after which he finished second in the Daily Express Triumph. His initial stay at Lambourn was intentionally brief for he was soon off to San Siro in Milan for the Corsa de Siepi dei Quattro Anni, a hurdle event worth £9,500 which he won easily by five lengths, and was due to remain in Italy. However, he fell on the roads, scraping his knees (the hair never regrew) and was returned to England where the Marquis believed he would get better treatment. When Henderson heard in July that See You Then was back at Stype Wood, up the road at Hungerford, he started making overtures about the horse's future.

A lengthy, rather angular, brown horse with a round action, See You Then possessed a devastating turn of foot which he put to good effect when winning at Ascot and Doncaster in his second season, but in between he was no match at levels for Browne's Gazette and Desert Orchid in the Christmas Hurdle, beaten 15 lengths and ten lengths into third. Brown's Gazette was the season's outstanding hurdler, having also collected the fighting Fifth and Bula (from Gaye Brief), and the prospect of See You Then improving 25 lengths in three months seemed unthinkable. Consequently, although he won the Champion Hurdle by seven lengths in record time (three minutes 51.70 seconds) there has to be an element of good fortune surrounding this first title since the 6/4 on favourite (there have been only seven shorter priced) swerved violently left as the tape rose, forfeiting almost 20 lengths, surely an impossible amount to recover in a race run at record pace.

'As we were lining up he almost took off and looked like charging the tape,' explained his jockey, Dermot Browne, 'so I turned him round and shouted to the starter but I was on the far side of him and other jockeys were also shouting – he can't have heard me because as I was turning round to my left he let them go.' Trainer Monica Dickinson saw things differently. 'He was caught napping. He should have charged the tape so there would have been a false start and they could have begun again. He'll remember this race for a long time.' (Browne went on to earn himself greater notoriety in the 1990s when he was named as 'The Needle Man' in a high-profile doping investigation; he was subsequently warned off for ten years after the Jockey Club found him to be in breach of six rules, including selling information to a bookmaker.) Browne's Gazette later gave the Champion Hurdle

THE CHAMPION HURDLE

third Stans Pride almost exactly the same beating in the Welsh Champion Hurdle as she had received from See You Then at Cheltenham, so it would have been a close-run thing.

As matters stood, however, the championship did not take much winning for in addition to the favourite's antics the effort of Gaye Brief (4/1 second favourite) fizzled out so rapidly on meeting the rising ground that a recurrence of some physical problem was feared (he'd recently been afflicted by a blood disorder), a view reinforced when he completed his only subsequent race in a very distressed state. Both placed horses, Robin Wonder and the mare Stans Pride, were no more than decent handicappers, as their starting prices of 66/1 and 100/1 amply indicated. 'Coming down the hill and jumping the second last, I stole a look round and I could hardly believe my eyes,' said See You Then's rider Steve Smith Eccles. 'Mine appeared to be the only runner still on the bridle.'

Smith Eccles's participation underlined the fact that the Browne's Gazette fiasco was not the only incident to capture the attention of a record first-day crowd of 27,880 before the Champion Hurdle was safely concluded. John Francome was See You Then's intended partner but in the previous race he took a nasty fall from The Reject, being 'hung up' by a stirrup for several strides. Badly shaken, he decided to forego the remainder of his rides and the mount was given to Steve Smith Eccles, a friend of his and the acknowledged 'wide-boy' of the weighing room. The stocky son of a Derbyshire miner, his riding experience was limited to a few bronco-busting jaunts on pit ponies until, at the age of 15, he went to Newmarket trainer Tom Jones on a month's trial. Smith Eccles first hit the headlines aboard the flying chestnut Tingle Creek and as his youthful, hunch-shouldered (he was always delivering coal on a Saturday as a schoolboy), relentlessly pushing style matured into that of a complete horseman, he began to rack up the winners and attract admirers. One of the latter was Nicky Henderson, latest in a long line of Old Etonians who found a life on the Turf a more attractive proposition than one in the City. He quit the lucrative haven of his father's stockbroking firm (tactfully bungling some vital exams) to learn at the knee of Fred Winter, a great friend of his late mother. 'Once I'd started riding out at Fred's there was no question of what I was going to do. It was fascinating! Wonderful!' After a three-year spell as Winter's assistant (during which time he booted home 69 winners as an amateur), Henderson set up shop at

THE CHAMPION HURDLE

Windsor House, Sir Hugh Nugent's old yard in Lambourn village, for the start of the 1978–79 season. The rosy cheeks, big saucer-shaped blue eyes and broad grin belie a self-confessed worrier. His first Festival winner would give him plenty of practice.

Like the last two five-year-olds to win the championship, Night Nurse and Persian War, See You Then successfully defended his title. On fast ground once more, the time was again quick (3.53.70) as See You Then, the 6/5 on favourite, humiliated his 22 opponents (11/1 bar him), the biggest field since 1967. There all similarity between See You Then's first two championships ends, because his preparation had presented Henderson with worry after worry. See You Then had summered so well that Henderson abandoned all hope of getting a run into him before Christmas, preferring to wait until 17 January and a thorough racecourse workout at Kempton Park instead. Viable opportunities were running short so Henderson elected to run him in the Oteley on 1 February. Understandably looking a trifle burly and ring-rusty, See You Then still accelerated on demand to beat Sabin du Loir and Tom Sharp without undue bother. With the condition of those legs, wrapped each morning like delicate porcelain, always in his thoughts, Henderson never planned to give See You Then many outings but the onset of freezing weather removed any possibility of another race before the Champion Hurdle. Consequently, Lambourn grew accustomed to the sound of Henderson's tractor harrowing the all-weather strip at two-hour intervals throughout the night so that See You Then could work in the morning. Henderson's tireless devotion to duty (he did much of the driving himself) was rewarded when not only the Champion Hurdler but also The Tsarevich and River Ceiriog achieved their Festival targets. As a result Henderson deservedly wound up topping the trainers' table for the first time, his 46 winners of £168,234 enabling him to pip his old boss Fred Winter by nearly £14,000.

Possibly the rumours concerning See You Then's fitness contributed to the large number of 'no-hopers' who entered the lists against him but, although three others crossed the second-last alongside him, only he and Gaye Brief were still on the bridle. Mrs Rimell's old champion had emerged from the doldrums of last spring to win at Ascot, lose honourably (at the weights) in the Bula and fall at the last in the Christmas Hurdle when assured of a place. He and See You Then took the last flight in identical fashion to

THE CHAMPION HURDLE

1985. Landing in unison, See You Then immediately asserted his usual authority to win by seven lengths, but at least Gaye Brief this year had the consolation of hanging on to second place. 'The race gave me no worries at all,' said Smith Eccles. 'There was never a moment when I was anything but convinced we would win and it all went absolutely as we had planned. Nicky was more of a worrier. When I'd walked into the parade ring, he was trying desperately to get a cigarette into his mouth with a hand that refused to stop shaking. It probably didn't help matters, but I said, "It's a bloody good job you're not riding him, boss."'

The champion was beaten in his next race, the Sandeman Aintree Hurdle, as much by the soft ground and additional five and a half furlongs as by the winner Aonoch (19th to finish in the Champion Hurdle), so the coveted third title, which had recently eluded Night Nurse, Monksfield and Sea Pigeon, remained within See You Then's compass as long as he stayed sound.

In October Henderson informed the press: 'A couple of runs before March and that may well be it. I do not want to overtax him before the big day.' By the end of January 'a couple of runs' appeared wildly optimistic for Henderson had virtually given up all hope of getting See You Then ready, and the newspaper sub-editors were having a field day with their obvious 'See You When' headlines. The main problem this year was a corn which caused inflammation to a foot, pastern and joint. 'If you have a problem like that the whole leg blows up. I was hopeful that the corn was the trouble, not the leg itself, though many didn't share my diagnosis! He didn't leave the yard for a month and just swam and swam.' At last, towards the end of February, Glyn Foster noticed a welcome change in the colour of the champion's coat. It began to go very black, a sure sign that he was coming right. Henderson was browbeaten into running him in the De Vere Hotels Hurdle at Haydock, 11 days before the Champion Hurdle. In soft ground, See You Then gave weight and a beating to his two opponents despite his 11 months of comparative inactivity. That completed the straightforward part of the operation. The tricky phase now ensued – how would those fragile forelegs react to the strain? It must have been inconvenient for Henderson and his staff to negotiate the following ten days with their fingers crossed, especially as they were 'leaping around from racecourse to racecourse and using other people's gallops' to get the horse fit to do himself justice, but it

THE CHAMPION HURDLE

proved worthwhile. See You Then was made 11/10 favourite to scale 'Mount Olympus'.

He had vanquished several of his 17 rivals in earlier years, notably the much-improved second favourite Nohalmdun. Peter Easterby's charge had won each of his three races, the Christmas Hurdle, Haydock's Trial and one at Ascot in which he defeated the Ladbroke winner Barnbrook Again. However, in the opinion of the cognoscenti, the one See You Then had to beat was Flatterer, who came not from Ireland, or even France, but from the USA.

Horses with American experience had competed in the Champion Hurdle before, Chenango of course being victorious, but Flatterer's participation was something different altogether since he was especially flown over four days prior to the race. Trained in Pennsylvania by Hertfordshire-born Jonathan Sheppard, the eight-year-old gelding numbered four Colonial Cups and two Temple Gwathmeys among his 22 victories (worth $500,000) and had won the Steeplechaser of the Year award four times in a row. Ocean-hopping was no novel experience for him as he had finished second in the 1986 French Champion Hurdle on a similar flying visit.

Neither the distance nor the obstacles, both unfamiliar, seemed to bother Flatterer in the race. He was up with the pace from the outset alongside Barnbrook Again, Corporal Clinger and See You Then's stablemate River Ceiriog. The champion himself was travelling ever so smoothly just behind them, however, filling Smith Eccles with confidence. 'I knew the opposition were not in the same class so I purposefully went middle to outer to steer clear of all traffic problems. We gave away ground that way but it made little difference. I woke up See You Then at the top of the hill but he pinged the second-last and got there too soon. I eased off going to the final flight and he blew up on the run-up but I was never worried.'

The same cannot be said for everyone watching, because after See You Then headed Barnbrook Again at the last, Flatterer, who had lost his place down the hill, renewed his challenge with the utmost zest. Had he and six times American champion jump jockey Jerry Fishback not misjudged the last – 'That cost us the prize – we were getting back at the end' – the winning margin of one and a half lengths would have been dramatically reduced. In the winner's enclosure Henderson hugged his wife Diana in a tangible gesture of relief and emotion. 'On what I'd been able to do with him he had

THE CHAMPION HURDLE

to blow up – it was a miracle he ran on really, and after the race I can tell you there wasn't another gallop in him. Haydock was the turning point. See You Then was getting too lazy and it was my head lad, Corky Browne, who talked me into running him there. Without that run he would not have won.'

If Henderson and his horse could endure the agony of another 364 days of torment the opportunity of matchless glory awaited them. The competition would be hot and the victor's laurels thus all the more noteworthy. Flatterer was due to return while two sons of Celtic Cone began the 1987–88 season very impressively, reviving the great Kinnersley–Uplands duels of yesteryear. Mercy Rimell's Celtic Chief won his four races with the aplomb of a future champion and in the last, the Lee Cooper Hurdle (the old Oteley) at Sandown, trounced Fred Winter's Celtic Shot, winner of his first four races, by a comfortable eight lengths to become 5/1 second favourite for the championship.

The noises emanating from Windsor House were sufficient to keep See You Then a firm favourite at 5/2. The champion was tearing up the gallops, giving every indication of being more forward than at this stage last year. On 7 February he did a nice piece of work over a stiff mile on the Faringdon Road gallop and Henderson decided to give him his championship warm-up in Wincanton's Kingwell Hurdle on 25 February. 'The Sandeman taught us he couldn't take three races, so we would have to do it in two. His final gallop at Manton was one of the most amazing I've ever seen. I jumped Rustle in, who's probably as good a workhorse as I've got, after seven furlongs. See You Then and the other two in the gallop had gone some lick beforehand. He kicked them aside and worked another seven furlongs with Rustle.'

When See You Then broke down at Wincanton the extent of Henderson's dismay was impossible to imagine because the damage occurred not in those perennially dodgy forelegs but the off-hind, a 'freak injury' according to Frank Mahon, who had seen only one similar in 20 years. See You Then had broken a splint bone and damaged the suspensory ligament, an extremely rare event in hind legs. Initial fears on the course that he might have to be put down were soon dispelled and he returned to Lambourn where, fitted with a specially made boot to support the fetlock, he commenced a lengthy period of recuperation. Ten wins in fifteen hurdle races (with only the last unplaced) for record earnings of £153,235 is a

THE CHAMPION HURDLE

career of which all connected with Windsor House could justifiably be proud – but the Champion Hurdle had not seen the last of See You Then.

With Flatterer forced into retirement after breaking down in the Breeders' Cup Steeplechase, any international flavour in this year's championship was going to originate from France. A few decades had passed since the last serious Gallic threat but in view of Nupsala's historic victory in the King George VI Chase, which rudely shattered the home side's chauvinistic attitude to jump racing, the news that France's top hurdler Marly River was being aimed at the Champion Hurdle whipped up a mighty wave of anticipation.

The half-bred Marly River was a five-year-old colt, not particularly handsome but particularly effective. He cost his owner, Christian-Serge Homeau, the equivalent of £3,000 and had won him nearly one hundred times that much in the course of nine consecutive victories over hurdles (he had fallen in one steeplechase), the last of which, needless to say, the Prix Juigne on 6 March, was microscopically examined by the British media. When introduced into the Champion Hurdle betting two months earlier, Marly River could be backed at 33/1 – by the time he had scooted home clear of a field which included the current French Champion Hurdler Claude Le Lorrain and the Breeders' Cup Chase winner Gacko, his odds had shrunk to 9/2. This would be no hit-or-miss expedition. His trainer Yann Porzier had taken the precaution of schooling him over three specially constructed English hurdles at his Lamorlaye stable and had arranged for his jockey, Jean-Yves Artu, to ride the championship course in the Waterford Crystal Supreme Novices' Hurdle an hour before the Champion Hurdle. However, most of Marly River's homework was done on sand over a perfectly flat surface on soft or heavy ground which suited a round-actioned horse such as himself. How would he handle Cheltenham's varied and testing topography?

It would not have been the Festival without traffic jams (seven miles from one direction) and rainstorms. The latter favoured not only Marly River (15/2) but also the Mullins's mudlark Cloughtaney (5/1), who was laid to lose over £250,000 by both Hills and Ladbrokes, and Celtic Shot (7/1), whom Uplands was convinced would reverse the form with Celtic Chief, the 5/2 favourite.

THE CHAMPION HURDLE

The 21 runners set off at a fierce gallop and Celtic Chief was never able to occupy the dominating position he had at Sandown. By contrast, Celtic Shot was always handily placed as first Floyd and Marly River, and then Juven Light did the spadework. The latter had cracked by the second last where Swingit Gunner came through to dispute the lead with Celtic Shot. His effort proved short-lived and rounding the bend it seemed the only danger to Celtic Shot was the 33/1 Irish outsider Classical Charm. He cannot have been more than a neck adrift up those final slogging 200 or so yards into the teeth of the wind but this was a day when good old-fashioned guts was an unbeatable currency and Celtic Shot's account was well in the black. Classical Charm gave his all but Celtic Shot stuck his neck out and battled on indefatigably to win by four lengths. Celtic Chief ran through tired horses to be third.

Celtic Shot's capture of the record £52,225 first prize confirmed racing is the stuff of which dreams are made. His success broke the ice in the race for Peter Scudamore, three times a runner-up on Broadsword, Cima and Gaye Brief, back from a three-week suspension with something to prove. He had not been happy with his riding of Celtic Shot at Sandown. 'Mr Winter did not have to say anything after Sandown – he just looked at me and I knew how he felt. I made more use of my fellow this time and the experience was obviously not lost on me. They always say practice makes perfect!'

The three times champion jockey was bred for the job, being the son of Michael Scudamore, winner of a National on Oxo, and at the age of eight he was writing in a school essay imagining life 20 years hence: 'I have been champion jockey for the past five seasons.' But he was never pushed into it. A studious, thoughtful (he admits to enjoying Kipling verse) and highly respected pupil at his public school, Belmont Abbey ('He had great depth and concentration and modesty,' its headmaster said of his former deputy head boy who left with two A-levels), Scudamore's mother fancied him as an estate agent rather than a jockey. Despite his seemingly compliant nature, the young Scudamore was made of strong stuff and knew his own mind. When he was 16, and his father refused to allow him to ride a disreputable animal in a point-to-point, he packed his bags and left home. He didn't get very far before his father picked him up in his car but the point had been made. Peter Scudamore was going to be his own man. After leaving school, he was dispatched

THE CHAMPION HURDLE

to Royston to spend six months with Willie Stephenson, and when this experience failed to rid him of his perilous intentions he went to Stephenson's nephew, David Nicholson. From there on it was onwards and upwards. Scudamore rode his first winner in 1978 and within four seasons won his first championship.

The victory also continued the love affair that had begun 20 years earlier when owner-breeder David Horton was smitten by a foal called Clay Duck, a half sister of Clear Cut, winner of the Mackeson and Topham. It took Horton two years to raise the £500 necessary to buy her and she did him proud, gaining a hurdle success in record time at Fakenham and throwing Clayside (winner of the 1981 Arkle Challenge Trophy) and Duckdown, a big mare who won twice over hurdles before producing Celtic Shot. As a yearling Celtic Shot had often been unruly and once gave Horton's daughter, Sue, who broke him, a particularly nasty moment. Going to be lunged one day, Charlie, as he was affectionately known, got slightly free and she was forced to give him too much rein. Charlie set off down the field with Sue in the unenviable position of being directly behind him when he accepted the chance of lashing out with both hind legs. Fortunately, she was quick enough to bring both her arms up to her face but in so doing broke one arm, the other elbow and her nose.

Celtic Shot was Fred Winter's seventh winner of the championship, three as a jockey and four as a trainer, and therein lay the real story of the 1988 Champion Hurdle for this living, breathing symbol of all that is integral to the sport of National Hunt racing was not present to witness one of his stable's greatest triumphs. Back in September he had suffered a stroke and fallen down the stairs back at Uplands. Winter sustained a fractured skull and damage to the left side of his brain. Recovery would be slow. Thanks to the teamwork and corporate pride Winter had instilled in them, the Upland staff carried on under his young assistant Charlie Brooks and head lad Brian Delaney, who had been with him since the start in 1964. 'Fred watched the whole race on television. He knew exactly what had happened and was absolutely thrilled,' said Diana Winter. 'We were all rather emotional afterwards.'

After surviving 319 bone-crushing falls during his riding career, Winter found the ravages of this one in his own home virtually impossible to beat. Speech and mobility became increasingly onerous. Not that Winter conceded defeat. 'Win if you can,' was the customary parting shot as he used to leg-up his jockey – and he

THE CHAMPION HURDLE

continued to practise as well as he preached. Such indefatigable and indomitable spirit ensures Fred Winter a home in the hearts and minds of every person remotely interested in racing.

14

Toby Takes on Newmarket

Fred Winter's enforced retirement meant Charlie Brooks assumed official control of Celtic Shot's defence of the championship. The champion's preparation amounted to four races and his single success came in a minor event at Leicester first time out. Nor had the other Celtic – Chief (who would be the last championship runner carrying the Rimell banner) – enjoyed an auspicious lead-up to the Festival, winning one of his three. Soft ground seemed essential for either of the Celtics to be seen to their best advantage at Cheltenham.

The new kid on the block was Kribensis and he represented the shape of things to come. His CV was Flat-racing through and through. Owned by Sheikh Mohammed and trained by Michael Stoute at Newmarket, he should have been gracing Royal Ascot (indeed he had run third in the 1987 King George V Handicap) instead of the National Hunt Festival but he could be a bit of a 'lad' temperamentally: returning from exercise one morning he decided to mount the horse ahead of him in the string, to the considerable consternation of the boy riding the unfortunate beast. He boasted an unbeaten record of six victories over timber which included the previous season's Daily Express Triumph Hurdle and the latest Christmas Hurdle, where his main victim was Floyd who had beaten Celtic Chief in the Fighting Fifth and would later add the Kingwell. However, no horse had achieved the Daily Express–Champion Hurdle double since Persian War (although Night Nurse, Monksfield and See You Then were Triumph losers) and at the age of five Kribensis might still not be sufficiently battle-hardened. 'The Triumph isn't a killer,' observed the wily Stoute, 'but most runners have had a busy Flat season as three-year-olds and never have a break. For a lot of them, the tank is nearly dry. The programme for Kribensis was very different. He did have a nice break.'

THE CHAMPION HURDLE

Grey skies disgorging plenty of rain provided a suitable backdrop to an opening day of shocks. The first two races went to 20 and 25/1 shots and the Champion Hurdle would fall to only the second 50/1 'no-hoper' in its history. Moreover, Beech Road was lucky to be alive, let alone lining up for the Champion Hurdle and eventually winning it. Like Blaris and, more recently, Salmon Spray, his preparation had involved outings over fences and on 2 January, at Cheltenham, he was given up for dead after falling horrifically at the last and staying down for fully ten minutes. 'I only watched the race on television but I remember fearing the worst,' said the seven-year-old's trainer Toby Balding, 'We decided to revert to hurdling after that fall even though his form did not flatter him. He's got a very delicate constitution and was a total lunatic when he first came over to us from Trevor Hallett, where apparently he was broken, ridden away and won all within the space of seven weeks. He was terribly revved up and it was a job to get him to eat. Even now he carries little condition.'

Unlike, some might say, his eloquent (always an active voice in racing politics) and ebullient trainer whose efforts to ride in point-to-points as a young man were soon stymied by the tyranny of the scales. Toby Balding (christened Gerald but nicknamed after a family friend to avoid confusion with his trainer-father) had held a licence for over 30 years, having taken command of Fyfield upon his father's premature death in 1957. Big and bespectacled, genial and gregarious, Balding (elder brother of Flat trainer Ian) had already won a Grand National in 1969 with Highland Wedding (and would succeed again a month later with Little Polveir), whilst Cool Ground's Gold Cup victory of 1992 enabled him to follow in the footsteps of the Anthony brothers (Jack and Owen), Briscoe, O'Brien, Price, Walwyn, Rimell, and Winter and become only the ninth trainer in history to collect all three of the brightest jewels in the National Hunt calendar.

Despite appearances to the contrary, however, Beech Road was clearly made of stern stuff and a mere seven weeks after his brush with death he won the National Spirit at Fontwell. It was originally planned that the next step would be a crack at either the Imperial Cup or the County Hurdle ('He's entered in the Champion but I think that's clutching at straws,' Balding had informed the press), but after consulting with the chestnut's owner, St Austell garage proprietor Tony Geake (who paid a mere 2,800 guineas for him as

THE CHAMPION HURDLE

a foal), the trainer elected to go for broke. Nor was Beech Road's partner deficient in the backbone department. If ever a jump jockey aspired to being his own man it was Richard Guest. The 23-year-old son of one jockey in Charlie and younger brother of another in Rae, was something of a firebrand: 'What's on my heart is on my tongue. I'm not the most diplomatic person, I say what I feel.' Guest, who once upon a time had ridden out Beech Road's sire Nearly A Hand in his school holidays, favoured a patient, quiet style of race-riding but this penchant often got him into hot water with those who wondered how hard he was trying and in 1998 resulted in him slinging his licence through the door of the stewards' room at Perth after being suspended under the 'non-triers' rule. 'It's like saying to an artist, "No, you can't use your brush like that any more, you've got to paint this way instead." What you do as a jockey is an art. And if you believe in what you do, but you are not allowed to do it your way, what's the point?' Opined Balding: 'Yes, he's an arrogant little bugger but that's half his ability.' Later on, the jockey's patient handling of sketchy jumper Red Marauder in the infamous Grand National slog of 2001 would also be rewarded with a memorable success.

Thus no one was in the least bit surprised to see Beech Road languishing at the tail of the field as Floyd cut out a sedate pace (the final time was three seconds slower than the Novices' Hurdle) on the first circuit, closely followed by Kribensis who, despite the rain promising a tougher contest than a five-year-old might conceivably relish, was sent off the 11/8 favourite. Kribensis made his challenge on the last bend but the horse approaching the last flight seemingly full of running was none other than Beech Road, and he came up the run-in with all guns blazing to repel the late thrusts of the two Celtics (both running on after being taken off their feet when the tempo quickened down the hill) and become, in the words of the *Racing Post*, 'The champion who came back from the dead.'

'He was taking lengths off every horse,' reported Guest. 'He was so good I even had to take a tug at the top of the hill, as we were getting there too soon. Can you imagine taking a pull in the Champion Hurdle? You wouldn't believe it!' For Kribensis, suffering his first defeat, the championship, reflected his trainer, may have come a year too early.

Beech Road demonstrated his success was no fluke by first of all going on to Aintree and winning the Sandeman Aintree Hurdle over

THE CHAMPION HURDLE

two and a half miles by seven lengths and then, in the course of a more orthodox run-up to the 1990 championship, adding two impressive victories at Cheltenham (both over the longer trip, it must be said) from four starts. Despite the continuing winning ways of Kribensis, whose victories in the Fighting Fifth, Christmas Hurdle and Kingwell improved his record to nine wins out of ten, the reigning champion was a warm order to retain his title. 'Personally I can see no reason why he shouldn't have a favourite's chance,' said Balding. 'I have no reason to think he's any worse than last year and some reason to think he might be a bit better. He's gone from being a total lunatic to being very relaxed and professional.'

Stoute's one-horse jumping yard was 'on' Kribensis to a man. The grey son of Derby winner Henbit was one year older and one year stronger, and the ground for the championship was going to be fast – favouring him, not Beech Road. This was no two-horse race, however. Balding fielded an interesting second string in Morley Street, a strapping six-year-old chestnut by champion jumping sire Deep Run. Said Balding: 'He was very much the dandy, an extremely good-looking horse. But for some reason you always have it in the back of your mind that with a horse that good-looking, if things don't go absolutely right for him he might not give it everything he's got.' Thus far, Morley Street had not done much wrong, winning six of his nine starts, including a prestigious novices' event at Aintree the previous spring.

There was further flat-race involvement courtesy of the 1988 Cesarewitch winner Nomadic Way, who sported the colours of Robert (The Minstrel, Alleged, Golden Fleece) Sangster and was trained by Barry Hills. The five-year-old entire had followed a good second place in the Bula with victory in the Wessel Cable Champion Hurdle at Leopardstown.

However, the choice for most popular winner was no contest. See You Then was back in the arena. Somehow Nicky Henderson had patched up his dodgy-legged reprobate triple champion, and two years after his Wincanton tumble had got him back on the track at Nottingham on 17 February, where he finished sixth of eight to Royal Derbi. 'The problem,' conceded Henderson, 'will be getting the killer instinct back into him. A lot of horses come back after a year off but I have not had one after such a long break and one that had been consciously retired and totally let down. It's one thing to make a comeback at seven or eight but at ten it is a different story.

THE CHAMPION HURDLE

It's a bit like asking me to run in the Olympics! We were under no illusions that we had to train him properly. There could be no pussyfooting around. We couldn't treat him like glass as we had done during his title-winning days. We schooled him round Wincanton, which was very special. A lot of the crowd stayed behind and SIS screened it live. He galloped round in eerie silence, jumping like a stag, and when he had jumped the last everyone applauded. I felt everyone who had stayed there had appreciated him for once. When he was champion he never had the popularity he deserved, considering what he had achieved, because he was this mystery horse that appeared at Cheltenham and that was all people saw of him. We had jokes about "See You When". Now he is an underdog and has captured people's imagination for this pipedream of a comeback and is more popular than he ever was when a star.'

Sadly, See You Then was to perform like the 25/1 shot he was, beating only one home in the championship he had once made his own. After another lacklustre display in the Scottish Champion Hurdle, his handler finally called time on a career which now read ten wins from nineteen starts over hurdles. 'He was the best I've trained,' Henderson stated, an opinion replicated by Steve Smith Eccles: 'See You Then was the classiest horse I have ridden, although I'd have to say Tingle Creek was the most exciting. I did ride Kribensis, too, first time out at Doncaster after schooling him at Newmarket, but then I was claimed to ride one of Nicky's and Richard came in for the ride and kept it. See You Then was a horse who could go fast at cruising pace and keep it going. He skimmed over hurdles, never breaking stride, and possessed the devastating ability to quicken up in a matter of strides. That's what made him so special.'

Once Balding's Forest Sun (in the Morley Street colours) had landed the opener, the trainer must have wondered whether his luck was in or used up. Certainly some modicum of fortune proved useful during eventful early moments. After one false start, Keith Brown (subsequently to star in a far more infamous starting gate fiasco at the 1993 Grand National) got them away and three of the nineteen participants departed over the first two flights as Sudden Victory led stablemate Nomadic Way left-handed into the back straight. As was his wont, Beech Road brought up the rear until the top of the hill when the 2/1 favourite could be spotted making his customary progress on the outside along with Kribensis. The final

THE CHAMPION HURDLE

hurdle saw four in a line – Beech Road, Past Glories, Kribensis and Nomadic Way – but on this slick surface it was the superior Flat-race speed of Kribensis that would turn out to be decisive. At the line he had three lengths to spare over Nomadic Way with Past Glories (at 150/1 the longest-priced horse ever to reach the places) and Beech Road ('Always flat-out and never travelling as well as last year on this ground,' according to Guest) a further three-quarter length and half length adrift. Kribensis had laid the 22-year-old Triumph Hurdle bogey and stopped the clock in a new record of 3 minutes 50.70 seconds.

The victorious connections were accustomed to winning championship events on the Flat with a string of famous names (Unite, Musical Bliss, Sonic Lady et al) but this amounted to something entirely different. Sheikh Mohammed had followed events via satellite television back home in Dubai but Stoute, the son of a Barbados chief of police whose path to training stardom was paved initially by losing out to Julian Wilson in an audition for a job as a BBC commentator, was present to savour the moment. Almost as renowned in Newmarket for his singing, whistling, humming and passion for cricket (he has a net complete with bowling machine in his back garden) as his gift for training blue-blooded thoroughbreds, Stoute grew up next door to the Garrison Savannah racetrack and would shin over the wall to assist an English ex-jockey named Freddie Thirkell who had set up as a trainer. 'I was only six but I knew absolutely then that I wanted to train racehorses. I didn't ride until I got on my father's police horses – it wasn't the riding, it was the racing I was after.' Luckily for the young Stoute, a friend of his father's – the Chief Justice, no less – knew the Yorkshire handler Pat Rohan and arranged for the budding trainer to join him at the age of 19. 'Michael has always been a natural with horses and a natural with people,' says Rohan. 'He seems to be able to judge a horse's ability from a very early age. He has great patience and, whatever he says, he always commands respect.' Stoute soon picked up the thread and after further stints with Doug Smith and Tom Jones he was ready to strike out on his own in 1972 at the age of 26 with a string of just 15 horses in a rented yard. Six years later he won his first Classic, the Oaks with Fair Salinia. The sky was the limit. Stoute proved time and again what a sorcerer he is with older horses by sending out the likes of Pilsudski and the Sheikh's own Singspiel to snaffle ultra-competitive international prizes such as the

THE CHAMPION HURDLE

Breeders' Cup Turf, Japan Cup and the Dubai World Cup: now he had worked the oracle with the single jumper in his 191-horse stable. 'There's been a tremendous build-up with Kribensis being the only jumper in the yard. It will have meant a great deal to everyone. I'm delighted for the horse as well as the staff because he's had his knockers and things didn't go right for him in the race last year. He wasn't man enough for the job last year, not tough enough. Up to then he'd found it easy, coming there on the bridle and winning the race, but in the Champion Hurdle they were stretching and increasing the pace from halfway and he just wasn't strong enough at that stage of his career. It was the first time he had ever carried 12 stone.'

Richard Dunwoody was likewise winning his first Champion Hurdle, thereby completing the 'big three' initiated by the 1986 Grand National (West Tip) and 1988 Gold Cup (Charter Party) and gaining membership of the exclusive club numbering just seven others: F.B. Rees, Leader, Cullinan (who did so in the same year, 1930), Wilson, Winter, Beasley and Robinson.

In equine terms, Dunwoody was a box-walker of massive proportions. 'I had been tensed up during the race because of the expectancy and because I know how often in racing the expected doesn't happen,' he confessed. 'The sensation of winning was as much a feeling of relief. I was a bit worried going away from the stands but I had got a good position by the time we were at the top of the hill, although we were taken wide round it. I then got a good lead from Nomadic Way and my horse battled on well up the hill.'

Although not yet a champion jockey he was fast becoming a complete jockey. 'Every jockey has a good point,' said Jonjo O'Neill, 'but every point Richard has is good. He's got style and class. He can ride any type of race, on any type of horse, and is always in control. He makes it look easy.' For his part, John Francome declared he had never seen anyone better. 'He's got it all, and he does the one thing in sport which is harder to do than anything else – and that is nothing. Like all top sportsmen he seems to create a bit more time, he anticipates things and never flaps, and fence-to-fence throughout the season he gets it right more often than anyone else.' Scudamore concurred: 'Richard is the supreme rider, completely unflappable. He doesn't unbalance horses; he gets the best out of them but doesn't try to make them go faster than

THE CHAMPION HURDLE

they're capable. And what sets him apart is his bravery and his toughness. He's a very tough man.'

If the Belfast-born Dunwoody belonged rather more to the Francome academy of artistry than the Scudamore school of effectiveness, it is nonetheless fair to say that he absorbed much of the current champion's singlemindedness – and more besides. Although Scudamore had introduced to the job of jump jockey a level of dedication and determination never seen before, Dunwoody revised the formula courtesy of a fanatical devotion to, and dissection of, all its components that found vivid expression in the title of his autobiography, *Obsessed*. He consulted dieticians and even a sports psychologist in order to secure that extra edge, over and above his God-given talent. 'It is not so much an obsession with winning,' he explained. 'I don't mind being beaten, provided I've done my best for the horse. I thought seeing someone might give me some sort of advantage. Mental attitude and preparation of the mind are very important. The key is to minimise the number of mistakes and to be better than the next person. For the likes of myself and Scu to get where we have, you can't be entirely normal.'

Dunwoody became fiercely competitive – according to one girlfriend, he even competed with her to see which of them could be first to get their key in the lock to his house. 'Down at the start you ask another jock what his is doing and he will tell you,' attests Jamie Osborne. 'Ask Richard and he will just mutter something unintelligible. He really cares that much.' Losing a race necessitated endless viewings of the video to check whether he'd been at fault and if the answer was in the positive his torment extended to physical self-abuse, banging himself into walls and doors. Dunwoody drove himself to the very brink of physical and mental exhaustion, often falling asleep at the dinner table. 'Winning was like a drug to me but I shouldn't have let the pressures get to me the way they did. If you're aiming for the top it's probably a requirement to become obsessed about the job but I found that's not a good trait.'

The son of a horseman father and a trainer's daughter, the seeds of fanaticism were sewn early. At the age of four he was unshipped by his donkey Seamus, picked himself up and boldly announced to his father that he had fallen off 'just like a jockey'. At school, near Cheltenham naturally, he began to starve himself for fear he'd become too heavy to fulfill his destiny; in the holidays he once travelled down to Newton Abbot armed with his new Polaroid

THE CHAMPION HURDLE

camera intent on snapping his hero, Peter Scudamore. He left school at 17 and had spells with Paul Kelleway and Tim Forster (famously riding a four-timer at Hereford as an amateur) before assuming Scudamore's mantle at David Nicholson's powerful stable. From there the rise of the jockey soon to be christened 'The Prince' was inexorable.

Dunwoody never did add to his Champion Hurdle tally but at his retirement in December 1999, brought about at the age of 35 owing to muscle wasting in an injured upper right arm, he topped the list of leading jump jockeys with a total of 1,699 British winners. These included a record ten century-seasons (though never a double-century like Scudamore: 197 was his best), three jockeys' championships and partnerships with equine stars of the calibre of Desert Orchid and One Man. Furthermore, in November 2001 a panel of experts comprising Mercy Rimell, David Nicholson and John Oaksey adjudged him to be the best postwar champion, ahead of Tony McCoy and Fred Winter – with John Francome astonishingly not in the top five.

There would be no title defence for Kribensis under the aegis of a new championship sponsor, Michael Smurfit's paper and packaging company. Kribensis had experienced a bleeding problem during the summer and was resting at the Sheikh's Kildangan Stud in Ireland. The Balding boys were back. Beech Road had won the Fighting Fifth but was increasingly more layabout than loony, and much prone, reported his trainer, 'to stopping at the foot of the gallops, looking up at the sky, and playing to the gallery'. Then, at Windsor, he did it on the racecourse and refused to take part. Despite the old champion being on his best behaviour when winning at Fontwell next time up, Morley Street was arguably now the principal Fyfield standard-bearer. Arguably, because Morley Street's most eyecatching performance had come over fences. After a running-on fifth in the Champion Hurdle he had gone to Aintree and won the Sandeman over the longer trip, and then, having warmed up by defeating a St Leger winner in Michelozzo on the Flat at Goodwood, he crossed the Atlantic to land the Breeders' Cup Steeplechase. However, a disastrous show over the stiffer obstacles at Kempton's Christmas meeting, where he jumped badly to the left and broke a blood vessel, prompted a complete break (herding sheep at Geoffrey Peate's Manor Farm Stud, near Tunbridge Wells in Kent, his customary summer holiday destination) and a subsequent return to

THE CHAMPION HURDLE

hurdles at Newbury. 'I think he must have frightened himself to death over fences,' mused Balding. 'He's always been as exciting a horse as I've ever had. He has everything – speed, stamina, physique, the whole lot – and he's such an athlete. The only worry I've ever had with him is he's just a bit of a playboy, a natural show-off and very pleased with himself, though he's matured a lot mentally, and there's no doubt he is best on good, fast ground, whereas Beech Road prefers wet, winter ground. I'd be very happy if either won and wouldn't be surprised if they were first and second.'

Not the strongest championship field in depth (albeit 24 in number equalling the record of 1964) it contained one fascinating participant in The Illiad, because the Irish would need a high security vessel to transport their winnings back home if he successfully completed the double initiated by Destriero in the Supreme Novices': backed from 18/1 to 11/2 he would take £10 million out of the ring.

The bookmakers were, as usual, rescued. The Illiad made a bad mistake at the fourth flight and trailed home last. Beech Road also struggled on the good ground and, for a moment at the top of the hill, it seemed his better-fancied stablemate (the 4/1 favourite) was about to come to grief. As Nomadic Way went past the tiring leader, Sondrio, he squeezed him up, causing Morley Street to clip the latter's heels and scrape the turf with his nose. 'After that I could almost hear Morley Street saying: "Right, boss, do you want to go for home? I'm going",' Morley Street's pilot Jimmy Frost later told the press. 'That was it, and we set sail. We were probably in front too long but then I remembered reading what Tim Molony had said: "If you want to go and win your race make sure you go at the second-last and don't worry about the final hill. That's where races are won at Cheltenham." Morley Street is becoming a man He always picks up the leaders in a matter of strides, he has so much speed – he'd win even over six furlongs. He'd had enough by the last and when I heard the noise I realised that something must be closing on me, but I just gave my fellow a crack and that was enough. This is better than winning the Grand National.'

For the long-legged Frost, who had won the 1989 National for Balding on Little Polveir, this was indeed the finest hour. After turning professional in 1983, success for the West Country farmer's son was mostly low-key (if one excludes his 'starring' role as stunt

THE CHAMPION HURDLE

rider and double in the movie *Run Wild, Run Free*, filmed on Dartmoor) until Balding went searching for someone 'with long legs and no brain' to partner his notoriously unreliable jumper Lucky Vane during 1986. Victory in the Champion Hurdle was also sweet for Morley Street's owner Michael Jackson, not least because as a paper manufacturer himself, taking money from a rival like Michael Smurfit was particularly pleasurable. On the debit side, the late thrust of Ruling, by far the strongest finisher in the race, did a man who had undergone three heart bypass operations no good whatsoever!

Morley Street looked a class act and immediately stamped his authority on the scene with another victory over the championship runner-up Nomadic Way in the Sandeman. Although Jackson's flat-race ambitions for a tilt at the Ascot Gold Cup did not come to fruition, Morley Street did contest the Doncaster Cup, failing by only a short head, before adding a second Breeders' Cup Steeplechase. Having won his first English start back over timber round Ascot, he gave championship opposition some hope when failing by a short head to concede Chirkpar 3lb in the Irish Champion Hurdle. Balding was undismayed: all he prayed for was a dry spring. His other champion would not line up at Cheltenham, having spent the season back over fences. Beech Road would add 7 chases to the 11 victories over hurdles before he was pensioned off in 1996 at the venerable age of 14. 'He has been amazing – a one-off,' declared his grateful trainer in tribute. 'He ended up being as near as good a chaser as he was a hurdler, and has been an absolute credit to everyone. It's been a joy to have him for ten years.'

Another absentee was Nomadic Way. After twice occupying second spot in the championship, he finally gave up the ghost and went instead for the Stayers' Hurdle – and won. Kribensis had returned to action, finishing second at Haydock a fortnight before the championship, but in truth it seemed Sheikh Mohammed boasted a better prospect in Royal Gait, trained by Michael Stoute's former assistant James Fanshawe, who had been largely responsible for the grey's day-to-day supervision in 1990 having won his National Hunt training stripes with Josh Gifford and his aunt Dinah's husband – who happened to be David Nicholson: 'I lived on nothing but cheese and whisky there because that's all he'd have in the larder!' Fanshawe belied his gangly six-foot-two-inch, eleven-stone frame (later immortalised via the skeleton adorned with his trademark

THE CHAMPION HURDLE

thick-rimmed spectacles that he adopted in a self-deprecatory advertising campaign entitled 'Hungry for More Winners') to ride successfully in point-to-points – 'I'd wanted to be a jump jockey but I grew like a pig' – before a fall broke his neck, necessitating six weeks in traction and four screws securing a metal halo to his head. In 1990, still only 27, Fanshawe took out a licence of his own to train at Newmarket's historic Pegasus Stables, whose original yard was completed by Fred Archer shortly before his death in 1886. After nearly eight years with a Flat-race master like Stoute, his attentions had to be similarly directed and he enjoyed instant Group 1 success with Environment Friend in the Eclipse Stakes but, he assured early press enquirers, 'if a horse like Kribensis came along I would be only too happy to have a go with him over the sticks'. Such a horse duly arrived within 18 months.

Royal Gait came to Fanshawe with quite a history. Conceived at the Limestone Stud of Doorknocker's owner Clifford Nicholson, the bay son of Eclipse winner Gunner B out of a mare tracing to the Vincent O'Brien-trained champion stayer Gladness was purchased as a somewhat 'stroppy' two-year-old for export to Spain, where, gelded, he won eight races on the Flat including three at Group level prior to collecting the Group 1 Prix du Cadran, the French equivalent of the Ascot Gold Cup. Transferred to John Fellows in France, he proceeded to win four more, notably the Group 1 Prix Royal-Oak in 1987, before attempting to add the Ascot Gold Cup the following summer. There ensued one of racing's most infamous *causes célèbres*. Royal Gait passed the post a comfortable five-length victor but, adjudged to have caused interference (even though his 'victim' was tiring badly and dropping out of contention), he was disqualified and placed last, the race being awarded to the favourite Sadeem, owned by Sheikh Mohammed. Royal Gait had been hard done by. Sheikh Mohammed subsequently bought him but the gelding had no opportunity for revenge, being struck down with an injury to his off-fore tendon that ensured lengthy recuperation at the Sheikh's Kildangan Stud in Ireland – where he demonstrated his future inclinations by constantly jumping out of his paddock. A plan for Henry Cecil to train him for the 1990 Ascot Gold Cup fell through and when he did return to Newmarket in November 1991 it was to Pegasus House with the Champion Hurdle as his target.

Recalls Fanshawe: 'He came to us fit from cubbing with the Belvoir in the hands of Emma Newton, who looked after the

THE CHAMPION HURDLE

hunters belonging to Sheikh Mohammed's racing manager Anthony Stroud. He loved jumping from the start, which was helped, I'm sure, by cubbing. We thought about running him on the Flat again but, being three years older, we thought he'd have lost some of his pace and that the pace of a hurdle race wouldn't be so intense.'

Fanshawe started Royal Gait off at Kempton on Boxing Day and the old boy ran the decent novice Travado to 3 and a half lengths. Three years *hors de combat* or no, Royal Gait was up and running and he soon won twice at Nottingham. Just 11 weeks into his comeback and début as a novice hurdler, he came to the sport's blue riband as the third favourite. 'With his history of leg problems and aged nine now,' concluded Fanshawe, 'we thought it might be a case of now or never.' No novice had won the championship in the 37 years since Doorknocker; and Royal Gait had been displaying the worrying trait of hanging left-handed under pressure in his hurdle races. There would be pressure a-plenty up the Cheltenham hill on 10 March.

Ironically, the strongest opposition to Morley Street appeared to come from his own brother Granville Again, who had finished second to Destriero in the previous season's Sun Alliance Novices' before winning all four of his starts this campaign. Both chestnuts were bred at the Boyne Bank Stud, near Trim in County Meath, by Marshall Parkhill (who also bred 1983 Grand National hero Corbiere) from the Straight Deal mare High Board, a granddaughter of Royal Alliance for whom he paid 120 guineas at the dispersal of Dorothy Paget's stock in 1960. 'The two brothers could not have been more different. Granville Again wasn't the nicest horse you could see, certainly not as nice as Morley Street, who was altogether bigger and more beautiful.' Needless to say, Toby Balding had shown interest in acquiring Morley Street's two years younger sibling but eventually demurred because 'he's nothing like as impressive an individual as my fellow and he had rather a high head carriage'.

Balding had other things on his mind as race day loomed. A fortnight before the championship Morley Street had suffered a leg infection: the enforced break from training, he sincerely hoped, would enable his champion to defend his crown a sharper and fresher horse. Nor was the weather forecast doing him any favours. Rain was due. 'If it's good to firm I couldn't see him getting beat,' he told the press. Unfortunately for Balding intermittent rain did

THE CHAMPION HURDLE

fall, keeping the going no faster than good. Even so, Morley Street faced the tape favourite at 2/1 from 7/2 with his brother at 9/2 and Royal Gait, who in his last piece of work apparently had gone badly for the only time in his life, at sixes.

The preliminaries were enlivened by a parade of former champions headed by Sea Pigeon but this excitement was as nothing compared to the drama of the race itself – or, should one say, its aftermath. For the first time in its 63 renewals there was a stewards' enquiry that raised the distinct possibility of the winner being thrown out. Furthermore, almost unbelievably, the horse in jeopardy was none other than the luckless Ascot victim of 1988, Royal Gait. For 20 anxious minutes history looked like repeating itself. Six horses had crossed the last with a chance. Almost immediately, Royal Gait seemed to collide with the rival to his right, Fidway, who dropped out abruptly to finish fourth, and in the course of battling on to beat Oh So Risky by half a length it was quite possible he had committed his usual sin of hanging left-handed and thus interfered with the third-placed Ruling. On this occasion the jury gave Royal Gait the benefit of the doubt and justice prevailed.

Royal Gait, for once, had enjoyed his fair share of luck. At the second-last and still going strongly, Granville Again crumpled on landing, while his elder brother 'just didn't sparkle, he felt like an ordinary horse today' according to Jimmy Frost. It was also a depressing day for supporters of Kribensis, who blundered at the third flight and came back with all the skin stripped off one of his hind legs from hock to fetlock joint.

Sheikh Mohammed was again in absentia but Fanshawe admitted to being 'very relieved and very happy. A lot of people have been giving me a hard time about running him in the wrong race, but he is already nine and he has always shown a lot of class. It's a tempting proposition to go back on the Flat with him but 2 and a half miles at Ascot is probably more of a strain on his legs than this game.' Successful jockey Graham McCourt insisted he had always been confident of victory, albeit not confident enough to say so beforehand. 'I steered wide to give him a good view of the first two flights but he jumped them so keenly that I had to cover him up again. He has such a high cruising speed that we were always going easily with time to think.' McCourt was another of those relatively unsung journeyman professionals who seemed to have been around

THE CHAMPION HURDLE

for ages (he won his first race at 16) without ever pulling up any spectacular trees until winning the 1990 Gold Cup on the 100/1 shot Norton's Coin. However, when he called it a day in 1996, McCourt had accumulated 921 winners gaining him sixth place (at that time) in the all-time list below only the acknowledged titans Scudamore, Dunwoody, Francome, Mellor and Winter, all of whom had been champion.

Royal Gait had earned himself a degree of immortality: a Champion Hurdle as a novice on only his fourth start over hurdles, the least experienced champion since Seneca in war-restricted circumstances of 1941. He was also the first Group 1 winner on the Flat to successfully make the transition. Alas, fate decreed Royal Gait would add nothing further to his entry in the annals of the Champion Hurdle other than the unwanted addendum of being the first reigning champion to die in action since Brown Tony way back in 1931. Seconds after finishing fourth on his seasonal reappearance in the Bookmakers' Hurdle at Leopardstown on 30 December, he suffered a massive haemorrhage and dropped dead from heart failure barely 100 yards past the winning post. He was buried at Kildangan.

15

Pipe Über Alles

Martin Pipe is a statistical phenomenon. His astonishing results took the sport by storm and shook its dyed-in-the-wool training establishment to the very tips of its deeply entrenched roots. He became Britain's most successful trainer by overtaking Arthur Stephenson's total with number 2,989 on 4 February 2000 (204 of them on the Flat) – having broken Stephenson's verifiable jumps record of 2,644 (that of Arthur Yates being unverifiable) earlier in the season – just 25 years after sending out his first: Stephenson took 46 years; he has a record 11 championships over jumps; most centuries – 16; most wins in a season (243 in 1999–2000); most prize money (£1,677,603 in 1999–2000); most wins at a single Cheltenham Festival – four in 1997 and 1998 (held jointly with Tom Coulthwaite). The only objective to prove elusive was going through a card; he got the first five one day at Exeter in 1991, but his odds-on representative in the last finished second.

How did Pipe do it? He had no right to rack up figures like these. He possessed no formal grounding in the sport (he rode one point-to-point winner at Bishopsleigh in 1973 and promptly retired), he looked as if he would be more at home behind the wheel of the fast cars he loved to drive in his youth (including a Triumph Stag into a tree on one occasion) and what's more, his father was a bookmaker with whom he had once worked. Hmm. Just what was he up to at Pond House Farm in far-flung Nicholashayne down on the Devon–Somerset border? In a nutshell, what Pipe was doing was rewriting the training manual and a lot of jumping folk found that a very unpalatable meal to digest, so much so that when his methods were scrutinised by television's investigative *Cook Report* in 1991 (Pipe spent £30,000 defending himself) there were some jaundiced souls who hoped for the worst. Jealousy was rife. He was blood-doping, 'changing blood' in the

THE CHAMPION HURDLE

manner of Finnish athletes. People trackside were heard to mutter: 'That one's had the injection.' No wonder he could be prickly with the press and maintain he was regarded as an outsider by the jumping establishment. Pretty soon, however, other trainers began to ape his methods. As one famous downland trainer testified after visiting Pond House, 'It turns out I have wasted 25 years of my life giving horses a holiday!' Through this climate of envy and spite, Pipe somehow retained his sense of humour – to the extent of sponsoring a race at Taunton named 'The Martin Pipe Am I Really That Difficult Hurdle.'

In his first six years holding a licence Pipe sent out the winners of a mere 31 races. 'When I took out a permit to train Dad's horses in the 1973–74 season my knowledge was lacking and my experience nil,' Pipe recalls in his autobiography. 'I can remember telling Dad the horses were mad fresh because it had been raining for days . . . and they couldn't go out in the rain! The horses were only pleasure for me and Dad; the betting office was our living. From 1975 up to 1980 people were entitled to say I was a complete idiot, a joke, and I did not object because it was true.'

Pipe set about acquiring for himself an equine education. As the proud owner of an enquiring mind he began to read a few books, commencing with *Modern Horse Management* by Major Reginald Timmis of the Royal Canadian Dragoons which he bought for £2 in a Taunton jumble sale. He'd attend the horses-in-training sales at Newmarket with which came free access to all the leading stables; Pipe would leave with samples of their hay and foodstuffs ready for analysis. 'I would love to have worked in a proper stable. Henry Cecil, Fred Winter and Vincent O'Brien are my heroes. Never having been in another trainer's yard I had nothing to compare my ideas with at that time. Buying horses was the main reason for being there, but observing what went on gave me every bit as much satisfaction. I didn't know who was doing things best, but some were attaining better ratios of winners to runners, and that interested me.' He attended seminars and lectures on all things equine and bumped into Michael Dickinson, his closest mirror image on the jumping scene who, after an unhappy period training on the Flat, departed for America where he was affectionately to be regarded as a 'mad genius'. The two got on like a house on fire and Pipe went over to the States to see Dickinson's new set-up at close quarters. Back at Pond House Pipe installed a solarium and a blood-

THE CHAMPION HURDLE

testing laboratory ('It won't tell you when the horse is going to win but it'll tell you when it's got no chance'), had a swimming pool put in and constructed a six-furlong, 20-feet wide all-weather wood-chip uphill gallop on which to condition his horses: breeze up it, stop, hack back down – repeat three times. 'Coming into racing from a bookmaking background, I am not blinkered by old beliefs handed down within horsey families. I am convinced that long steady cantering makes horses slow,' he explains. 'Ours never come off the bridle at home, although they do quicken up over short distances. The way I tell when a horse is ready to run is purely by listening to its breathing and monitoring its recovery rate. I have a particular place by the strip where I stand to listen and I often close my eyes to sharpen my hearing. The fitter a horse is, the quicker he stops blowing and his heart rate returns to normal.'

Pipe's horses proceeded to become the fittest runners ever seen in the history of National Hunt racing. They ran as fast as they could for as long as they could – which tended to be faster and longer than most. Others may claim to have developed 'interval training' for racehorses, but they merely dabbled; Pipe turned it into a science. During his second six years, Pipe trained 219 over the sticks, including his breakthrough at the Cheltenham Festival, Baron Blakeney, a 66/1 shocker in the 1981 Daily Express Triumph Hurdle. The following six-year period saw the balloon really lift off. Pipe's totals soared: 106, 129, 208, 224, 230 and 224 in the 1991–92 season. Along the way Pipe had lost none of the savvy epitomised by the story surrounding his very first winner, Hit Parade, at Wincanton on 9 May 1975. Intending to make all the running, jockey Len Lungo walked the course beforehand loosening the second section from the rail of each flight of hurdles in order to ease his mount's passage. Pipe was so pleased he gave Lungo the prize money – all of £272! Nevertheless, lest one think Pipe some sort of automaton, he had the frailties and foibles of ordinary mortals: while he organised the lives of his horses, his own life was organised to the minutest detail by his wife Carol, who would lay out his clothes, tell him where he was going and even order his meals in restaurants, and at tracks where he enjoyed notable successes his superstition extended to standing in the same place in the parade ring!

Once Pipe had primed them it was up to Peter Scudamore to deliver the goods on the racecourse. The pair first met in Taunton

THE CHAMPION HURDLE

Hospital: amateur rider Mr P. Scudamore had been brought in concussed to find Pipe had been there for six months with a broken thigh after one of his many riding mishaps. 'I didn't know him, he didn't know me. We just talked about racing,' recalled Pipe. 'Between us we represented opposites but he never had an ego to feed, which meant the loser of an argument could take the decision in good grace. Only rarely did we hurt each other's pride, despite the thousands of decisions which were made each week.' Scudamore had been champion jockey with both David Nicholson and Fred Winter, but from 1986 he acted as Pipe's foil at the sharp end of proceedings – or as he put it, 'I'm just the goal hanger. Martin keeps lobbing them over and I kick them in the net.' On 792 occasions, as it happened, at a strike-rate of 37 per cent (compared to an overall career percentage of 22). It was that straightforward. Moreover, if anyone was going to be aware of skullduggery at Pond House it would be Scudamore, yet this champion of unquestioned integrity vehemently defended Pipe against the persistent smear campaigns: 'I can put my hand on my heart and tell you that all the rumours are complete and utter rubbish. I watched it happening with Michael Dickinson and now it's happening again. I think it's a sort of compliment really. Nothing is going on. They're just training horses differently to anything I've been used to. The first horse I rode for him, in 1985, was the fittest horse I rode all that season. It kicked every hurdle out of the ground and still won. Martin is just a very, very good trainer and that's it.'

Pipe and Scudamore constituted a statistical double act without peer in the history of the sport, truly a marriage made in heaven. 'Martin and I stand and fall by each other,' continued the jockey. 'The greatest asset we have between us is we're always looking to improve. We both do our groundwork and try to be honest. To some people, if things go wrong, you're a bloody idiot. With us, if things go wrong, you're a bloody idiot, but it's OK. If I make a mistake he's very cross, but we don't fall out about it.'

Scudamore was making fewer and fewer mistakes. The years of dedication to his craft and its constant analysis were paying off. 'My approach to race-riding is to make the most of my talents by eliminating as many mistakes as I possibly can both in the saddle and out of it. I have been called a perfectionist, and if that is being a perfectionist, then that is what I am. There must be application to go with the talent. This game is about consistent concentration,

THE CHAMPION HURDLE

something I have got better at with age. You exercise with practice. Nothing annoys me more than missing out through lack of proper thought application.' Winners rolled in: 1,678 of them by the time Scudamore retired in April 1993, a new record 540 better than that set by John Francome, his former adversary with whom he was always unfavourably compared. Other records tumbled. The most wins in a season, 221 in 1988–89 (158 of them for Pipe at a strike-rate of 44 per cent); the most championships – eight; the biggest margin of superiority – 129 in 1988–89; the most centuries – eight; the fastest 50, 100, 150 and 200 in a season. One needed an abacus to keep up. Scu's place in the jump jockeys' hall of fame was assured.

Although Scudamore was adamant Granville Again had been an unlucky horse when knuckling over two out in the 1992 championship, he wasn't convinced that Morley Street's brother represented his best chance of lifting the title in 1993. Yes, he had demonstrated his worth by running away with the Scottish Champion Hurdle after that Festival misfortune but the current campaign had brought disappointment. Elder brother Morley Street (who had duly collected his third straight Aintree Hurdle at the previous season's back end) outsprinted him on his reappearance before both finished behind Halkopous in the Bula. The video of the Bula was seen by Michael Dickinson when he came over to visit his mother. He thought he detected a problem. He advised Pipe to forget the horse's next intended run in the Irish Champion Hurdle and suggested a training strategy aimed solely at the Champion Hurdle. With the plan in place, Dickinson invested £100 at 7/1 on Granville Again to lift the title. However, the fact that he had not run for 78 days caused Scudamore to lean toward partnering the front-running Valfinet, a good winner of the Kingwell. 'Granville Again had been working well, unholdable almost, and when they work so well at home it's always a worry.' Pipe wanted Scudamore on Granville Again and kept chipping away at his jockey to agree, and after a final spin the day before the championship Scudamore's name was finally inserted alongside Granville Again's.

Despite Granville Again's travails only Flown (7/2), the previous year's winner of the Novices', was backed to beat him in a championship run back over an extended distance of two miles and 110 yards. Of the old guard neither Kribensis (virtually white at the age of nine) nor Morley Street were pulling up trees nowadays, and

THE CHAMPION HURDLE

of the Flat-race dilettantes it was the sponsor's Vintage Crop, who had a Cesarewitch (and soon an Irish St Leger and a Melbourne Cup) to his credit that held most appeal for each-way punters.

There were to be no mistakes from Granville Again this year. After Flown had taken over from Valfinet going to the third-last, Scudamore began to take closer order and once over that tricky obstacle at the bottom of the hill he headed towards the final flight with only Halkopous and Royal Derbi as threats. 'If he dropped the bridle as he left the starting gate, you knew he was going to go well within himself,' Scudamore confided afterwards, 'and as the tape flew up he did just that. Everything kept opening up for me as it does when you are going well, though at the top of the hill I started to get a little concerned that he might have been too relaxed. Naturally I was pleased to get over the second-last after last year. After that he went right just like his brother, and went on to win just like his brother. I was particularly pleased for Martin as critics had said that he could train quantity but not quality – and this success comprehensively gave the lie to that.' Though perhaps not finding as much as expected up the run-in, Granville Again emulated his brother comfortably enough. They were the first pair from the same mare to make the frame since Song of Essex and Hill Song (out of Cradle Song) in the 1930s and, of course, the first brothers to win. Their sire Deep Run also made his mark, joining Jackdaw as the only stallion with three individual winners. The smile on the face of owner Eric Scarth, a builder from Haltwhistle in Northumberland who bought Granville Again as a replacement for his Scottish Champion Hurdle winner of 1990 Sayparee, suggested his plan to recoup last year's losses by backing his horse at 14s, 12s and 8s had borne considerable fruit. All that remained was for Pipe to relay the news to Dickinson with whom he'd kept in constant touch throughout the preceding two months: 'You've trained numerous winners but this must be the first one by fax! Well done and thanks.'

Granville Again's victory provided an upbeat finale to Scudamore's career which, despite all the records, was noticeably lacking in the sport's most prized jewels such as the Gold Cup, Grand National, King George VI Chase or Whitbread Gold Cup. Scudamore retired on a winner (Sweet Duke at Ascot) a month after Granville Again's victory and a matter of days after the starting gate shambles of the National-that-never-was robbed him of a final stab at emulating his father's success aboard Oxo.

THE CHAMPION HURDLE

Finishing just over eight lengths behind the triumphant Granville Again was the seven-year-old mare Flakey Dove. The 5lb allowance capitalised upon by Dawn Run had attracted only eight females since 1984 but Flakey Dove was always liable to be one such because the race was in her blood: back in 1963 her grandam Red Dove ran unplaced behind Winning Fair. Flakey Dove ran in the name of Herefordshire farmer Tom Price and was trained on his 400-acre Eaton Hall property, straddling the River Lugg, near Leominster, by son Richard, assisted by younger brother Andrew, known to one and all as Ernie. The mare was the latest advertisement for one of jumping's most popular and enduring dynasties which resulted from one day in the early 1950s at Ludlow Market when Tom Price's father spent £25 acquiring Cottage Lass II, thereby saving this Irish-bred, winning Welsh pointer from the knacker's yard. The mare's plebeian origins excluded her from the General Stud Book but that didn't stop her daughter Red Dove, trained by Tom's brother Gordon, winning sixteen races and granddaughter Shadey Dove a further nine: all told, it was estimated that the Cottage Lass dynasty had amassed something close to 90 wins if one included point-to-points. It was a 1985 mating with Derby third Oats, who stood locally at the Cobhall Court Stud, which produced Flakey Dove, whose winning tally going into the 1993 championship had stood at a bumper and six hurdle races. Price believed Flakey Dove to have been nowhere near her best on her Champion Hurdle début owing to her early season preparation being held up by a foot injury.

Since Cheltenham, however, the mare had really begun to fire. She won a decent hurdle race at Uttoxeter, broke her maiden on the Flat in October and then recorded a tremendous hat-trick comprising Haydock's Champion Hurdle Trial (despite turning out lame on the morning of the race), the Grade 1 Cleeve Hurdle at Cheltenham and the Berkshire Hurdle round Newbury. 'She's so laid-back, she wouldn't turn a hair,' averred Richard Price of the star resident among his dozen boxes at Eaton Hall Farm. 'After she'd won at Cheltenham, you wouldn't have known she'd been in a race. She hardly broke sweat. She switched off as soon as she went past the post. Walking back in, she had her head between her legs, the job done. She's a real professional now. When the season began, we thought we'd go for the Stayers' Hurdle but she didn't appear to stay when we tried her over the trip at Wetherby. Then she had a bit of a virus and coughed. Come the New Year she was OK and

THE CHAMPION HURDLE

she ran well at Windsor to finish second to Absalom's Lady, giving weight away. She was 90 per cent that day but when everything is right she's top class, as she's been proving of late, and like a lot of her family, she's improving with age.'

Although Price could be satisfied with his mare's preparation for the championship, he could not say the same about riding plans. Richard Dunwoody, Flakey Dove's victorious partner in the recent hat-trick, was currently banned (and in any case would have had to ride Granville Again for his new retainer, Martin Pipe); another former partner Jamie Osborne was committed to Large Action; and the next choice, Norman Williamson, also went and got himself suspended. Price had to search high and low. Fourth choice was Mark Dwyer. However, Price was hardly scraping the bottom of the barrel. Dwyer was top-class and had been for ten years or so. Possessed of no racing heritage (surprising enough for a scion of County Meath), Dwyer's boyhood ambition to become an airline pilot soon evaporated once he developed a passion for the small string of horses trained near his home by a German farmer. At the age of ten he was taught to ride by Paddy Woods – regular work-rider of the peerless Arkle – and the thrill of competition was fuelled and fanned by a weekly dose of pony racing. On leaving school (illegally prior to his 15th birthday), he served his apprenticeship with that notably hard taskmaster Liam Browne (father of Dermot) who knocked off the youngster's rough edges (Dwyer actually won a Group race on the Flat for his master) before, gaining weight, he crossed the Irish Sea in 1982 to join Jimmy Fitzgerald's predominant jumping yard in Malton. Dwyer's cool brain and long-reined smoothness in the saddle stood out a mile. Three years later Dwyer won the Gold Cup for Fitzgerald on Forgive 'N Forget ('He was so strong, the 12 apostles wouldn't hold him,' said a colleague, 'but Mark made him look easy.') and in 1993 he won a second on Peter Beaumont's Jodami, favourite to retain his crown in 1994. Flakey Dove would constitute some hors d'oevre to the meeting's main course. 'I've picked up a plum in Flakey Dove,' Dwyer told readers of the *Racing Post*. 'You'd have to put her right in the reckoning in a race where so many runners have an "if" attached to them.'

There was no 'if' against the name of one former champion in Kribensis, who after failing to win since his day of glory in 1990, had retired to his trainer's yard where he continues to do sterling

THE CHAMPION HURDLE

service as a hack for either Stoute's assistant Patrick Prendergast or his head lad Stuart Messenger. Even though the title-winning brothers Morley Street ('We have to live with the fact that he's an intermittent bleeder,' said Balding, a comment which punters now interpreted less charitably) and Granville Again (not seen out since finishing in the ruck in January's Irish Champion Hurdle) did come to the table once more, all the aces – or at least three of them – seemed to be held by David Elsworth, a trainer who had won everything worth winning (notably with the princely Desert Orchid) except the Champion Hurdle in which he had saddled two seconds, a third and a fourth: 'I ought to know better after all these years, but I'm nervous and I've got the gee-up.' Muse had won the Christmas Hurdle and the Oteley, Absalom's Lady took Flakey Dove's scalp at Windsor, and Oh So Risky, runner-up in the 1992 championship (since gelded) after winning the Triumph and a Group 3 winner on the Flat, had run the novice Large Action (receiving 20lb) to a short head in the Tote Gold Trophy (formerly the Schweppes) with Flakey Dove third (receiving 13lb) – form which saw him sent off the 9/4 favourite upon the defection of main market rival, Michael Smurfit's Irish Champion Hurdle winner Fortune And Fame, at 7 a.m. on the morning of the race owing to a bruised near-hind.

The course was bathed in bright sunshine as Dwyer was legged up onto Flakey Dove's back for the very first time in the paddock. 'She gave me no sort of feel at all going to the start, and I thought I had no chance. She went down like nothing. She was so switched off I thought I was going to end up pulling her up. How wrong can you be! Once we jumped off she was a different horse.' Valfinet dragged the field through the first three-quarters of the contest until headed by Large Action approaching the second last. However, Dwyer was priming Flakey Dove for a devastating run on the novice's outside which he delivered jumping the final hurdle with the favourite in his slipstream. Try as he might up the hill, that dastardly 5lb concession was too much for Oh So Risky to pull back against an adversary with the stamina to have won over 2 and a half miles, and he had to be content with second spot yet again – an unenviable record of near-and-yet-so-far that he shared with Anarchist (1941–42), Quita Que (1956–57) and Nomadic Way (1990–91).

'Flakey Dove's is a much more romantic tale than old Elzee

189

THE CHAMPION HURDLE

making a few quid,' said a chivalrous David Elsworth. How true. Coming amidst victories for Newmarket Flat stables and the big battalions of a Balding or a Pipe, success for the 'Plain Jane who simply would not be denied', in the words of Brough Scott in the *Racing Post*, was a throwback to the old days of the Champion Hurdle. Eaton Hall Farm was a jumping set-up which those earlier denizens of the Welsh Marches Arthur Jones and Stan Wright would both recognise and appreciate, not to mention Uncle Gordon who had sent out the mare Stans Pride to finish third in 1985 from his base at nearby Hamnish Farm. Seventy-year-old Tom Price preferred to avoid the hurly-burly of Cheltenham and watched events unfold on television at home, but son Richard was relishing the limelight: 'I'm very proud. Tell me that this is not all a dream. I was lambing ewes at 6.15 this morning and here I am standing in the winner's enclosure after a Champion Hurdle! We've always had faith in Flakey Dove. Everybody keeps saying how tough she is but she's classy as well. We suspect she was in season in the Tote, it shows when the pressure is on, and we reckon that was the trouble that day. All my friends have had 66/1 about her but I haven't had a bet – me and betting don't get on. I don't know whether she'll be covered or what we'll do with her now, but I may retire and go to stud myself after this!'

The story of the next two championships is dominated by one horse – and he didn't win either renewal. But then again Danoli didn't need to win a Champion Hurdle to earn immortality because Danoli was the latest in a long line of Irish racing icons who transcended anything actually achieved on the racecourse. 'Danoli Delirium' and 'Dan-holy' were just two of the headlines testifying to the quasi-religious fervour (the gelding even raced wearing a St Benedict medal on his bridle) generated during the roller-coaster career of this bay son of The Parson who sported one white sock behind and a smudgy white thumb print between the eyes. Just consider the following. Having landed an almighty Irish gamble in the 1994 Sun Alliance Novices', he goes to Aintree and trounces his elders and betters by eight lengths in the Martell Hurdle (a performance which arguably made him the best hurdler of the season), and defies a broken fetlock to win a second 12 months later; a miraculous recovery ensues – to be sure, wasn't the Pope supposed to have said a Mass for the stricken horse? Eventually Ireland's darling goes over fences; wins, falls, wins, falls – and again

THE CHAMPION HURDLE

rises like Lazarus to vanquish a pair of Cheltenham Gold Cup winners in the 1997 Hennessy Cognac Gold Cup, Ireland's equivalent. Tears, cheers, thrills, spills; the Danoli saga had the lot.

Danoli was bred by Willie Austin, a dairy farmer from Cloughjordan in Tipperary, and acquired privately by another farmer, Tom Foley of Aughabeg Farm, near Bagenalstown in County Carlow, for IR7,000 guineas on behalf of local bonesetter Danny O'Neill, who named the horse after himself and his wife Olive. Foley – quickly dubbed 'Popeye without the pipe' by one wag – made even Paddy Mullins appear a raging extrovert. 'When I started out, I just sort of made it up as I went along. Everyone thought it was a bit of a joke because I knew nothing about the business. We sort of learned from making mistakes. We're very, very small country people. We act what we are and I reckon that's why the horse gets all the publicity he does. I'm the little man taking on the giants.' Within two months Foley was being offered a 100 per cent profit on his promising-looking animal. No sale. Danoli won all three of his bumpers in 1992–93 and three of his five hurdle races (plus running second to Fortune And Fame in the AIG (Europe) Irish Champion as a raw novice on his fourth start) prior to the famous Sun Alliance–Martell double of 1994, prompting Foley to suggest: 'I reckon he's too good for me to say how good he is.' Two wins and a surprising reverse at Leopardstown (all at odds on) preceded his title bid, but Danoli, who had exacted revenge to the tune of eight lengths over Fortune And Fame in the Martell, had not run since Christmas and warmed up for the championship with a public workout round Leopardstown. Only Granville Again's 78 days and Sea Pigeon's 115 and 122 constituted longer lay-offs for an eventual winner, while at the other extreme Flakey Dove enjoyed a mere ten-day break and the likes of Morley Street and See You Then, eleven. Nevertheless, Foley's main worry concerned his own dubious ability to survive the inaugural flight in an aeroplane! 'Danoli carries the hopes of a nation,' declared the *Racing Post* headline with little or no exaggeration.

Who could stop him? Not the reigning champion, for Flakey Dove had been retired in February after injuring her off-fore tendon on the gallops without managing to add another victory to her record. She quickly adjusted to motherhood, and if ever a foal was bred to win a Champion Hurdle it must be her third, a filly by Alderbrook. Morley Street had also called it a day as far as the

THE CHAMPION HURDLE

championship was concerned, though he raced on till 1995. Life as a hack with Geoffrey Peate's son Ed in Newmarket failed to enthuse Morley Street and he was returned to Manor Farm Stud where he happily shares a paddock with his old Fyfield mucker Forest Sun. His brother Granville Again would contest a fourth championship, only to finish tailed-off. Like Kribensis and Flakey Dove, he failed to win another race of any description after his championship, eventually leaving Martin Pipe and returning, via Muriel Naughton in Richmond, to live with Eric Scarth's daughter Anne Oliver at Oakwell House, Henshaw, in Northumbria. A heart murmur had put paid to the hoped-for career over fences but Granville Again enjoyed the odd day out hunting with the Haydon until Mrs Oliver's other hunters and show ponies were all sold. The old champion grew lonely and depressed without company so he was sent to rejoin his former groom Linda Kent in nearby Whitfield, where he is regularly ridden out alongside his new stablemates.

Fortune And Fame would get to represent sponsor Michael Smurfit this March, having won his only race, the Irish Champion at the end of January. Best of the home side was Large Action, last year's third, who was seeking his fifth straight win of the season. Yet, given the significant roles recently played by crack Flat-racers in recent championships, the intriguing candidate had to be Alderbrook, a six-year-old entire by Ardross out of a mare related to the decent chaser Sybillin (who had run unplaced in the 1991 Champion Hurdle), whose two runs over hurdles divided by 27 months paled when set beside his successes for Julie Cecil on the level which featured the Group 3 Select Stakes at Goodwood and the Group 2 Prix Dollar at Longchamp. 'If this was a Flat race Alderbrook would be 6/4,' said Norman Williamson, who, like the horse's trainer Kim Bailey, had never enjoyed any success at the Festival and was still smarting from the loss of Flakey Dove's championship. Alderbrook had won the Kingwell nicely. 'I've never seen a horse go so fast over hurdles in my life,' commented Bailey. 'I'm not worried by his inexperience because I know he jumps brilliantly. The biggest worry is that he has never made a mistake, so we don't know whether he can put himself right. He had been with us for only six weeks before Wincanton so he is bound to improve. I've taken 50/1 about him!'

For the first occasion in seven years the ground rode soft on the Festival's opening day, paradoxically the exact conditions

THE CHAMPION HURDLE

appreciated by all the leading contenders. The market could not separate Danoli and Large Action (both drifters) on 4s, closely followed by Fortune And Fame at 5/1 and Alderbrook, backed into 11/2 from 13/2 via some hefty wagers, including one of £35,000 to £7,000; and there was some sentimental each-way money for Mole Board, at 13 the oldest horse ever to contest the championship.

The mare Mysilv went off like the clappers as usual and quickly had the field stretched out. Three flights from home she was still in front, though the two joint favourites were closing and Alderbrook was travelling with ominous ease in behind. Danoli hit the hurdle hard (returning with a bruised knee; 'He hung like a bitch after that,' muttered Tom Foley), leaving Large Action to wrest the advantage from Mysilv running to the last. However, it was as plain as a pikestaff to any sane observer that Alderbrook, cruising at Large Action's quarters, would win comfortably once Williamson finally let him loose. And so he did, by five lengths, with Danoli a further two behind Large Action. Bearing in mind his classy Flat credentials, there seemed no limit to what the new champion might achieve over hurdles and, just three runs or no, Timeform awarded the first entire to lift the title since Monksfield a rating (174) not exceeded in a dozen years. Mind you, it could have all ended so differently. It later emerged that three days before the race Alderbrook's lad, Chris Robinson, had been offered a £3,000 bribe by a man convicted of illegal bookmaking, one half of a duo known locally as the 'Lambourn Mafia', to help 'stop' the horse. Robinson reported the approach to Bailey and stayed up with the horse every night until he'd won.

This first Festival success for Williamson was especially tasty given the events of the previous March. Dubbed 'Stormin Norman' after America's Gulf War general of that christian name, the 25-year old from Mallow had been three-times champion pony rider in Ireland before starting out as an amateur with Dermot Weld. Lured across the Irish Sea to ride as stable jockey to Herefordshire trainer John Edwards, Williamson's career really blossomed when he linked up with Bailey in 1993, for his tally of winners almost trebled overnight. 'Mr Bailey has been the key figure in things picking up for me as they have. There are a lot of other jockeys in the weighing room who are good enough to reach this level. The biggest thing is just a lot of luck and jumping on the right horse. Alderbrook has

THE CHAMPION HURDLE

so much speed it's unbelievable. He was always cantering and I knew early on that he'd win if he kept jumping and got the trip!'

Kim Bailey, the son of trainer Ken (a kiss from whom reduced him to tears in the winner's enclosure), had spent his formative years with jumping legends Tim Forster and Fred Rimell (during the Comedy of Errors period) before striking out on his own in 1977. In 1990 he had won a Grand National with Mr Frisk, and 48 hours after Alderbrook's victory Master Oats secured for him and Williamson the coveted Festival double – only the fifth team so to do following Anthony/Cullinan (1930), Briscoe/Leader (1932), Briscoe/Stott (1933) and O'Brien/Brabazon (1949 and 1950) – and thus made him the tenth member of the select group to have trained the winners of National Hunt racing's three principal events.

Bailey had been fortunate to get Alderbrook. Owner Ernie Pick, a retired North Yorkshire garage proprietor, had contemplated keeping him with Julie Cecil for his hurdling career, but when the moment came to grasp the nettle the Newmarket trainer was away on holiday. 'Mr Pick came to the yard and, over a cup of coffee, said he wanted to win the Champion Hurdle. It's unbelievable for Alderbrook to do that in eight weeks. I gave the horse one out of ten for trying and Yogi Breisner, who helps us iron out our jumping problems, thought we had no chance of getting him ready in time. He actually jumped his first hurdle ten days before he won the Kingwell. This isn't a bad way to break your Festival duck!'

Perhaps Bailey used up all his luck with Alderbrook in 1995 because the following 12 months were fraught ones. Things began well enough as Alderbrook picked up where he left off on the Flat by running second in the Group 1 Prix Ganay (finishing in front of French Derby winner Hernando) and a Group 2 at Baden-Baden (taking the scalp of a German Derby winner in Lando). However, in high summer, Pick announced his horse would not be returning to Bailey for the defence of his crown but would remain with Mrs Cecil: 'Last time it was a spur-of-the-moment thing. Now that we've got a bit more time Julie deserves the chance to train him. She knows the horse better than anyone and I think it's maybe fairest to let Julie have a go.' Fortunately, Pick eventually saw sense and Alderbrook returned to Lambourn, but not before a bout of coughing and an operation to remove two bone chips from his near-fore. 'He always did walk like a crab – moving with his right front leg and his right hind leg at the same time – and when you walk

THE CHAMPION HURDLE

or trot him, you feel like you're driving a car with four flat tyres,' observed Bailey. Alderbrook gingerly took the first steps to recovery on Bailey's water treadmill with an eye to a possible return in the New Year. Soft ground was now more than ever a prerequisite. Then, to cap it all, Bailey lost his jockey when Williamson dislocated his right shoulder shortly before Alderbrook's intended comeback in the Kingwell. Bailey went searching for a top rider who might also be free on Champion Hurdle day should Williamson not recover in time. He rang Graham Bradley.

Bradley had long been one of the weighing room's most stylish practitioners, but he carried a lot of baggage. The 35-year-old Wetherby-born jockey came to the fore on the back of the Dickinson training dynasty, partnering all manner of top chasers to win big races for them such as Bregawn (Hennessy/Gold Cup), Righthand Man (Welsh National) and Wayward Lad (King George VI Chase), and when Toby Balding was seeking someone to work the oracle on the increasingly canny Morley Street in his later years it was Bradley who produced the ride of the season to win the 1993 Aintree Hurdle on the old stager; one day he even got a ride on Desert Orchid. However, controversy and the self-styled 'Wayward Lad' (according to the title of his autobiography) or 'Bad Boy Brad' (according to one tabloid) were never far apart. Bradley was Richard Guest with knobs on: riding with such patience that unsuccessful efforts attracted the attention of stewards and punters alike and wearing his heart on his sleeve with typical Yorkshire pride and disregard for the consequences. Occasionally even his greatest supporters must have winced at his naivety; he once forfeited his licence after striking a bet at Cartmel still decked out in his riding gear! In 1999 he was one of five jockeys (and Charlie Brooks) arrested in connection with alleged race-fixing – all of whom were absolved from any wrong-doing before the case (which collapsed) came to court. 'It all started with that Cartmel incident. I made a couple of human errors and it all escalated. There were lots of hiccups, the kinds of things that can happen to anyone, like dropping my hands and getting beaten a short head – only in my case it would end up on the front page of racing papers. I was unlucky but people said there's no smoke without fire. But you can't put a price on the experiences I've had, and for all the ups and downs I don't regret any of them and I wouldn't change a thing.'

One of Bradley's less memorable moments was to miss a ride at

THE CHAMPION HURDLE

Worcester because he was asleep in the car park. On Sunday, 18 February 1996, that particular 'hiccup' came back to haunt him. He was due to partner Alderbrook in a 10 a.m. gallop – in the presence of owner and the media – prior to the champion's reappearance at Kempton the following Saturday (the Kingwell having been lost to the weather). The previous night had seen Bradley attend a bucolic birthday binge for colleague Dean Gallagher and he didn't get home until 1.30 in the morning. Having duly set his electric alarm clock for 9.45, the 'Wayward Lad' hit the hay – to wake up at 10.20. Bradley had been undone by a power cut! A frantic call to Bailey explaining the reason for his non-appearance cut no ice. Bradley had lost the mount on the Champion Hurdle favourite – who reinforced his market status with a fluent Kempton success in the hands of Richard Dunwoody. However, as Bradley's experiences amply testified, when one door closes another tends to open. With Jamie Osborne committed to Mysilv, he could accept Jim Old's offer to ride Collier Bay on whom he had won the Agfa (Oteley) Hurdle.

Dunwoody kept the ride on Alderbrook in the championship because no sooner had poor Williamson made it back into the saddle than he promptly dislocated the selfsame shoulder whilst out schooling for Bailey. It would be a miracle of training were Alderbrook to triumph – but a victory for Danoli would be a monument to the power of a nation's prayers and would crown the greatest comeback since Ali bounced off the Kinshasa ropes to flatten George Foreman. Danoli quickly overcame the bruised knee sustained in the 1995 Champion Hurdle to register a second Aintree Hurdle despite passing the post with a broken fetlock joint; so damaged was the bone that, in Tom Foley's opinion, he would have been dead in another half-furlong. Two months elapsed after an operation to insert three screws in the shattered leg at Liverpool's Leahurst Veterinary College before Danoli was fit to return to Aughabeg. Danoli swam, walked and trotted, and, nine months on from his life-threatening accident, he was ready to see action in the AIG (Europe) Irish Champion Hurdle. Danoli brought the house down by finishing a gallant third behind Collier Bay and Hotel Minella. Foley had put six weeks of work into Danoli inside a fortnight to get him half-ready to do himself justice, but a further month's input got 'The People's Champion' cherry-ripe for the Red Mills Trial Hurdle at Gowran Park which he proceeded to win with

THE CHAMPION HURDLE

some élan, in the words of the *Racing Post*, 'on the day Ireland went Danoli mental'.

Rain greeted the arrival of Festival week (Cleeve Hill was carpeted with snow and gale-force winds ripped the roof off one of the temporary stands), just the ticket for Alderbrook and Danoli – not forgetting Collier Bay. Bradley went off to play a round of golf at The Belfry on the Monday afternoon and drew encouragement from every drop that fell, albeit pondering his latest faux pas which was to inform the *Racing Post* that Alderbrook was his 'banker' of the meeting. Small wonder he received a phone call from Collier Bay's owner Wally Sturt asking: 'You're not going to stop him, are you?' Bradley assured the anxious London property developer that nothing was further from his mind and the placated owner concluded the conversation by promising him a bonus of £6,000 if Collier Bay won.

In the circumstances, a two and a half length victory for Collier Bay (a drifter in the market) over the heavily backed odds-on favourite amounted to pure theatre. Bradley rode back in triumph, outrageously playing to the gallery by pointing to the invisible watch on his wrist in reference to the oversleeping escapade that had worked out very nicely thank you in the end; an ecstatic Sturt stumped up the bonus; Collier Bay's avuncular trainer and avid devotee of Churchillian oratory, Jim Old (second with Sturt's Cima and a perennial contestant with Mole Board), who had been the under-bidder when Alderbrook was acquired by Ernie Pick, fought back the tears celebrating his first Festival victory: 'This means everything in the world to me. It's all I've ever dreamed of. The Gold Cup is a dream factory and the Grand National a lottery but the Champion always looked possible. Approaching the last I knew we had it because up the hill Collier Bay was certain to explode like a cork popping out of a bottle'; and the aggrieved Osborne was to be heard 'effing and blinding' at his wretched misfortune as Bradley and Collier Bay swept past Mysilv on the home turn. Nor were Pick ('100 per cent confident he would win') and Bailey (ironically the under-bidder when Old purchased Collier Bay) exactly over the moon – both reckoned Dunwoody had left the favourite (who lost a shoe) with too much to do. Dunwoody analysed the video over and over again, but could not agree. 'I wanted to be a bit closer but the horse kept pulling out in front of me and he didn't travel downhill like he had the previous year.' (A month later the pair

THE CHAMPION HURDLE

reunited to win the Scottish Champion Hurdle.) Danoli ran his heart out to finish fourth, and after running third in the Aintree Hurdle his attentions were turned to fences – and several more chapters in the Danoli legend before his eventual retirement at the age of 12 in August 2000.

Although Danoli exited the arena on his shield, he was in one piece – as was Alderbrook when he left to take up stud duties at Cobhall Court after a ligament injury, adding to the general wear-and-tear to his fragile legs, curtailed his hurdling adventure the following January. Others were not so fortunate. As many as ten competitors had met their deaths at the Festival, four of them over hurdles, including Mack The Knife in the Champion Hurdle itself. A subsequent Jockey Club inquiry concluded that 'no single factor, or indeed combination of factors' was to blame for this sad occurrence. Of course, there had been always been the occasional death in the championship, from Teddy's Double way back in 1935 through Wilhelmina Henrietta (1965) and Dondieu (1972) to Northern Trial (1985) and Chesham Squire (1989). Unofficially, others pointed to the preponderance of Flat-bred stock (Collier Bay himself was by the sprinter Green Desert out of a High Top mare belonging to Lord Derby) competing at speeds prejudicial to their safety. Whatever the case, Cheltenham's hurdles were loosened as a precautionary measure prior to the 1997 Festival.

Mack The Knife was trained by Martin Pipe. The Wizard of Nicholashayne had continued, of course, to churn out winners by the score since Granville Again's Champion Hurdle of 1993 but Pridwell's recent third to Collier Bay was as close as he'd come to a repeat in hurdling's blue riband. This minor blip was corrected in 1997 with the aid of a horse who had been winning a maiden hurdle at Newton Abbot less than a year earlier and the assistance of a jockey who seemed on a different planet even in comparison to the greatest of his predecessors.

On Peter Scudamore's retirement in 1993 no one in their wildest dreams envisaged his fistful of records being remotely challenged in the foreseeable future, let alone broken, and certainly not by an 18-year-old Irish kid, nearly six foot tall, from County Antrim, who had yet to ride in a jumps race of any description and was presently recuperating from a broken leg after being thrown on the gallops. When the kid in question entered a British weighing room for the first time minus boots, he was handed a pair to the

THE CHAMPION HURDLE

put-down, 'Borrow these. They are Scu's old boots . . . you will never be able to fill Peter Scudamore's boots.' However, within four years every old hand from O'Neill and Francome to Scudamore and Dunwoody was singing the praises of the best jockey they had ever seen and were ever likely to see.

On this occasion the star was to be seen in the west, not the east, and its rising caught everyone completely unawares. Anthony Peter McCoy struck National Hunt racing like a whirlwind. At the age of 12, 'Wee Authnay' used to duck school and pedal his bike the ten miles to Billy Rock's yard in Cullybackey from his father's village store in Moneyglass and tame the fieriest animal the trainer had to offer, thereby making himself £100 a week. Bodybuilding teenage hormones ruled out any feasible career for McCoy on the Flat, and he arrived at Toby Balding's yard in 1994 armed with a 7lb claim and a burning desire to add to the 13 winners he had accumulated to date. The first in Britain, on 7 September 1994, at Exeter, started him on the road to beating Adrian Maguire's record for a conditional rider with a total of 74, and the very next season he collected the jockeys' championship itself with 175 winners at the tender age of 22 – a year older than Josh Gifford in 1962–63.

McCoy has been champion ever since, and it is impossible to think of him losing the title to anything other than injury or a major reassessment of priorities. 'One day I'd like to be the same as Richard Dunwoody was and ride just the good ones, but that's still a long way off,' he conceded in 1999. The champion has positively chewed up the existing records and spat out new ones in a feeding frenzy that saw him in breach of the whip regulations on too many occasions for comfort in the early years. In 1997–98 he amassed a scarcely credible 253 winners to shatter Scudamore's seasonal record. He is the fastest jump jockey to 1,000 winners, taking just five years – Scudamore and Dunwoody reached that mark in ten and the mould-breaking Stan Mellor in all of 17 – and already has Scudamore's total of 1,678 in his sights, having rocketed past John Francome (1,138) into third place in the all-time winners' list. At this rate Dunwoody's record is liable to fall some time in 2003. 'This fellow could set standards no one will ever match,' conceded Scudamore.

In any quest for the human embodiment of 'mind over matter' one need look no further than McCoy. In the annals of jump jockeys his only point of reference is himself – in the Turf's eternal

THE CHAMPION HURDLE

weighing room only Fred Archer keeps him company. McCoy rides not just like a man possessed but like one bordering on the demented. His mounts have no option but consent to do his bidding. He makes each and every one of them 'an offer it can't refuse'; they are compelled to jump, accelerate or resist any challenge entirely at his behest. 'Tony's some jockey and he seems to be getting better,' says Pipe. 'Scu was brilliant but Tony really is the best ever. He's got everything. He's young and very keen and he's got a brain – that's crucial for a jockey. He wins lots of races which no other jockey would have won. He tries in every race whether it's the Champion Hurdle or a seller. He's a good horseman and great at everything. Look how determined he is with his weight. He doesn't drink, he doesn't even eat!' That is not quite true, even if McCoy's food intake was another instance of him exercising mind over matter in order to pare down his lanky frame to ten stone whenever the chance of a decent winner materialised. Allegedly, he existed on a diet of KitKats and Diet Coke; according to his biographer, 'If you gave AP champagne, he'd probably wash the car with it.'

McCoy's meteoric rise could not have transpired without the aid of the Pond House winner factory. Not every jockey saw eye to eye with Pipe. Although Richard Dunwoody stayed three seasons, he never really developed the rapport with his boss that Scudamore had enjoyed. McCoy played it cool. 'A lot of the lads have found it hard working for Pipey but I do genuinely get on with the man. We have our rows, usually because I'm angry at being on the wrong horse when he has more than one runner in a race, but we've established a deep mutual respect that I know will overcome any problem. If he sacked me tomorrow I'd still say he's the best trainer you could ever ride for. People don't realise the work he puts into it – he's a workaholic nutter! He'll not waste time talking about his achievements; it's always about how he can improve. He's fascinated by the mental side, it's not about galloping them 50 times a day. Any health and fitness programme on TV and he's watching it. He wants to know what made Ali so exceptional, how Emil Zatopek could sprint after all that distance and what turned Linford Christie from being average into an Olympic champion. Most of all, he wants to know why he can't do the same with some selling hurdler!'

With Make A Stand, Pipe more or less did 'do the same'. He

THE CHAMPION HURDLE

bought the gelding as a four-year-old for a mere £8,000 out of a Leicester claimer on the Flat in August 1995. Once the Pipe wand had been suitably waved and the magic words suitably incanted, the chestnut son of Master Willie came on by leaps and bounds. Post Newton Abbot he added seven more successes, culminating in an all-the-way charge to win the Tote Gold Trophy a month before the championship. The novice's handicap mark had now risen by nearly three stone inside six months. Injury deprived Make A Stand of McCoy's assistance at Newbury but nothing was going to keep the champion out of the saddle once the Festival came around.

Make A Stand went to post fourth best in the market behind Large Action (unbeaten in three this season), Collier Bay (winner of his only start, at Towcester) and one of seven Irishman, Space Trucker (winner of his last three, including one verdict over Make A Stand back in November). The size of the task facing Make A Stand was reflected in the fact that were this a handicap he would be receiving 11lb from the favourite and all of 23lb from the champion. Bradley was reunited with Collier Bay after missing the Towcester race due to suspension, but there was to be no fairytale ending to a horrific period in Jim Old's training career, which had been triggered by someone deliberately setting fire to his stables on the night of 16 September, razing them to the ground. The going proved far too firm for Collier Bay ('If it wasn't the Champion Hurdle we wouldn't have run,' remarked Old) and after blundering the first hurdle in the back straight Bradley pulled him up with three flights still to be jumped. However, Bradley later stated he'd heard from several friends who had watched the race from Wally Sturt's box that the owner repeatedly called his integrity into question. 'Wally was convinced I'd stopped Collier Bay,' wrote Bradley in his autobiography. He never rode Collier Bay again.

Collier Bay wasn't the only fancied horse in the wars; Jamie Osborne pulled up Large Action after just two flights, having felt the favourite go lame approaching the first. None of this bothered McCoy, because he didn't see another horse until turning Make A Stand at the top of the track after passing the post five lengths clear of Theatreworld in a new course record of 3 minutes 48.40 seconds. The clock bore ample testimony to their stunning performance. McCoy took the race by the throat down the far side, setting Make A Stand alight over the three flights to leave everything feeling the pinch by the time he began the sweep for home. He had

THE CHAMPION HURDLE

nothing to fear bar a fall, but he continued to belie his novice status by flicking over the obstacles efficiently and professionally to gallop resolutely into the record books alongside Night Nurse, Victor Norman and Blaris as a winner of the championship to have made every yard of the running. 'I rode as if there was nothing else in the race, as that's the way to ride him,' observed McCoy, 'I wondered early on if we were going fast enough but down the back he went from hurdle to hurdle and had stretched them so much that I could give him a breather at the top of the hill. He was there to be shot at but they just couldn't catch him.'

Although Make A Stand, the third novice (of nine) to lift the title in six years, eased in the market on the day, he was William Hill's only loser in its ante-post book. Owner Peter Deal had additional reason to thank his trainer. He was a member of the syndicate who lost the gelding after that Leicester claiming race, but later on he was able to persuade Pipe to sell half the horse back to him: 'Thank God Martin let me back in. Martin Pipe is pure genius and the horse is a star.' The trainer, who had been convinced his 'star' was going to stop up the hill and be caught, quietly gathered three more winners to equal Tom Coulthwaite's Festival record of 1923. And as for McCoy, well, he went out two days later to become the tenth jockey to achieve the Champion Hurdle–Gold Cup double with another faultless performance on the big chestnut Mr Mulligan, and raise his Festival total to five, thereby equalling the record of Fred Winter (1959) and Jamie Osborne (1992). Several champion jockeys – Gifford, Davies, Stack, Barry, Mellor even – never rode five in their entire careers.

Neither McCoy nor Pipe was the kind of man to accept second best. 'Winning is a drug for me,' said the trainer, echoing his jockey's very own sentiments. 'My appetite is insatiable, and I'm never fully satisfied. That's why I carry on.' Despite possessing a young champion of seemingly limitless horizons, Pipe already had due reason to look over his shoulder. Twenty-four hours after the Champion Hurdle a promising Irish horse landed a huge patriotic punt in the Royal SunAlliance Novices' Hurdle which took £250,000 out of the ring. The 1998 Champion Hurdle was to be his target. His name was Istabraq. He was trained by a young man called Aidan O'Brien.

16

'O-le, O-le, O-le, O-le . . .'

There are some who will promote Istabraq as not only the greatest-ever winner of the championship but also the greatest exponent of the hurdling art: better than his four triple-champion predecessors, superior to a Night Nurse or the unbeaten Trespasser. Of course, one cannot make meaningful comparisons between horses separated by up to eight decades, but during the thirty-nine years that Timeform has awarded a seasonal rating to the winner of the Champion Hurdle only Night Nurse (182 in 1976–77) has received a higher figure than Istabraq's 180 of 1999–2000. What can be said in Istabraq's cause is that he dominated his contemporaries like no other: his aggregate superiority over three championships amounted to 19½ lengths compared to 15½ for See You Then, 12½ for Hatton's Grace, 9½ for Persian War and 5 for Sir Ken. Istabraq's championship campaigns encompassed 11 other races, of which he lost only 2: Persian War lost 10 of his 12, Hatton's Grace 4 of his 7 and Sir Ken 3 of his 11; See You Then lost just the once, but he did only run 3 times. Istabraq was sent off odds-on for every one of those 11 races. On the other hand, like See You Then, he never tested his superiority in a handicap, a fact which, however unfairly, does seriously undermine his credentials in an era when top-class opposition was thin on the ground. The best of his contemporaries – Limestone Lad, Lady Rebecca or Baracouda for instance – tended to be staying hurdlers not two-milers, and all too many potential rivals met with injury (Monsignor; Barton), went over fences (Best Mate; Sackville) or were never at their peak in the spring (Dato Star). In all honesty, come Champion Hurdle day, Istabraq desperately needed someone to play National Spirit to his Hatton's Grace, Lanzarote to his Comedy of Errors or Monksfield to his Sea Pigeon if he was to win universal acclaim as the supreme champion of champions.

THE CHAMPION HURDLE

Be that as it may, Istabraq is Ireland's latest patron saint. He receives regular visits from parties of schoolchildren – rather than 'three kings' – and his races are attended by members of the Istabraq fan club decked out in his emerald green-and-gold colours. He glories in his own hymn of praise, composed and frequently performed on track by singer-comedian Brendan Grace. Whenever he runs, road signs miraculously appear marking the equine Pilgrims Way. Istabraq has earned this canonisation whilst housed in a yard boasting all manner of Flat-race bluebloods ranging from Galileo and Giant's Causeway to Stravinsky and Mozart, yet it is he, and he alone, who is treated like an equine god. One day, for example, he was enjoying a snooze when his owner paid a visit; he was told in the politest of terms to come back 90 minutes later because Istabraq couldn't be disturbed. Istabraq is the only inmate of Ballydoyle who gets his own box straight back rather than suffer a routine stay in an isolation box when he has been away at the races – all of his neighbours are moved instead. 'He lives on the edge,' says his trainer. 'If you shout at him in the stable, he breaks into a sweat. The slightest change to his routine upsets him and he is inclined to fret. So he does the same work every day. He starts with a hack canter to loosen him up; that's over a couple of furlongs. Then he works over a mile and a furlong. The same two pieces of work every day. He is a natural athlete and a very clean-winded horse who does not take a lot of work. As the Champion Hurdle draws near, he goes a bit faster, but a lot of that is to do with the ground drying. We have to mind him a lot because he is a highly-strung horse who we have to make sure is well protected all the time. It's between keeping him right and spoiling him. If we did the latter, we would have to correct him – and we obviously don't want to have to do that. So we try not to let him have too high an opinion of himself. He is just on the right side of toppling over onto the wrong side and the closer to a race we get the closer he is to toppling.'

An equine marvel of this magnitude needed a trainer to match. O'Brien is not exactly an uncommon surname in Ireland. Even so, one might not expect two men owning this most Irish of names to excel in the same sport to the same exalted degree. Vincent O'Brien and Aidan O'Brien are not related except in terms of their uncanny ability to train racehorses better than their peers. Like his namesake, Aidan O'Brien takes the most extraordinary pains to get things spot-

THE CHAMPION HURDLE

on, right down to the tiniest scintilla of detail. When Istabraq and chums travel over to Cheltenham, for instance, they are accompanied not only by their own feed (which tends to be *de rigueur* these days) but also by O'Brien's own electrician, who ensures the dust-control system for their boxes is correctly installed. Genius is an accolade often bestowed too casually. In this particular history it has been applied, guardedly, to a few individuals: Vincent O'Brien, Ryan Price and Fulke Walwyn, for instance. It may be hard to offer a precise definition of 'genius' but one knows it when one sees it. And Aidan O'Brien has been blessed with it in spades. Were trainers awarded Timeform ratings O'Brien would be up there nudging Arkle's 212.

By the time Istabraq made his 28-year-old handler the championship's youngest winning trainer by securing his first Champion Hurdle in 1998, O'Brien had held a licence for five years and was widely viewed as some sort of wunderkind, having been Ireland's leading jumps trainer throughout that period. Since the slight, bespectacled, fresh-faced O'Brien looked at least ten years younger than his actual age and frequently punctuated responses to press enquiries with 'please God', quite a few people reckoned he could pass for a novice priest or, at the very least, an eager sixth-former attending a university interview. However, the fact that O'Brien neither drank nor smoked ('I was brought up as a Pioneer') rather scotched the former notion and the instant success he had enjoyed suggested he was more of a Harry Potter than the ordinary student. In addition to plundering titles and major events over jumps (the 1996 Whitbread Gold Cup, for example), O'Brien had also made his mark on the Flat by winning the Irish 2000 Guineas, 1000 Guineas and Derby of 1997. Pretty soon he was collecting Classics all over Europe as if they were going out of fashion.

One of six children from a farming and point-to-point background in Killegney, near Clonroche in County Wexford, O'Brien began his working life at the age of 16 weeding strawberries before transferring to the local Co-op where he won promotion from the equally attractive occupation of floor-sweeper to fork-lift truck driver. Eight months of this was enough to convince O'Brien that his future lay in racing. A brief stay with P. J. Finn prefaced 3 and a half years with Jim Bolger during which time he began to gain attention as an amateur rider. It was down at the start of a race at Galway that he first set eyes on Anne-Marie

THE CHAMPION HURDLE

Crowley. O'Brien won the race and, ultimately, the heart of (third-placed) Miss Crowley who, despite possessing the looks to have dabbled in modelling, took over the training stable of her father Joe in 1991. O'Brien left Bolger to assist his new wife at Carriganog, Owning Hill, near Piltown in County Kilkenny, and the partnership proved successful on more than one front. In 1992–93 his wife was the first-ever woman to become champion jumps trainer and in 1993–94 he became champion amateur rider. And, lest anyone be fooled, behind the shy, boyish, wire-rimmed-spectacled façade lurked an innately ferocious will-to-win that often got him into hot water with the stewards for excessive use of the whip!

O'Brien assumed control of Carriganog from his wife in the summer of 1993, sending out his first winner at Tralee, on the Flat, on 7 June. Failure was never going to be an option. 'He is very hard working, reliable and a very pleasant fellow to get on with,' stated former boss Jim Bolger before adding crucially: 'And it's a fact that you can't work without your brains.' O'Brien duly set a prize money record in his maiden jumps season; became the first trainer in Ireland to win 100 races in his first year; and in 1994 established an Irish record of 176 wins (Flat and jumps combined) in a calendar year – which he's since bettered. Such was the instant impact he had made on the Irish scene that when Vincent O'Brien retired just over a year later and sold Ballydoyle to his son-in-law, Coolmore Stud supremo John Magnier, it was he who was immediately approached to take over from his illustrious namesake. O'Brien agreed, so long as he could keep his jumping yard at Piltown, which was a good 20-mile drive away. Magnier was not about to argue. 'When Vincent retired, Coolmore lost its supplier of proven champions,' he said. 'We believe Aidan can fill this gap. He showed that he could train ordinary horses to win an extraordinary number of races.'

Some 18 months before O'Brien decided to concentrate almost exclusively on the Flat in 1998, he had taken charge – in the most tragic circumstances – of one horse who was to prove indubitably out of the ordinary. And so he should, for Istabraq was bred in the purple, being a son of multiple champion Flat-sire Sadler's Wells out of the Secretariat mare Betty's Secret – and thus a half brother to 1984 Derby winner Secreto. However, there was to be no Derby for Istabraq in 1995. Although a good-looking individual – a hard bay boasting an elongated heart-shaped star and white socks –

THE CHAMPION HURDLE

Istabraq never raised Classic expectations for his owner-breeder Sheikh Hamdan Al Maktoum and, after registering 2 wins from 11 tries in the care of John Gosden, he was sent up to the Newmarket July Sales of 1996. Istabraq fell to a bid of 38,000 guineas (the highest on the opening day) from John Durkan, a young man about to set up in Newmarket as a trainer. Durkan never got the opportunity to emulate his father Bill, who prepared the champion two-mile chaser Anaglog's Daughter, by training the champion he had purchased because within months he had developed the leukaemia which was to claim his life in January 1998. In the opinion of Istabraq's new owner there was now only one man for the job.

Istabraq's new owner was J. P. McManus, the legendary 'Sundance Kid' of the betting world. Despite dodging his lessons at every opportunity and claiming to have passed through school 'unnoticed', John Patrick must have learned something at his Limerick alma mater before he left to begin driving a bulldozer for his father ('I used to earn a tenner a week and spent most of it in Alf Hogan's betting shop') because by the age of 20 he was making a name for himself as both a bookmaker ('I went skint a couple of times') and a punter. McManus's attentions shifted toward owning horses (not to mention lucrative dealings in financial markets), and the mare Cill Dara, sporting the emerald green-and-gold livery of East Limerick's South Liberties Gaelic Athletic Association of which he'd once been chairman, landed the Irish Cesarewitch in both 1976 and 1977. Although McManus had been drawn to the Cheltenham Festival since 1975, his best jumper, Jack of Trumps (second in two King Georges and the vehicle of another spectacular betting coup in the 1979 Irish Cesarewitch), fared poorly, coming to grief in both the 1978 National Hunt Chase and the 1980 Gold Cup, while he could only manage sixth in the 1981 renewal shortly before meeting his death at Aintree. Mr Donovan finally worked the oracle for McManus in the 1982 Sun Alliance Hurdle. Istabraq raised McManus's level of commitment to another plain altogether. 'He's my life, my family's, a lot of my friends' lives. Whenever he runs, whatever Istabraq is doing, I'm there. I'll never take my holidays to miss anything he's doing.'

Istabraq's new jockey was certainly no stranger to success at the Festival and had twice been leading rider. Indeed, until a clash of loyalties one day at Leopardstown in 1996, Charlie Swan had been

THE CHAMPION HURDLE

the regular partner of none other than Danoli and it was he who helped 'The People's Champion' land that monstrous gamble in the Sun Alliance Novices', one of the 11 victories (all bar one over hurdles) he had accumulated at the meeting since his first visit in 1987. Born in Ireland to British parents, Swan was the first jump jockey to ride a century during an Irish season (1992–93) and the first to reach 1,000 winners. He had been Irish champion for seven seasons (adding two more titles before ceasing to ride over fences) when he was introduced to the horse whose ability – if not necessarily his fame – surpassed even Danoli's. Swan was said 'to look like a choirboy and ride like the devil', which was no surprise given that his father was a dashing army officer and amateur rider who once acted as the Grand National 'hare' aboard Zimulator in 1975 and his mother was a descendant of Tom Chaloner, who won ten English Classics including the Derby of 1863 on Macaroni. When Richard Dunwoody left Martin Pipe in 1995, Swan turned down what many regard as the best job in the sport. Swan's love for his homeland was rewarded with Istabraq. 'I might have given up riding if Istabraq had not been around, but he has rejuvenated me.'

Bearing in mind the astonishingly rapid and dynamic impact he had made on the sport in general, Aidan O'Brien was positively lethargic at the Cheltenham Festival. It took three visits and 14 runners before Urubande obliged in the 1996 Sun Alliance Novices', and in the Champion Hurdle itself Hotel Minella could only manage ninth behind Collier Bay while Theatreworld had chased home Make A Stand in the latest renewal. Indeed, the Festival had thrown up a couple of eminently forgettable moments as far as O'Brien was concerned. He had intended to run Hotel Minella in the Coral Cup 24 hours after the Champion Hurdle but was forced to withdraw the top-weight, causing the weights to stay down. The horse had run on consecutive days in the past but on this occasion he declined to eat or drink overnight. The stewards took a dim view of O'Brien's explanations and referred him to the Jockey Club: 'ridiculous' and 'disgrace' were two of the printable words uttered by the visibly disgruntled trainer. Then, after Istabraq's Royal SunAlliance victory, he'd been on the verge of forcible eviction from the winner's enclosure by Cheltenham manager Edward Gillespie because, lacking the correct badge, he resorted to vaulting the rail to gain access; diplomatic intervention by trainer and broadcaster Ted Walsh fortunately saved the day.

THE CHAMPION HURDLE

Istabraq came to his first Champion Hurdle at the age of six with overpowering credentials. Although meeting defeat on his hurdling début at Punchestown on 16 November 1996, he marched unbeaten through his next 9 races – a pre-championship streak matching Lanzarote's of 1974, though trailing Bula's 11 in 1971 and Sir Ken's 15 in 1953. The reigning champion Make A Stand was on the sidelines injured, while Collier Bay had gone over fences (winning a couple before finally bowing out in April 2001). The principal danger seemed to rest with last year's fourth I'm Supposin' (winner of the Kingwell), the Haydock Trial winner Dato Star and last season's winner of the Supreme Novices' Hurdle and Scottish Champion Hurdle, Shadow Leader. Some doubting Thomases pointed to the fact that since Istabraq had contested the longer novices' event last March he might be disadvantaged by the shorter trip – and he'd failed to impress every onlooker when beating the novice His Song in his championship prep, the AIG (Europe) Irish Champion Hurdle. O'Brien was quick to pour cold water on any such misgivings. Istabraq ran in the Royal SunAlliance because McManus had another runner for the shorter race, and as for this season 'his races have really been part of his work and schooling – we deliberately left plenty to work on and we have got serious with him only since the Irish Champion Hurdle, which was run at a messy pace that didn't suit him'.

Thus, in his characteristically understated way, O'Brien oozed confidence: ground, distance, temperament, the necessary speed. Worries there were none. Ballydoyle knew that at one and a half miles or more Istabraq regularly proved himself at home to be every bit as fast as any of its elite Flat horses. And it was St Patrick's Day. What could go wrong? McManus treated himself to a bet of £90,000-£30,000 with Victor Chandler and settled down to watch his horse annihilate the opposition with a clinical exhibition rarely witnessed in the history of the Champion Hurdle.

Istabraq slaughtered his field to the tune of 12 lengths, a margin not seen since Insurance beat Song of Essex (and just one other) in 1932. 'Aidan told me he would destroy them and he did destroy them,' gasped Swan. 'They went too slow early on for him but when he quickened again turning in I couldn't believe it. Sixty yards after the final flight I looked to my right and I couldn't believe I was so far clear.' Nothing got in a blow. Dato Star nearly slipped up at the fourth and poor Shadow Leader broke his neck at the last.

THE CHAMPION HURDLE

Theatreworld filled the runner-up spot for the second year, in so doing once again landed the £250 each-way bet (at 40s, too, not the starting price of 20/1) O'Brien had placed on behalf of his staff on its Ballydoyle 'selected'. Both first and second were progeny of Sadler's Wells, which provided a notable first for both the Coolmore stallion and O'Brien – the only other trainer to have had even two horses in the frame was Peter Easterby when Sea Pigeon and Night Nurse filled the minor places behind Monksfield in 1978. It proved a mighty afternoon for Ireland, and the roars of 'King Aidan' which rang round the winner's enclosure soon metamorphosed into chants of 'St Aidan' and, eventually, a full-throated chorus of the Irish soccer team anthem, 'O-le, O-le, O-le, O-le . . .'

Although Istabraq's winning streak came to an abrupt end on his very next start at the hooves of Pridwell in Aintree's Martell Hurdle (ironically over the 2 and a half mile trip pre-Champion Hurdle wisdom insisted he preferred), the opposition standing between him and a successful defence of his title in 1999 harboured less threat than that he'd dispatched to win it. Heavier (15 kilos), stronger and, according to O'Brien, quicker than ever before ('We just hope he gets the trip,' he quipped), the only one of the 13 to confront him that started shorter than 16/1 was French Holly (11/2) with whom he had toyed in the Irish Champion, the last of his four wins during the current campaign. 'The only thing that can beat Istabraq is his temperament,' conceded rails bookmaker Victor Chandler. 'If it wasn't the Champion Hurdle, he'd be 4s on.' Even Martin Pipe agreed: 'Istabraq is home and hosed.' One of Pipe's two runners did warrant some attention, however, because Blowing Wind enabled Richard Dunwoody to edge past Fred Winter and Peter Scudamore with a record 14th (and last) mount in the championship.

A record crowd for a Festival opening day of 46,470 crammed into Prestbury Park to witness Istabraq (9/4 on) retain his crown with the minimum of fuss and bother. Although the second-shortest-priced favourite in history (to Sir Ken's 5/2 on in 1953) had again proved slightly edgy and sweating during the preliminaries, normal service swiftly resumed once the tape rose. Electing to stalk the steady pace set by City Hall, Swan waited until French Holly tried to forge clear coming down the hill before allowing Istabraq to take command at the second-last. At this stage another considerable

THE CHAMPION HURDLE

margin of victory looked on the cards but Istabraq did not stretch away up the hill on this occasion and he crossed the line just 3 and a half lengths in front of the perennial bridesmaid Theatreworld, who thus won a dubious form of immortality for himself as the first horse to achieve a hat-trick of second places – again burdened with the staff's each-way money (at 25/1 instead of 16s). O'Brien blamed the good-soft ground, which he described as 'a bit tacky, it wouldn't be in his favour', although he quickly added, 'He's probably more relaxed than he's ever been. We didn't have to go to the bottom of the barrel this year.' Nor was the pace as quick as Istabraq would have liked, being some 3 and a half seconds slower over the first 6 flights than the novices' contest won by Hors la Loi III an hour earlier. Nevertheless, Istabraq was immediately installed as short as 5/4 to lift his third title in 2000 when he would meet, among others, the up-and-coming Hors la Loi III who had won the Supreme Novices' by 17 lengths in a faster time than his own.

Back in Ireland, Istabraq found he had a rival for the affection of his countrymen. When all was said and done, Istabraq was born with a silver spoon in his mouth and had resided in the equivalent of five-star hotels. By comparison, Limestone Lad had been equipped with a wooden ladle and had lived his life in a log cabin. He was, in other words, another homespun hero in the Danoli mould whom the Irish race-going public tends to clasp to its bosom as no other. The solitary racehorse housed (and bred) at the Bowe family's farm at Gathabawn, near Johnstown in County Kilkenny, had been beaten twice by Istabraq in 1999 over two miles, but in November the seven-year-old sensationally lowered the champion's colours over the half-mile longer trip of the Hatton's Grace Hurdle at Fairyhouse to offer a glimmer of hope to every Champion Hurdle aspirant. Limestone Lad was unlikely to be one of them, despite promotion to third favourite. He was a trailblazing stayer. Only hock-deep mud could entice him to the Champion Hurdle, and once Istabraq exacted emphatic revenge in the AIG back at the championship distance, the attentions of Limestone Lad (at 177 rated only 3lb inferior to Istabraq in Timeform's *Chasers and Hurdlers*) were directed toward the Stayers' Hurdle over three miles.

Istabraq's immediate predecessor Make A Stand would re-enter the lists but it was almost three years since his last run, in the Martell, and he could not be seriously considered. A variety of

THE CHAMPION HURDLE

breathing and bleeding problems meant the French-trained Hors La Loi III had failed to fulfil his promise of the previous March and his trainer, the astute Francois Doumen, did not think he was really ready for a race like the championship. Conversely, the Yorksire-trained Dato Star did come to the championship in fine fettle for once and was due a change of luck. Quietly fancied in 1998, Malcolm Jefferson's pride and joy had torn a huge flap of skin off a leg at an early flight and never hurdled fluently thereafter; and then there had been a ligament operation and traces of a heart murmur. This season he had won the Fighting Fifth, the Christmas Hurdle and the Haydock Trial to confirm his status as the best of the home contingent. However, it had been a wet winter. Dato Star loved it soft. Unfortunately for him, conditions began to dry up as the Festival neared.

The championship seemed all over bar the shouting. Ireland's two big bookmaking firms, Paddy Power and Cashmans, even took the novel step of announcing they would pay out all ante-post bets on Istabraq before the race was run. A little extra something was sorely needed to inject a bit of genuine pep into proceedings. Right on cue one materialised. In the course of one of his final pre-Festival interviews Aidan O'Brien had confided, 'It has been a case of so far, so good, but you never know what will happen.' At 4.30 on the afternoon before the Champion Hurdle that comment came back to haunt him. O'Brien took a call in his Ballydoyle office from Pat Keating, his travelling head lad, who had gone on ahead with Istabraq to Cheltenham to be told there was a trickle of fresh blood coming down one of the horse's nostrils. He had just enjoyed a roll in his box, so he may have only banged himself. That would be nothing to worry about. But, far more seriously, Istabraq may have haemorrhaged – in which case he could not be raced. O'Brien alerted McManus and Swan, and then the media. 'Istabraq is a very excitable horse and we are hoping the blood has come from a vessel in the nostril and not from further down. He did have blood showing from a nostril once before when we moved him from one box to another. Then, he scoped clear – but this time we won't be able to have him scoped so close to the race because he'd need to be sedated and the medication would still be in his system when he raced. He'll have his breakfast as usual and then a bit of exercise, as he usually would. Then we'll look at him and make a decision.'

Although veterinary opinion decreed bleeding from one nostril

THE CHAMPION HURDLE

suggested some localised source in the head rather than a more dangerous source in the lungs, there 'wasn't much sleep in the house' according to Anne-Marie O'Brien as her husband contemplated the early-morning helicopter flight to Cheltenham and the repercussions it would bring. Ballydoyle vet John Halley was asked to accompany O'Brien on a chopper ride more stomach churning than usual. Halley examined Istabraq thoroughly and could find nothing amiss. O'Brien took all necessary counsel and at around 11.30, barely three hours before race-time, he informed the media that Istabraq would run unless anything untoward arose in the interim. Inwardly, O'Brien was bleeding as much as he hoped his horse was not. 'In many ways I felt we were doing the wrong thing by running him,' he later confessed, 'but it was a team decision to run and we all stood by it. What influenced us was that he was never going to get another chance to win a third successive Champion Hurdle. If it had been an ordinary race, we would not have run him.'

The kudos of hurdling's championship had never been more graphically illustrated. Thankfully, the outcome was one that all connected with Istabraq both desired and deserved. Although Istabraq's relatively generous price of 15/8 on at the off reflected the nerve-jangling news emanating from the racecourse stables (he'd been 7/2 on before the scare), the race itself threw up no problems whatsoever. Make A Stand set off at the speed of an angry wasp in an attempt to replicate his successful tactics of 1997 and soon established a huge lead. However, the former champion had shot his bolt by the fifth flight, at which point the Henderson-trained pair of Katarino and Blue Royal set sail on a long run for home. But, on their inside, loomed the unmistakable figure of Istabraq cruising along as happy as a child in a sweet shop. 'I tried to blot the nosebleed out of my mind and ride a normal race,' said Charlie Swan, whose season had started so inauspiciously when he had broken both his arms in a fall at Roscommon. 'I'd walked the course and decided to race up the inner. I was happy where I was – I'd seen Make A Stand looking keen going down to the start, so no one was going to lay up with him. Istabraq ran a bit lazily at the top of the hill but when I shook the reins at him he suddenly came alive and I knew we were going to win.'

Once every whip bar Swan's could be spotted fully employed rounding the final turn, the cheering swelled by an octave or two,

THE CHAMPION HURDLE

troubling a high 'C' as Istabraq crossed the final obstacle. Swan let out a reef and Istabraq responded with the fastest sprint up the run-in since the final flight was relocated in 1980: a fraction of 16.91 seconds – the only other mark even below 18 seconds in the previous 20 years was See You Then's 17.80 of 1985. At the line he had four lengths to spare over Hors la Loi with Blue Royal a neck behind, setting a new track record of 3 minutes 48.10 seconds on ground no faster than good (one of four on the day – by huge margins, in the main – leading some to wonder whether race distances had been on the 'short' side).

The relief was palpable. 'After today I won't feel pressure any more,' whispered O'Brien. 'It was like walking on air coming into the winner's enclosure. I don't think he was at his very best but the long and the short of it is that he's so superior to other horses. There's such an engine there.' Istabraq's record over hurdles now stood at 21 victories and three seconds from 24 starts. He had matched the feat of Golden Miller and Arkle by winning at four successive Festivals. The *Racing Post*'s headline summed him up just fine: 'Immortal'.

An unprecedented fourth title seemed a formality, notwithstanding the 2000–01 campaign opening disastrously – almost catastrophically – when he took a horrific cartwheeling fall at the last flight of the Hatton's Grace that might have killed him. The conditions were well-nigh unraceable and it was only in deference to the vast turnout of Istabraq pilgrims who had defied the foul weather and trekked to Fairyhouse that he was finally allowed to participate. In truth, Istabraq looked dog-tired and beaten when he fell. However, O'Brien had been giving his charge kid-glove treatment with just that fourth Champion Hurdle in mind. He stripped a lot fitter for his fourth AIG (Europe) Irish Champion Hurdle a month later and duly became the first jumper to pass the £1 million mark in prize money courtesy of a victory bearing all the customary Istabraq trademarks.

Even as Istabraq resumed his winning ways at Leopardstown, his prospects of achieving a fourth title were being threatened by something far more dangerous than any rival. Britain had been struck by a virulent outbreak of foot-and-mouth disease. For some time it appeared the Festival might survive but six days before it was due to start the axe fell once it was discovered that a local farmer had breached new Ministry of Agriculture guidelines by

THE CHAMPION HURDLE

grazing some sheep on the course within 28 days of a meeting. Ironically, his flock grazed near the Champion Hurdle starting gate. A rescheduled Festival in April was ultimately abandoned, giving rise to the only total peacetime wipe-out in the Festival's 99-year history excepting the frost-plagued year of 1931.

However sad the decision was for the twin communities of jump-racing and farming, it proved just as well for the credibility of Cheltenham's various championships. Istabraq would not have won a fourth title because he would not have lined up. Like all Irish trainers, O'Brien had acceded to the wishes of his own Minister of Agriculture and agreed to minimise the risk of the disease reaching Ireland by keeping his horses at home. Instead, Istabraq contested the Shell Champion Hurdle at Leopardstown on 27 April, sustaining a crashing fall at the very same flight (albeit an assured winner on this occasion) that had almost killed him in December.

Istabraq repaired to McManus's Martinstown Stud for his annual summer holiday. He will still only be nine-years-old when the 2002 Champion Hurdle comes round, an age at which Free Fare, Our Hope, Solford, Royal Gait and fellow legend Hatton's Grace were winning their first championships – and Sea Pigeon had yet to start. It was hard to believe that Istabraq's occupation of a pedestal all to himself in the Champion Hurdle's hall of fame had been nothing other than delayed.

EPILOGUE: 2002

And so it came to pass that Festival history was not to be made. In one of the most dramatic renewals of the Champion Hurdle ever staged, triple champion and 2/1 favourite Istabraq was pulled-up after less than 60 seconds of his attempt at a record fourth title and the Pipe-McCoy representative Valiramix (whom sentimental money had seen the reigning champion displace as favourite barely minutes before the off) came down on the flat when going to the second last looking as if he was on the verge of trotting up.

All the mishmash of rumours surrounding Istabraq's physical well-being – for him to win required 'a miracle', according to Aidan O'Brien, and Irish bookie Paddy Power offered 8/1 that he would not finish – seemed confirmed once the stiffness he had reportedly been suffering from increasingly as the year progressed, struck with a vengeance the moment he left the tape. Charlie Swan did not feel he took the first hurdle too fluently and after giving him the opportunity of a second chance – and finding no encouragement – the sympathetic Swan elected for the safest option, by which time Aidan O'Brien had already walked off the grandstand in anticipation of the inevitable. The Cheltenham faithful applauded Istabraq in the paddock and, bizarre as it is to envisage 51,000 punters saluting a favourite pulled out of a big race before it has really even begun, that is precisely what transpired as Swan and his champion forlornly made their way to the side of the track.

Istabraq had run only the once since his second fall at Leopardstown, recording an unconvincing head victory in a conditions event from the handicapper Bust Out, who received just 10 of the 49lb to which he was properly entitled. 'It was a difficult decision to run him,' conceded O'Brien upon greeting his fallen champion. 'He has been very stiff this year. We took the chance for the horse's sake but there was to be no risk. If Charlie was in any

THE CHAMPION HURDLE

doubt he was to pull him up. There's no doubt the missed year cost him his best chance of winning it again.'

So, the path lay open for a new champion to be crowned. The identity of that new title-holder looked no contest. By the penultimate hurdle at the bottom of the hill, the imposing grey shape of Valiramix could still be spotted tucked in behind the leaders, contentedly lobbing along waiting for McCoy to flip the switch.

Opinions vary as to whether Valiramix clipped the heels of the fading Ansar but the six-year-old took one false step and then another to crash spectacularly and horrifically. He left the track in the horse ambulance but was found to have broken a shoulder and was put-down – the third fatality (and to the second Pipe horse) in the last six championships.

The remainder of the race couldn't avoid being anticlimactic – unless you were a supporter of Hors La Loi, on whom Dean Gallagher's elbows were already in motion when Valiramix made his sad exit. Those urgings reaped their reward, however, since no one around him was travelling any better turning into the straight. The only horse to make significant inroads up the final incline was the French mare Bilboa (who had lost her pitch on the descent to the second last) but Hors La Loi (10/1 fourth best in the field of 15) was never in danger of being caught by her or the 25/1-shot Marble Arch who won the battle for second by ½ length, three lengths adrift of the winner.

For Dean Gallagher this victory marked a step back from the brink. In January 1998 he was one of four jockeys arrested as part of police investigations into allegations of race-fixing and in July 2000 he received a six-month ban following a positive test for cocaine. No charges were eventually brought in the former case, but Gallagher was obliged to sell his house to cover the cost of his defence. As for the latter indiscretion, a comprehensive programme of rehabilitation was necessary before Gallagher's licence was returned at the beginning of 2001.

Trainer James Fanshawe – whose two Champion Hurdles had come courtesy of the two lowest-rated winners (Royal Gait at 164 and Hors La Loi at a provisional 161) in the 40 years Timeform had been awarding a figure – wore the smile of a bemused man. Last season he could get no tune whatsoever out of the winner of the 1999 Supreme Novices and the 2000 championship runner-up, one

THE CHAMPION HURDLE

of just two jumpers in his yard. 'By the end of last year the horse and I had rock-bottom confidence in each other. He couldn't go past the slowest horse in the yard. I was pleased to see the back of him when he went off for his summer holiday and hoped I'd seen the last of him.'

The championship had seen the last of Istabraq. As expected, he was quickly retired. 'He is like an ice cube – when he melts away there will never be another one like him,' said O'Brien, echoing the thoughts of every hurdling enthusiast.

Hurdling's holy grail of a fourth success in the Champion Hurdle remains as elusive as ever and it will take 'another one like him' to have the remotest chance of realising the quest.

Appendix 1

Results

1927
WEDNESDAY, 9 MARCH
1 **BLARIS** (b g Achtoi–Opplinger)
2 Boddam (b h Ultimus–Princess Longniddry)
3 Harpist (b g Hapsburg–Harmonica)
Owner: Mrs H. Hollins
Trainer: B.W. Parr
Also ran: Labrador
4 ran

SOFT   £365
6-12-0   G. Duller 11/10f
8-12-0   W. Speck 7/2
6-12-0   F.B. Rees 9/4
Distances: 8 lengths and 1
Time: 4 min 13.60

1928
THURSDAY, 15 MARCH
1 **BROWN JACK** (br g Jackdaw–Querquidella)
2 Peace River (br h Cygnus–Isle of the Blessed)
3 Blaris (b g Achtoi–Opplinger)
Owner: Sir H. Wernher
Trainer: A. Hastings, Wroughton
Breeder: G. Webb
Also ran: Zeno, Killia, Rathrueen
6 ran

GOOD   £680
4-11-0   L.B. Rees 4/1
5-11-0   T. Leader 5/1
7-12-0   G. Duller 2/1f
Distances: 1½ lengths and 6
Time: 4 min 5.00

1929
TUESDAY, 12 MARCH
1 **ROYAL FALCON** (ch h White Eagle–
       Queen Mother)
2 Rolie (br g Rivoli–Accisia)
3 Clear Cash (b c Dibs–Proud Issue)
Owner: Miss V. Williams-Bulkeley
Trainer: R. Gore, Findon
Breeder: National Stud

GOOD   £675
6-12-0   F.B. Rees 11/2

8-12-0   W. Stott 4/1
4-11-0   G. Pellerin 7/4f
Distances: 4 lengths and 5
Time: 4 min 1.20

THE CHAMPION HURDLE

Also ran: Blancona, Fenimore Cooper, Helter Skelter
6 ran

1930

TUESDAY, 11 MARCH	SOFT £670
1 **BROWN TONY** (br g Jackdaw–Lady Peary)	4-11-0 T. Cullinan 7/2
2 Clear Cash (b c Dibs–Proud Issue)	5-11-0 G. Pellerin 6/4f
3 Peertoi (br g Achtoi–Lady Peroe)	5-11-0 S. Ingham 7/2
Owner: Mrs J. de Selincourt	*Distances*: Head and short head
Trainer: J. Anthony, Letcombe Regis	*Time*: 4 min 20.20

Breeder: S. Slocock
Also ran: Promptitude, Arctic Star
5 ran

1931
No Race

1932

TUESDAY, 1 MARCH	GOOD–FIRM £670
1 **INSURANCE** (b g Achtoi–Prudent Girl)	5-11-10 T. Leader 4/5f
2 Song of Essex (br g Essexford–Cradle Song)	6-12-0 W. Parvin 5/4
3 Jack Drummer (b g Jackdaw–Drummin)	4-11-0 T. Cullinan 33/1
Owner: Hon. D. Paget	*Distances* 12 lengths and Bad
Trainer: B. Briscoe, Longstowe	*Time*: 4 min 12.30

Breeder E.J. Hope
3 ran

1933

TUESDAY, 8 MARCH	SOFT £670
1 **INSURANCE** (b g Achtoi–Prudent Girl)	6-12-0 W. Stott 10/11f
2 Windermere Laddie (b g Bachelors Double–Passing Show)	9-12-0 S. Ingham 4/1
3 Indian Salmon (b c Salmon Trout–Voleuse Aga)	4-11-0 G. Pellerin 100/8
Owner: Hon. D. Paget	*Distances*: ¾ length and 8
Trainer: B. Briscoe, Longstowe	*Time*: 4 min 37.60

Breeder: E.J. Hope
Also ran: Song of Essex, Tees Head
5 ran

THE CHAMPION HURDLE

1934

TUESDAY, 6 MARCH	GOOD–SOFT £670
1 **CHENANGO** (b g Hapsburg–Will Return)	7-12-0 D. Morgan 4/9f
2 Pompelmoose (b c Pommern–Mahonia)	4-11-0 P. Fitzgerald 9/2
3 Black Duncan (bl g Grand Parade– Lochranza)	4-11-0 T. Cullinan 20/1

Owner: G.H. Bostwick
Trainer: I. Anthony, Wroughton
Breeder: C. Prior
Also ran: Song of Essex, Brunel
5 ran

Distances: 5 lengths and 6
Time: 4 min 17.0

1935

TUESDAY, 12 MARCH	GOOD–FIRM £670
1 **LION COURAGE** (b/br g Jackdaw – Lullaby)	7-12-0 G. Wilson 100/8
2 Gay Light (b h Flamboyant–Lone Star)	9-12-0 S. Ingham 9/4f
3 Hill Song (br g Spion Kop–Cradle Song)	6-12-0 G. Pellerin 3/1

Owner: R. Fox-Carlyon
Trainer: F.A. Brown, Bourton-on-the-Hill

Distances: ½ length and ¾
Time: 4 min 0.20 (race record)

Breeder: M.J. Gleeson
Also ran: Victor Norman, Flaming, Latoi, Patrimony, Enchanter, New Era, Heartbreak, Teddy's Double
11 ran

1936

TUESDAY, 10 MARCH	SOFT £670
1 **VICTOR NORMAN** (gr g King Sol – Tickits)	5-11-10 H. Nicholson 4/1
2 Free Fare (ch g Werewolf–Bachelors Fare)	8-12-0 G. Pellerin 5/2f
3 Cactus II (b h Guido Ressi–Conossa)	6-12-0 G. Wilson 20/1

Owner: Mrs M. Stephens
Trainer: M. Blair, Ewhurst
Breeder: W.J. Peek
Also ran: Armour Bright, Patrimony, Swift and True, Wheatley, Hill Song
8 ran

Distances: 3 lengths and 1½
Time: 4 min 14.40

THE CHAMPION HURDLE

1937

TUESDAY, 9 MARCH	SOFT	£670

1 **FREE FARE** (ch g Werewolf – Bachelors Fare) 9.12.0   G. Pellerin 2/1f
2 Our Hope (gr g Son and Heir – 8.12.10
        Here's Hoping)   Capt. P. Harding 100/8
3 Menton (ch g Papyrus – Nice)   5.11.10   S. Ingham 11/2
Owner: B. Warner   *Distances*: 2 lengths and a
Trainer: E. Gwilt, Lambourn   short head
Breeder: A. Lawry   *Time*: 4 min 19.20
Also ran: Patriot King, Citadel, Victor Norman, Wardley
7 ran

1938

TUESDAY, 8 MARCH	FIRM	£745

1 **OUR HOPE** (gr g Son and Heir –   9-12-0   Capt. P. Harding 5/1
        Here's Hoping)
2 Chuchoteur (b/gr h Chubasco–   6-12-0   M. Plaine 9/2
        La Belladeuse)
3 Lobau (ch h Mon Talisman–Lybienne) 6-12-0   H. Nicholson 100/6
Owner: R. Gubbins   *Distances*: 1½ lengths and 10
Trainer: R. Gubbins, Lambourn   *Time*: 4 min 4.80
Breeder: W.E. Robinson
Also ran: 1/2f Free Fare, Up Sabre
5 ran

1939

TUESDAY, 7 MARCH	STICKY	£720

1 **AFRICAN SISTER** (ch m Prester John–Meloa) 7-12-0   K. Piggott 10/1
2 Vitement (gr g Prestissimo–Jaylight) 6-12-0   E. Vinall 20/1
3 Apple Peel (ch g Apelle–White Coral) 9-12-0   S. Ingham 100/8
Owner: H.J. Brueton   *Distances*: 3 lengths and ½
Trainer: C. Piggott, Cheltenham   *Time*: 4 min 13.60
Breeder: A. Baker
Also ran: 3/1f Iceberg II, Mask and Wig, Prudent Achtoi, Santayana, Our Hope, Lobau, Solford, Bahuddin, Free Fare, Argentino
13 ran

1940

WEDNESDAY, 13 MARCH	SOFT	£410

1 **SOLFORD** (b g Soldennis–Margaret Beaufort) 9-12-0   S. Magee 5/2f

THE CHAMPION HURDLE

2 African Sister (ch m Prester John–Meloa)	8-12-0	K. Piggott 8/1
3 Carton (ch g Lemon Car–Tonsil)	5-11-10	F. Rickaby 3/1

Owner: Hon. D. Paget
Trainer: O. Anthony, Letcombe Bassett
Breeder: J.P. Hartigan
Distances: 1½ lengths and 4
Time: 4 min 13.40
Also ran: Aldine, Bahuddin, Lemanaghan, Fairfax, Patrimony
8 ran

1941

WEDNESDAY, 19 MARCH   GOOD   £410

1 **SENECA** (ch c Caligula–Facette)	4-11-0	R. Smyth 7/1
2 Anarchist (b c Taj ud Din–Fontaine Francaise)	4-11-0	M. Jones 33/1
3 Ephorus (ch g Apelle–Esla)	5-11-10	H. Nicholson 8/1

Owner: Sir M. McAlpine
Trainer: V. Smyth, Epsom
Breeder: Sir M. McAlpine
Distances: Head and 2 lengths
Time: 4 min 9.00
Also ran: 4/7f Solford, African Sister, Luncheon Hour
6 ran

1942

SATURDAY, 14 MARCH   GOOD   £495

1 **FORESTATION** (b g Felicitation– Woodciss)	4-11-0	R. Smyth 10/1
2 Anarchist (b c Taj ud Din–Fontaine Francaise)	5-11-10	T. Isaac 100/8
3 Southport (gr g Portlaw–Majority Calling)	6-12-0	F. Rickaby 9/2f

Owner: V. Smyth
Trainer: V. Smyth, Epsom
Breeder: Sir W. Burbridge
Distances: 3 lengths and 3
Time: 4 min 10.40
Also ran: 9/2f Interlaken, Jamaica Inn, Milk Bar, Verbatim, Carton, Fir Cone, Mickie Bulger, Tragedian, Poetic Licence, Luncheon Hour, Red April, Easy Chair, Going Gay, Kuela, Kentucky, Ephorus, Farther West
20 ran

1943 and 1944
No Race

1945

SATURDAY, 31 MARCH   GOOD   £340

1 **BRAINS TRUST** (ch g Rhodes Scholar– Easter Bonnet)	5-11-10	T. Rimell 9/2
2 Vidi (br c Umidwar–Lodge Park)	4-11-0	D. Butchers 100/6

THE CHAMPION HURDLE

3 Red April (b g April the Fifth–Red Maru)   8-12-0   D. Jones 10/1
Owner: F. Blakeway   *Distances*: ¾ length and ¾
Trainer: G. Wilson, Andoversford   *Time*: 4 min 9.40
Breeder: Hon. D. Paget

Also ran: 2/1f Triona, Prince Florimonde, Radiance, Port O' London, Pythagoras, Firoze Din, Chesterholme, Clansman, Rosencranz, Bravona, Stipendiary, Tourist, Forestation

16 ran

1946

TUESDAY, 12 MARCH   GOOD   £980
1 **DISTEL** (b g Rosewell–Laitron)   5-11-10   R. O'Ryan 4/5f
2 Carnival Boy (br h Colombo–Sharp Tor)   5-11-10   T. Rimell 7/2
3 Robin O'Chantry (b g Robin Goodfellow –   6-12-0   J.Goodgame 100/6
     Lady Champ)
Owner: Hon. D. Paget   *Distances*: 4 lengths and ½
Trainer: M. Arnott, Clonsilla, Co. Dublin   *Time*: 4 min 5.00
Breeder: A.J. and I.J. Blake

Also ran: The Diver, Mytholm, Abbot of Knowle, Fariaco, Odette

8 ran

1947

SATURDAY, 12 APRIL   YIELDING   £1,035
1 **NATIONAL SPIRIT** (ch g Scottish Union–   6-12-0   D. Morgan 7/1
     Cocktail)
2 Le Paillon (b h Fastnet–Blue Bear)   5-11-10   A. Head 2/1f
3 Freddy Fox (ch g Foxhunter–Her Eminence)   8-12-0   R. Smyth 8/1
Owner: L. Abelson   *Distances*: 1 length and 2
Trainer: V. Smyth, Epsom   *Time*: 4 min 3.80
Breeder: L. Abelson

Also ran: Triona, Sammy Rock, Shining Penny, Gay Scot, Austerity, Oregon, Sabry, Distel, Mask & Brush, Inspired, General Factotum

14 ran

1948

TUESDAY, 2 MARCH   GOOD   £2,068
1 **NATIONAL SPIRIT** (ch g Scottish Union–   7-12-0   R. Smyth 6/4f
     Cocktail)
2 DUKW (b g Precipitation–Aquatic)   5-11-10   J. Maguire 5/1
3 Encoroli (b g Olibruis–Veuve Joyeuse)   5-11-10   M. Connors 20/1

THE CHAMPION HURDLE

Owner: L. Abelson
Trainer: V. Smyth, Epsom

Breeder: L. Abelson

Distances: 2 lengths and ¾
Time: 3 min 54.80 (race record)

Also ran: Swift Flight, Hatton's Grace, Dame Street, Robinson, Budore, Urgay, Hells Bells, Stirling Castle, Point of Law
12 ran

1949

TUESDAY, 8 MARCH	GOOD	£2,299
1 **HATTON'S GRACE** (b g His Grace–Hatton)	9-12-0	A. Brabazon 100/7
2 Vatelys (b g Vatellor–Yssel II)	9-12-0	R. Bates 10/1
3 Captain Fox (ch c Nearco–White Fox)	4-11-0	K. Mullins 100/9

Owner: Mrs M. Keogh
Trainer: M.V. O'Brien, Churchtown, Co. Cork
Breeder: J.W. Harris

Distances: 6 lengths and 1
Time: 4 min 0.60

Also ran: 5/4f National Spirit, Anglesey, Shining Gold, Benedictine, Ballindine, Secret Service, Admiral John, Tant Pis, School Treat, Gallant Scot, Wolfschmidt
14 ran

1950

TUESDAY, 7 MARCH	HEAVY	£2,427
1 **HATTON'S GRACE** (b g His Grace–Hatton)	10-12-0	A. Brabazon 5/2f
2 Harlech (b h Owen Tudor–Grand Duchesse)	5-11-12	M. Molony 9/2
3 Speciality (b h Scottish Union–Tabaret)	5-11-12	K. Mullins 100/6

Owner: Mrs M. Keogh
Trainer: M.V. O'Brien, Churchtown, Co. Cork
Breeder: J.W. Harris

Distances: 1½ lengths and 2
Time: 3 min 59.60

Also ran: National Spirit, Desir, DUKW, Vatelys, School Treat, Sylvian III, Pretence, Lady Baby, Fil d'Or II
12 ran

1951

TUESDAY, 6 MARCH	HEAVY	£3,615
1 **HATTON'S GRACE** (b g His Grace–Hatton)	11-12-0	T. Molony 4/1
2 Pyrrhus II (b g Barreveldt–Patala)	8-12-0	A. Gill 11/2
3 Prince Hindou (b h Louqsor–Dail)	5-11-12	M. Larraun 9/2

Owner: Mrs M. Keogh
Trainer: M.V. O'Brien, Churchtown, Co. Cork
Breeder: J.W. Harris

Distances: 5 lengths and ½
Time: 4 min 11.20

THE CHAMPION HURDLE

Also ran: 11/4f Average, National Spirit, Speciality, Secret Service, Noholme
8 ran

1952

TUESDAY, 4 MARCH	STICKY £3,632
1 **SIR KEN** (b g Laëken–Carte Grise II)	5-11-12 T. Molony 3/1f
2 Noholme (br g Bakhtawar–Acornut)	5-11-12 B. Marshall 100/7
3 Approval (b g Dubonnet–Applause)	6-12-0 D. Dillon 9/1
Owner: M. Kingsley	*Distances*: 2 lengths and 4
Trainer: W. Stephenson, Royston	*Time*: 4 min 3.20
Breeder: M. Chenorio	

Also ran: Hatton's Grace, National Spirit, Telegram II, Wye Fly, Fellah II, Average, Royal Oak IV, Chasseur, Penny on the Jack, Cloncan, Hunza, Richard Louis, Farad
16 ran

1953

TUESDAY, 3 MARCH	GOOD £3,479
1 **SIR KEN** (b g Laëken–Carte Grise II)	6-12-0 T. Molony 2/5f
2 Galatian (ch g Way In–Ankara)	6-12-0 B. Marshall 4/1
3 Teapot II (b g Nepenthe–Gris Perle)	8-12-0 P. Taaffe 100/9
Owner: M. Kingsley	*Distances*: 2 lengths and 1½
Trainer: W. Stephenson, Royston	*Time*: 3 min 55.40
Breeder: M. Chenorio	

Also ran: Nuage Dore, Campari, Flush Royal, Assunto
7 ran

1954

TUESDAY, 2 MARCH	GOOD £3,657
1 **SIR KEN** (b g Laëken–Carte Grise II)	7-12-0 T. Molony 4/9f
2 Impney (b g Torbido–Ansley)	5-11-12 M. Pumfrey 9/1
3 Galatian (ch g Way In–Anakara)	7-12-0 P. Taaffe 10/1
Owner: M. Kingsley	*Distances*: 1 length and 3
Trainer: W. Stephenson, Royston	*Time*: 4 min 11.00
Breeder: M. Chenorio	

Also ran: Rendoz Vous III, Lively Lord, Kipling Walk, Tifas, Pintail, Boy David, Tracassian, Pasfort, Assynt, Florestan
13 ran

THE CHAMPION HURDLE

1955

WEDNESDAY, 9 MARCH	SOFT	£3,717
1 **CLAIR SOLEIL** (br g Maravedis–La Divine)	6-12-0	F. Winter 5/2f
2 Stroller (b g Casanova–Bathing Love)	7-12-0	T. Burns 7/2
3 Cruachan (b g Tartan–Lass O' Kilcash)	7-12-0	G. Slack 50/1
Owner: G. Judd	*Distances*: Head and 4 lengths	
Trainer: H.R. Price, Findon	*Time*: 4 min 12.80	
Breeder: F. Dupre		

Also ran: Sir Ken, Prince Charlemagne, Quita Que, Assynt, Flame Royal, Impney, Syrte, Greystown, Bandit King, The Pills, Straight Quill, Kenure, Toremo, Shilford, Sassanian Monarch, Tasmin, Brunel II, Terrible Turk
21 ran

1956

TUESDAY, 6 MARCH	GOOD	£3,300
1 **DOORKNOCKER** (ch g Cacador–Shady Girl III)	8-12-0	H. Sprague 100/9
2 Quita Que (br g Mustang–Selection)	7-12-0	Mr J. Cox 33/1
3 Baby Don (b g Donatello II–Baby Blue)	6-12-0	T. Molony 100/8
Owner: C. Nicholson	*Distances*: ¾ and 4 lengths	
Trainer: W. Hall, Towton	*Time*: 4 min 2.20	
Breeder: P. Mangan		

Also ran: 2/1f Stroller, Clair Soleil, Flame Royal, Ingoe, Bold Baby, Impney, Toreno, Boltown Comet, Vindore, Noholme, Archie
14 ran

1957

TUESDAY, 12 MARCH	SOFT	£3,729
1 **MERRY DEAL** (b g Straight Deal–Merryland)	7-12-0	G. Underwood 28/1
2 Quita Que (br g Mustang Selection)	8-12-0	Mr J. Cox 15/2
3 Tout ou Rien (ch h Anemos–Triple Couronne)	5-11-12	R. Emery 100/8
Owner: A. Jones	*Distances*: 5 lengths and 5	
Trainer: A. Jones, Oswestry	*Time*: 4 min 7.40	
Breeder: Hon. D. Paget		

Also ran: 7/4f Clair Soleil, Rosati, Flame Royal, Ivy Green, Caesars Helm, Nanjula, Straight Jacket, Plainsman, Solatium, Curling Iron, Winning Hit, Peggy Jones, Francette
16 ran

THE CHAMPION HURDLE

1958

TUESDAY, 11 MARCH	GOOD	£4,812
1 **BANDALORE** (b g Tambourin–Smart Woman) 7-12-0		G. Slack 20/1
2 Tokoroa (b g Flamenco–Habiba)	7-12-0	D. Dick 5/1f
3 Retour de Flamme (b g Samaritain– Reine du Bearn)	5-11-12	J. Lindley 11/2

Owner: Mrs D. Wright *Distances*: 2 lengths and 3
Trainer: S. Wright, Leintwardine *Time*: 3 min 56.00
Breeder: Mrs A. Warman

Also ran: Merry Deal, Grey Magic, King, Skate Up, Dunnock, Fare Time, Chamanna, Owens Image, Nanjula, Rosati, Straight Lad, Baby Don, Wayward Bird, Flame Royal, Roma Festival

18 ran

1959

TUESDAY, 3 MARCH	GOOD	£4,587
1 **FARE TIME** (b g Thoroughfare–Septime)	6-12-0	F. Winter 13/2
2 Ivy Green (ch m Flyon–Hedge Law)	9-12-0	P. Taaffe 40/1
3 Prudent King (b g Roi d'Egypte–Prudent Still)	7-12-0	T. Burns 13/2

Owner: G. Judd *Distances*: 4 lengths and 1
Trainer: H.R. Price, Findon *Time*: 4 min 7.80
Breeder: Mrs C. Macdonald-Buchanan

Also ran: 9/4f Tokoroa, Friendly Boy, Merry Deal, Bandalore, Straight Lad, King, Havasnack, Retour de Flamme, Pundit, Camugliano, Wigmore

14 ran

1960

TUESDAY, 8 MARCH	GOOD	£4,290
1 **ANOTHER FLASH** (b g Roi d'Egypte– Cissie Gay)	6-12-0	H. Beasley 11/4f
2 Albergo (br g Dante–Bill of Fare)	6-12-0	D. Page 11/2
3 Saffron Tartan (b/br g Tartan– Kellsboro Witch)	9-12-0	T. Burns 3/1

Owner: J. Byrne *Distances*: 2 lengths and 3
Trainer: P. Sleator, Grange Con, Co. Wicklow *Time*: 3 min 55.00
Breeder: A. Duncan

Also ran: Tokoroa, Articeelagh, Bandalore, Laird O' Montrose, Langton Heath, Commutering, Merry Deal, Pearl Island, Retour de Flamme

12 ran

THE CHAMPION HURDLE

1961

WEDNESDAY, 8 MARCH	GOOD £5,211
1 **EBORNEEZER** (b h Ocean Swell–Priory Princess)	6-12-0 F. Winter 4/1
2 Moss Bank (ch g Mossborough–Gamesmistress)	5-11-12 J. Rafferty 7/4f
3 Farmer's Boy (b g Hyperbole–Bashful)	8-12-0 D. Nicholson 8/1
Owner: Dr B. Pajgar	*Distances*: 3 lengths and 1½
Trainer: H.R. Price, Findon	*Time*: 4 min 10.00
Breeder: Dr B. Pajgar	

Also ran: Quelle Chance, Merry Deal, Albergo, Costa Brava, Silver Reynard, Stenquill, Branca Doria, Mosstrooper of Chantry, Morning Coat, Birinkiana, Tonnerre de Brest, Articeelagh, Green Light, Benton's Row
17 ran

1962

WEDNESDAY, 14 MARCH	GOOD £5,143
1 **ANZIO** (ro g Vic Day–Lido Lady)	5-11-12 G. Robinson 11/2
2 Quelle Chance (br g Flush Royal–Quellenize)	7-12-0 D. Dick 11/2
3 Another Flash (b g Roi d'Egypte–Cissie Gay)	8-12-0 H. Beasley 11/10f
Owner: Sir T. Ainsworth	*Distances*: 3 lengths and 1½
Trainer: F.T. Walwyn, Lambourn	*Time*: 4 min 0.20
Breeder: Harwood Stud	

Also ran: Greektown, Beau Normands, Fidus Achates, Fare Time, Farmer's Boy, Settlement, Drakestone, Commandeer, Water Skier, Sibour
14 ran

1963

WEDNESDAY, 13 MARCH	VERY SOFT £5,585
1 **WINNING FAIR** (bl/br g Fun Fair–Winning Hazard)	8-12-0 Mr A. Lillingston 100/9
2 Farmey Fox (ch g Archive Foxy Jane)	8-12-0 P. Powell 10/1
3 Quelle Chance (br g Flush Royal–Quellenize)	8-12-0 B. Wilkinson 100/7
Owner: G. Spencer	*Distances*: 3 lengths and a neck
Trainer: G. Spencer, Thurles, Co. Tipperary	*Time*: 4 min 15.50
Breeder: P. Finn	

Also ran: 5/2f White Park Bay, Catapult II, Old Mull, Ross Sea, Stirling, Greektown, Height O' Fashion, Pawnbroker, Narratus, Moonsun, Drakestone, French Fox, Flights Orchid, Eastern Harvest, Grainspur, Tenerville, Red Dove, Princess Sobranie
21 ran

THE CHAMPION HURDLE

1964

FRIDAY, 6 MARCH	GOOD	£8,161
1 **MAGIC COURT** (br g Supreme Court–Blue Prelude)	6-12-0	P. McCarron 100/6
2 Another Flash (b g Roi d'Egypte–Cissie Gay)	10-12-0	H. Beasley 6/1f
3 Kirriemuir (br g Tangle–Jonquille II)	4-11-4	G. Robinson 100/6

Owner: J. McGhie

Trainer: T. Robson, Greystoke

Breeder: T. Lilley

Distances: 4 lengths and ¾

Time: 4 min 8.00

Also ran: London Gazette, Salmon Spray, Old Mull, Farrney Fox, Pawnbroker, Height O' Fashion, Chase the Shadow, Winning Fair, Catapult II, Sun Hat, Black Diamond, Jim's Boy, Wilhelmina Henrietta, Sainte Levantine, Sailaway Sailor, Tripacer, Running Rock, Cash Pediment, Clerical Gray, Malfaiteur

24 ran

1965

WEDNESDAY, 10 MARCH	GOOD	£8,042
1 **KIRRIEMUIR** (br g Tangle–Jonquille II)	5-11-12	G. Robinson 50/1
2 Spartan General (ch h Mossborough–Grecian Garden)	6-12-0	T. Bidddlecombe 8/1
3 Worcran (ch g Worden II–Cranseuse)	7-12-0	D. Nicholson 8/1

Owner: Mrs D. Beddington

Trainer: F.T. Walwyn, Lambourn

Breeder: Mrs F. Watkins

Distances: 1 length and 1½

Time: 4 min 6.60

Also ran: 11/4f Magic Court, London Gazette, Salmon Spray, Exhibit A, Wilhelmina Henrietta, Water Skier, Baridi, Nosey, Crown Prince, Orchardist, Running Rock, Lars Porsena, KO, Raphael, Rushing Waters, Aviator

19 ran

1966

WEDNESDAY, 16 MARCH	GOOD	£7,921
1 **SALMON SPRAY** (ch g Vulgan–Fly Book)	8-12-0	J. Haine 4/1
2 Sempervivum (b g Sayajirao–Veronica Franchi)	8-12-0	J. King 20/1
3 Flyingbolt (ch g Airborne–Eastlock)	7-12-0	P. Taaffe 15/8f

Owner: Mrs E. Rogerson

Trainer: R. Turnell, Ogbourne Maisey

Breeder: W. Corry

Distances: 3 lengths and ¾

Time: 4 min 10.20

Also ran: Kirriemuir, Burlington II, Robber Baron, Spartan General, Red Tears, Makaldar, Compton Martin, Silver Moss, Gypsando, Talgo Abbess, Tamerosia,

THE CHAMPION HURDLE

Aviator, Lanconello, Albatros
17 ran

1967
WEDNESDAY, 15 MARCH	FIRM £8,857
1 **SAUCY KIT** (b h Hard Sauce–Reckitts)	6-12-0 R. Edwards 100/6
2 Makaldar (ch g Makalu–La Madouna)	7-12-0 D. Mould 11/4f
3 Talgo Abbess (b g Talgo–Mount Abbess)	8-12-0 F. Carroll 100/8
Owner: K. Alder	Distances: 4 lengths and 1
Trainer: M.H. Easterby, Great Habton	Time: 4 min 11.20
Breeder: Sassoon Studs	

Also ran: Beaver II, Sempervivum, Kirriemuir, Sir Thopas, Aurelius, Johns-wort, Desacre, Rackham, Blue Venom, Specify, Interosian, Worcran, Robber Baron, Samothraki, Originator, New Liskeard, Albinella, Nikko, High Sheriff, Autobiography

23 ran

1968
WEDNESDAY, 20 MARCH	FIRM £7,798
1 **PERSIAN WAR** (b g Persian Gulf–Warning)	5-11-12 J. Uttley 4/1
2 Chorus (b g Beau Sabreur–May)	7-12-0 A. Turnell 7/2f
3 Black Justice (bl g Jock Scot–Triangle)	6-12-0 B. Scott 100/6
Owner: H. Alper	Distances: 4 lengths and 5
Trainer: C. Davies, Chepstow	Time: 4 min 3.80
Breeder: Astor Studs	

Also ran: Saucy Kit, Le Vermentois, Salmon Spray, Sempervivum, Talgo Abbess, Johns-wort, Mugatpura, Commander-in-Chief, Inyanga, Secret Venture, Cool Alibi, Severn Bore, Straight Point

16 ran

1969
WEDNESDAY, 19 MARCH	HEAVY £7,876
1 **PERSIAN WAR** (b g Persian Gulf–Warning)	6-12-0 J. Uttley 6/4f
2 Drumikill (b g Pampered King–Owenbeg)	8-12-0 B. Brogan 100/7
3 Privy Seal (ch h Privy Councillor–Requisite)	5-11-12 J. Cook 33/1
Owner: H. Alper	Distances: 4 lengths and 2½
Trainer: C. Davies, Chepstow	Time: 4 min 41.80
Breeder: Astor Studs	

Also ran: L'Escargot, Into View, Sempervivum, Celtic Gold, New Liskeard, Supermaster, Black Justice, Secret Venture, Ebony King, Early Settler, Tanlic,

THE CHAMPION HURDLE

Bobby Moore, Boat Man, England's Glory
17 ran

1970
WEDNESDAY, 18 MARCH	YIELDING £7,739
1 **PERSIAN WAR** (b g Persian Gulf–Warning)	7-12-0 J. Uttley 5/4f
2 Major Rose (br g March Past–Rosefield)	8-12-0 J. Gifford 8/1
3 Escalus (b h Lord of Verona–Singing Hinny)	5-11-12 D. Mould 25/1
Owner: H. Alper	*Distances*: 1½ lengths and 1
Trainer: C. Davies, Chepstow	*Time*: 4 min 13.80
Breeder: Astor Studs	

Also ran: Coral Diver, Tanlic, Solomon II, Drumikill, Celtic Gold, Colonel Imp, Normandy, Scamp, Mugatpura, Orient War, Bobby Moore
14 ran

1971
WEDNESDAY, 17 MARCH	SOFT £7,466
1 **BULA** (b g Raincheck–Pongo's Fancy)	6-12-0 P. Kelleway 15/8f
2 Persian War (b g Persian Gulf–Warning)	8-12-0 J. Uttley 9/2
3 Major Rose (br g March Past–Rosefield)	9-12-0 T. Biddlecombe 4/1
Owner: Capt. E. Edwards-Heathcote	*Distances*: 4 lengths and 1
Trainer: F.T. Winter, Lambourn	*Time*: 4 min 21.20
Breeder: C. Purcell	

Also ran: Bowie's Brig, Lockyersleigh, Geologist, Dondieu, Moyne Royal, Varma
9 ran

1972
WEDNESDAY, 15 MARCH	SOFT £15,648
1 **BULA** (b g Raincheck–Pongo's Fancy)	7-12-0 P. Kelleway 8/11f
2 Boxer (b g Hard Ridden–China Sarah)	5-11-12 J. Uttley 25/1
3 Lyford Cay (ch g Alcide–Sonata)	8-12-0 D. Cartwright 66/1
Owner: Capt. E. Edwards-Heathcote	*Distances*: 8 lengths and 3
Trainer: F.T. Winter, Lambourn	*Time*: 4 min 25.20
Breeder: C. Purcell	

Also ran: Hardatit, Kelanne, Varma, Coral Diver, Flower Picker, St Patrick's Blue, Dondieu, Canasta Lad, Garnishee
12 ran

THE CHAMPION HURDLE

1973

WEDNESDAY, 14 MARCH	GOOD	£14,563
1 **COMEDY OF ERRORS** (br g Goldhill–Comedy Actress)	6-12-0	W. Smith 8/1
2 Easby Abbey (b g Narrator–Memoire Cheri)	6-12-0	R. Barry 20/1
3 Captain Christy (b g Mon Capitaine–Christy's Bow)	6-12-0	H. Beasley 85/40

Owner: E. Wheatley
Trainer: T.F. Rimell, Kinnersley
Breeder: Miss E. Sykes
Distances: 1½ lengths and 2
Time: 4 min 7.70
Also ran: 5/6f Bula, Brendans Road, Mon Plaisir, True Luck, Invincible
8 ran

1974

WEDNESDAY, 13 MARCH	SOFT	£14,023
1 **LANZAROTE** (b/br g Milesian–Slag)	6-12-0	R. Pitman 7/4
2 Comedy of Errors (br g Goldhill–Comedy Actress)	7-12-0	W. Smith 4/6f
3 Yenisei (gr g Mellay–Grey Flash)	7-12-0	H. Beasley 100/1

Owner: Lord H. de Walden
Trainer: F.T. Winter, Lambourn
Breeder: Lord Howard de Walden
Distances: 3 lengths and 8
Time: 4 min 17.70
Also ran: Moonlight Bay, St Columbus, Calzado, Brantridge Farmer
7 ran

1975

WEDNESDAY, 12 MARCH	HEAVY	£14,459
1 **COMEDY OF ERRORS** (br g Goldhill–Comedy Actress)	8-12-0	K. White 11/8f
2 Flash Imp (bl g Bing II–Double Magnum)	6-12-0	T. Stack 12/1
3 Tree Tangle (b g Mandamus–La Belle au Bois)	6-12-0	A. Turnell 10/1

Owner: E. Wheatley
Trainer: T.F. Rimell, Kinnersley
Breeder: Miss E. Sykes
Distances: 8 lengths and a head
Time: 4 min 28.50
Also ran: Mr Straight, Ribosaint, Bumble Boy, Lanzarote, True Song, Ashendene, Supreme Halo, Calzado, Hardatit, Psalm
13 ran

THE CHAMPION HURDLE

1976

WEDNESDAY, 17 MARCH	GOOD–FIRM £14,530
1 **NIGHT NURSE** (b g Falcon–Florence Nightingale)	5-12-0 P. Broderick 2/1f
2 Bird's Nest (ch g Entanglement–Fair Sabrina)	6-12-0 A. Turnell 100/30
3 Flash Imp (bl g Bing II–Double Magnum)	7-12-0 R. Mann 40/1
Owner: R. Spencer	*Distances*: 2½ lengths and 8
Trainer: M.H. Easterby, Great Habton	*Time*: 4 min 5.90
Breeder: Cloghran Stud	

Also ran: Comedy of Errors, Lanzarote, Dramatist, Lord David, Tree Tangle

8 ran

1977

WEDNESDAY, 16 MARCH	HEAVY £18,147
1 **NIGHT NURSE** (b g Falcon–Florence Nightingale)	6-12-0 P. Broderick 15/2
2 Monksfield (b h Gala Performance–Regina)	5-12-0 T. Kinane 15/2
3 Dramatist (br g David Jack–Doone Valley)	6-12-0 W. Smith 6/1
Owner: R. Spencer	*Distances*: 2 lengths and 2
Trainer: M.H. Easterby, Great Habton	*Time*: 4 min 24.00
Breeder: Cloghran Stud	

Also ran: 9/2f Bird's Nest, Sea Pigeon, Beacon Light, Master Monday, Flying Diplomat, Winter Melody, True Lad

10 ran

1978

WEDNESDAY, 15 MARCH	GOOD £21,332
1 **MONKSFIELD** (b h Gala Performance–Regina) 6-12-0	T. Kinane 11/2
2 Sea Pigeon (br g Sea Bird II–Around the Roses) 8-12-0	F. Berry 5/1
3 Night Nurse (b g Falcon–Florence Nightingale) 7-12-0	C. Tinkler 3/1f
Owner: Dr M. Mangan	*Distances*: 2 lengths and 6
Trainer: D. McDonagh, Moynalty, Co. Meath	*Time*: 4 min 12.70
Breeder: P. Ryan	

Also ran: Beacon Light, Dramatist, Master Monday, Bird's Nest, Meladon, Prominent King, Decent Fellow, Kybo, Koiro Scott, Levaramoss

13 ran

THE CHAMPION HURDLE

1979

WEDNESDAY, 14 MARCH	HEAVY	£22,730
1 **MONKSFIELD** (b h Gala Performance–Regina) 7-12-0		D. Hughes 9/4f
2 Sea Pigeon (br g Sea Bird II–Around the Roses) 9-12-0		J. O'Neill 6/1
3 Beacon Light (b g Relko–Illuminous)	8-12-0	J. Francome 22/1
Owner: Dr M. Mangan	*Distances*: ¾ length and 15	
Trainer: D. McDonagh, Moynalty, Co. Meath	*Time*: 4 min 27.90	
Breeder: P. Ryan		

Also ran: Within the Law, Bird's Nest, Connaught Ranger, Major Thomson, Western Rose, Kybo, River Belle

10 ran

1980

TUESDAY, 11 MARCH	SOFT	£24,972
1 **SEA PIGEON** (br g Sea Bird II–Around the Roses)	10-12-0	J. O'Neill 13/2
2 Monksfield (b h Gala Performance–Regina)	8-12-0	D. Hughes 6/5f
3 Bird's Nest (ch g Entanglement–Fair Sabrina)	10-12-0	A. Turnell 11/1
Owner: P. Muldoon	*Distances*: 7 lengths and 1½	
Trainer: M.H. Easterby, Great Habton	*Time*: 4 min 6.00	
Breeder: Greentree Stud		

Also ran: Royal Boxer, Pollardstown, Connaught Ranger, Norfolk Dancer, Broadleas, Paiute

9 ran

1981

TUESDAY, 17 MARCH	SOFT	£32,260
1 **SEA PIGEON** (br g Sea Bird II–Around the Roses)	11-12-0	J. Francome 7/4f
2 Pollardstown (b g Lord Gayle–Mear-Aille)	6-12-0	P. Blacker 9/1
3 Daring Run (ch g Deep Run–Kertina)	6-12-0	Mr T. Walsh 8/1
Owner: P. Muldoon	*Distances*: 1 length and a neck	
Trainer: M.H. Easterby, Great Habton	*Time*: 4 min 11.20	
Breeder: Greentree Stud		

Also ran: Starfen, Slaney Idol, Celtic Ryde, Bird's Nest, Going Strait, Heighlin, Badsworth Boy, Martie's Anger, Meladon, Mount Harvard, Ivan King

14 ran

THE CHAMPION HURDLE

1982

TUESDAY, 16 MARCH	HEAVY	£37,044
1 **FOR AUCTION** (b g Royal Trip–Wrong Decision)	6-12-0	Mr C. Magnier 40/1
2 Broadsword (b h Ack Ack–Cutting)	5-12-0	P. Scudamore 100/30
3 Ekbalco (b g Deep Run–Wingalong)	6-12-0	D. Goulding 7/2

Owner: F. Heaslip
Trainer: M. Cunningham, Kildalkey, Co. Meath
Breeder: Mrs P. Finegan

Distances: 7 lengths and 1½
Time: 4 min 12.40

Also ran: 9/4f Daring Run, Pollardstown, Gaye Chance, Holemoor Star, Donegal Prince, Another Story, Migrator, Potato Merchant, Heighlin, Homeson, Derring Rose

14 ran

1983

TUESDAY, 15 MARCH	DEAD	£34,865
1 **GAYE BRIEF** (b g Lucky Brief–Artiste Gaye)	6-12-0	R. Linley 7/1
2 Boreen Prince (b g Boreen–Santa Luna)	6-12-0	N. Madden 50/1
3 For Auction (b g Royal Trip–Wrong Decision)	7-12-0	Mr C. Magnier 3/1f

Owner: Sheikh Ali Abu Khamsin
Trainer: Mrs M. Rimell, Kinnersley
Breeder: P. Sweeney

Distances: 3 lengths and 7
Time: 3 min 57.44

Also ran: 3/1f Ekbalco, Broadsword, Sula Bula, Heighlin, Cima, Daring Run, Fane Ranger, Donegal Prince, Royal Vulcan, Migrator, Lulav, Brave Hussar, Miller Hill, Comedian

17 ran

1984

TUESDAY, 13 MARCH	GOOD	£36,680
1 **DAWN RUN** (b m Deep Run–Twilight Slave)	6-11-9	J. O'Neill 4/5f
2 Cima (br g High Top–Lemon Blossom)	6-12-0	P. Scudamore 66/1
3 Very Promising (b g The Parson–No Hitch)	6-12-0	S. Morshead 16/1

Owner: Mrs C. Hill
Trainer: P. Mullins, Goresbridge, Co. Kilkenny

Distances: ¾ length and 4
Time: 3 min 52.60
(race record)

Breeder: J. Riordan
Also ran: Buck House, Fredcoteri, Cut a Dash, Amarach, Boreen Prince, For Auction, Robin Wonder, Desert Orchid, Sula Bula, The Foodbroker, Fine Sun

14 ran

THE CHAMPION HURDLE

1985
TUESDAY, 12 MARCH   GOOD – FIRM   £38,030
1 **SEE YOU THEN** (br g Royal Palace–Melodina) 5-12-0   S. Smith Eccles 16/1
2 Robin Wonder (b g Dawn Review–Rainbow   7-12-0   J. O'Neill 66/1
    Wonder)
3 Stans Pride (ch m Celtic Cone–Columba)   8-11-9   S. Morshead 100/1
Owner: Stype Wood Stud   *Distances*: 7 lengths and 3
Trainer: N. Henderson, Lambourn   *Time*: 3 min 51.70
Breeder: Ribblesdale Stud   (race record)
Also ran: 4/6f Browne's Gazette, Gaye Brief, Fredcoteri, Ra Nova, Centroline, Amarach, Passage Creeper, Statesmanship, Miller Hill, Northern Trial, Desert Orchid
14 ran

1986
TUESDAY, 11 MARCH   GOOD – FIRM £41,435
1 **SEE YOU THEN** (br g Royal Palace–Melodina) 6-12-0   S. Smith Eccles 5/6f
2 Gaye Brief (b g Lucky Brief–Artiste Gaye)   9-12-0   P. Scudamore 14/1
3 Nohalmdun (b g Dragonara Palace–Damsel)   5-12-0   J. O'Neill 20/1
Owner: Stype Wood Stud   *Distances*: 7 lengths and 1½
Trainer: N. Henderson, Lambourn   *Time*: 3 min 53.70
Breeder: Ribblesdale Stud

Also ran: Prideaux Boy, Humberside Lady, Bonalma, First Bout, Kesslin, Herbert United, Cima, Out of the Gloom, Ra Nova, Robin Wonder, Tom Sharp, Voyant, Ararun, Jamesmead, Asir, Aonoch, Glazepta Again, Stans Pride, Bruges, Corporal Clinger
23 ran

1987
TUESDAY, 17 MARCH   GOOD   £43,205
1 **SEE YOU THEN** (br g Royal Palace–Melodina) 7-12-0   S. Smith Eccles
                                                                           11/10f
2 Flatterer (br g Mo Bay–Horizontal)   8-12-0   J. Fishback 10/1
3 Barnbrook Again (b g Nebbiolo–Single Line)   6-12-0   S. Sherwood 14/1
Owner: Stype Wood Stud   *Distances:* 1½ lengths and 1
Trainer: N. Henderson   *Time*: 3 min 57.60
Breeder: Ribblesdale Stud

Also ran: Deep Idol, Stepaside Lord, Prideaux Boy, Herbert United, Nohalmdun, Jimsintime, Mrs Muck, Corporal Clinger, Bonalma, Ra Nova, Brunico, River Ceiriog, Saffron Lord, Comandante, I Bin Zaidoon
18 ran

THE CHAMPION HURDLE

1988
TUESDAY, 15 MARCH	SOFT	£52,225
1 **CELTIC SHOT** (b g Celtic Cone–Duckdown)	6-12-0	P. Scudamore 7/1
2 Classical Charm (b g Corvaro–Mahe Reef)	5-12-0	K. Morgan 33/1
3 Celtic Chief (b g Celtic Cone–Chieftain's Lady)	5-12-0	R. Dunwoody 5/2f

Owner: D. Horton
Trainer: F.T. Winter, Lambourn
Breeder: D. Horton

Distances: 2 lengths and 8
Time: 4 min 15.50

Also ran: Nohalmdun, High Knowl, Swingit Gunner, Tartan Tailor, Floyd, Deep Idol, Marly River, Aldino, Cloughtaney, Juven Light, Osric, Past Glories, Grabel, Pat's Jester, Convinced, Private Audition, Tradehimin, William Crump
21 ran

1989
TUESDAY, 14 MARCH	GOOD–SOFT	£50,207
1 **BEECH ROAD** (ch g Nearly a Hand–North Bovey)	7-12-0	R. Guest 50/1
2 Celtic Chief (b g Celtic Cone–Chieftain's Lady)	6-12-0	G. McCourt 6/1
3 Celtic Shot (b g Celtic Cone–Duckdown)	7-12-0	P. Scudamore 8/1

Owner: A. Geake
Trainer: G.B. Balding, Weyhill
Breeder: J. Tilling

Distances: 2 lengths and 1
Time: 4 min 2.10

Also ran: 11/8f Kribensis, Floyd, Vagador, Mole Board, Cloughtaney, Chatham, Condor Plan, Wishlon, Grey Salute, Cashew King, Chesham Squire, Sprowston Boy
15 ran

1990
TUESDAY, 12 MARCH	GOOD–FIRM	£50,047
1 **KRIBENSIS** (gr g Henbit–Aquaria)	6-12-0	R. Dunwoody 95/40
2 Nomadic Way (b h Assert–Kittyhawk)	5-12-0	P. Scudamore 8/1
3 Past Glories (b h Hittite Glory–Snow Tribe)	7-12-0	J. Quinn 150/1

Owner: Sheikh Mohammed
Trainer: M.R. Stoute, Newmarket
Breeder: M. Ryan

Distances: 3 lengths and ¾
Time: 3 min 50.7
(race record)

Also ran: 2/1f Beech Road, Morley Street, Jinxy Jack, Island Set, Vagador, Deep Sensation, Elementary, Don Valentino, Space Fair, Sudden Victory, Redundant Pal, See You Then, Dis Train, Bank View, Cruising Altitude, Persian Style
19 ran

THE CHAMPION HURDLE

1991

TUESDAY, 12 MARCH	GOOD £81,790
1 **MORLEY STREET** (ch g Deep Run–High Board)	7-12-0 J. Frost 4/1f
2 Nomadic Way (b h Assert–Kittyhawk)	6-12-0 R. Dunwoody 9/1
3 Ruling (b h Alleged–All Dance)	5-12-0 P. Niven 50/1
Owner: M. Jackson Bloodstock	*Distances*: 1½ lengths and a head
Trainer: G.B. Balding, Weyhill	*Time*: 3 min 54.31
Breeder: M. Parkhill	

Also ran: Mole Board, Voyage Sans Retour, Bradbury Star, Wonder Man, Beech Road, Royal Derbi, Deep Sensation, Jinxy Jack, Athy Spirit, Rare Holiday, Vayrua, Philosophos, Riverhead, Danny Harrold, Vestris Abu, Major Inquiry, Sondrio, The Illiad, Black Humour, Fidway, Sybillin
24 ran

1992

TUESDAY, 10 MARCH	GOOD £80,065
1 **ROYAL GAIT** (b g Gunner B–High Gait)	9-12-0 G. McCourt 6/1
2 Oh So Risky (b h Kris–Expediency)	5-12-0 P. Holley 20/1
3 Ruling (b h Alleged – All Dance)	6-12-0 P. Niven 20/1
Owner: Sheikh Mohammed	*Distances*: 2 lengths and a short head
Trainer: J.R. Fanshawe, Newmarket	*Time*: 3 min 57.2
Breeder: I. Wills	

Also ran: 2/1f Morley Street, Fidway, Bank View, Chirkpar, Prospero, Minorettes Girl, Winnie the Witch, Royal Derbi, Mardood, Shu Fly, Kribensis, Granville Again, Valiant Boy
16 ran

1993

TUESDAY, 16 MARCH	GOOD–FIRM £84,734
1 **GRANVILLE AGAIN** (ch g Deep Run–High Board)	7-12-0 P. Scudamore 13/2
2 Royal Derbi (b g Derrylin–Royal Birthday)	8-12-0 M. Perratt 50/1
3 Halkopus (b g Beldale Flutter–Salamina)	7-12-0 A. Maguire 9/1
Owner: E. Scarth	*Distances*: 1 length and 2½
Trainer: M.C. Pipe, Nicholashayne	*Time*: 3 min 51.60
Breeder: M. Parkhill	

Also ran: 7/2f Flown, King Credo, Oh So Risky, Vintage Crop, Flakey Dove,

THE CHAMPION HURDLE

Jinxy Jack, Kribensis, Morley Street, Coulton, Athy Spirit, Duke of Monmouth, Valfinet, Staunch Friend, Ruling

18 ran

1994

TUESDAY, 15 MARCH	GOOD–SOFT £99,933
1 **FLAKEY DOVE** (b m Oats–Shadey Dove)	8-11-9 M. Dwyer 9/1
2 Oh So Risky (b g Kris–Expediency)	7-12-0 P. Holley 9/4f
3 Large Action (b g The Parson–Ballyadam Lass)	6-12-0 J. Osborne 8/1
Owner: J.T. Price	*Distances*: 1½ lengths and ¾
Trainer: R.J. Price, Leominster	*Time*: 4 min 2.00
Breeder: J.T. Price	

Also ran: Mole Board, Absalom's Lady, Muse, Granville Again, Shawiya, Halkopus, Valfinet, High Baron, King Credo, Land Afar, Merchant House, Morley Street

15 ran

1995

TUESDAY, 14 MARCH	SOFT £103,690
1 **ALDERBROOK** (b h Ardross–Twine)	6-12-0 N. Williamson 11/2
2 Large Action (b g The Parson–Ballyadam Lass)	7-12-0 J. Osborne 4/1jf
3 Danoli (b g The Parson–Blaze Gold)	7-12-0 C.F. Swan 4/1jf
Owner: E. Pick	*Distances*: 5 lengths and 2
Trainer: K.C. Bailey, Lambourn	*Time*: 4 min 3.00
Breeder: J.H. Stone	

Also ran: Fortune And Fame, Mysilv, Absalom's Lady, Atours, Mole Board, Montelado, Jazilah, Destriero, Granville Again, Bold Boss, Land Afar

14 ran

1996

TUESDAY, 12 MARCH	GOOD–SOFT £127,966
1 **COLLIER BAY** (b g Green Desert–Cockatoo Island)	6-12-0 G. Bradley 9/1
2 Alderbrook (b h Ardross–Twine)	7-12-0 R. Dunwoody 10/11f
3 Pridwell (b g Sadler's Wells–Glowing With Pride)	6-12-0 C. Maude 33/1
Owner: W.E. Sturt	*Distances*: 2½ lengths and 6
Trainer: J.A.B. Old, Wroughton	*Time*: 3 min 59.00
Breeder: Stanley Estate and Stud Co.	

THE CHAMPION HURDLE

Also ran: Danoli, Squire Silk, Mysilv, Boro Eight, Staunch Friend, Hotel Minella, Land Afar, Chief Minister, Right Win, Kissair, Absalom's Lady, Mack the Knife, Muse
16 ran

1997
TUESDAY, 11 MARCH	GOOD	£124,138
1 **MAKE A STAND** (ch g Master Willie–Make a Signal)	6-12-0	A.P. McCoy 7/1
2 Theatreworld (b g Sadler's Wells–Chamonis)	5-12-0	N. Williamson 33/1
3 Space Trucker (b g Komaite–Seat of Learning)	6-12-0	J. Shortt 9/2
Owner: P.A. Deal		*Distances*: 5 lengths and ¾
Trainer: M.C. Pipe, Nicholashayne		*Time*: 3 min 48.40 (race record)

Breeder: I. Allen, K.C. Choo and Calogo Bloodstock Ag.
Also ran: 7/2f Large Action, I'm Supposin, Hill Society, Sanmartino, Pridwell, Moorish, Cockney Lad, Mistinguett, Zabadi, Dardjini, Bimsey, Dreams End, Guest Performance, Collier Bay
17 ran

1998
TUESDAY, 17 MARCH	GOOD–SOFT	£137,420
1 **ISTABRAQ** (b g Sadler's Wells–Betty's Secret)	6-12-0	C.F. Swan 3/1f
2 Theatreworld (b g Sadler's Wells–Chamonis)	6-12-0	T.P. Treacy 20/1
3 I'm Supposin (b h Posen–Robinia)	6-12-0	R. Dunwoody 6/1
Owner: J.P. McManus		*Distances*: 12 lengths and 1
Trainer: A.P. O'Brien, Cashel, Co. Tipperary		*Time*: 3 min 49.10

Breeder: Shadwell Estate Co. Ltd.
Also ran: Pridwell, Kerawi, Mistinguett, Shooting Light, Graphic Equaliser, Relkeel, Cadougold, Marello, Sanmartino, Dato Star, Grimes, Lady Daisy, Bellator, Red Blazer, Shadow Leader
18 ran

1999
TUESDAY, 16 MARCH	GOOD–SOFT	£138,000
1 **ISTABRAQ** (b g Sadler's Wells–Betty's Secret)	7-12-0	C.F. Swan 4/9f
2 Theatreworld (b g Sadler's Wells–Chamonis)	7-12-0	T.P. Treacy 16/1
3 French Holly (b g Sir Ivor–Sans Dot)	8-12-0	A. Thornton 11/2
Owner: J.P. McManus		*Distances*: 3½ lengths and 2½
Trainer: A.P. O'Brien, Cashel, Co. Tipperary		*Time*: 3 min 56.80

THE CHAMPION HURDLE

Breeder: Shadwell Estate Co. Ltd.
Also ran: Mister Morose, Nomadic, Tuitchev, Bellator, City Hall, Lady Cricket, Midnight Legend, Grey Shot, Upgrade, Blowing Wind, Zafarabad
14 ran

2000

TUESDAY, 14 MARCH		GOOD	£145,000
1 **ISTABRAQ** (b g Sadler's Wells–Betty's Secret)	8-12-0		C.F. Swan 8/15f
2 Hors la Loi III (b g Cyborg–Quintessence)	5-12-0		D. Gallagher 11/1
3 Blue Royal (b g Dauphin Du Bourg–Before The Flag)	5-12-0		M.A. Fitzgerald 16/1

Owner: J.P. McManus   *Distances*: 4 lengths and a neck
Trainer: A.P. O'Brien, Cashel, Co. Tipperary   *Time*: 3 min 48.10 (race record)
Breeder: Shadwell Estate Co. Ltd.
Also ran: Ashley Park, Stage Affair, Dato Star, Make A Stand, Katarino, Mr Percy, Theatreworld, Alka International, Balla Sola
12 ran.

2001

No Race

2002

TUESDAY, 12 MARCH		GOOD-SOFT £156,600
1 Hors La Loi III (b g Cyborg–Quintessence III)	7-12-0	D. Gallagher 10/1
2 Marble Arch (b g Rock Hopper –Mayfair Minx)	6-12-0	R Walsh 25/1
3 Bilboa (b m Phantom Breeze–Maisonnaise)	5-11-9	T Doumen 14/1

Owner: P.Green   *Distances*: 3 lengths and ½ length
Trainer: J.R. Fanshawe, Newmarket   *Time*: 3 min 53.80
Breeder: F.Cottin
Also ran: 2/1f Istabraq, Geos, Landing Light, Ansar, Mr Cool, Mister Morose, Liss A Paoraigh, Chimes At Midnight, Rostropovich, Regal Exit, Penny Rich, Valiramix
15 ran

Appendix 2

Records

MOST WINS BY A HORSE:
3 – **Hatton's Grace** 1949, 1950, 1951
   Sir Ken 1952, 1953, 1954
   Persian War 1968, 1969, 1970
   See You Then 1985, 1986, 1987
   Istabraq 1998, 1999, 2000

NB: when trying for a fourth title, Hatton's Grace was fifth in 1952; Sir Ken fourth in 1955; Persian War second in 1971; and See You Then fifteenth in 1990; while Istabraq was pulled up in 2002.

GREATEST MARGINS:
12 lengths – **Insurance** 1932; **Istabraq** 1998
 8 lengths – **Blaris** 1927; **Bula** 1972; **Comedy of Errors** 1975

SMALLEST MARGINS:
head – **Brown Tony** 1930; **Seneca** 1941; **Clair Soleil** 1955

OLDEST WINNERS:
11 – **Hatton's Grace** 1951; **Sea Pigeon** 1981
10 – **Hatton's Grace** 1950; **Sea Pigeon** 1980

YOUNGEST WINNERS:
4 – **Brown Jack** 1928; **Brown Tony** 1930; **Seneca** 1941; **Forestation** 1942

WINNING MARES:
3 – **African Sister** 1939; **Dawn Run** 1984; **Flakey Dove** 1994

WINNING ENTRIES:
6 – **Royal Falcon** 1929; **Seneca** 1941; **Eborneezer** 1961; **Saucy Kit** 1967; **Monksfield** 1978/1979; **Alderbrook** 1995

THE CHAMPION HURDLE

WINNING NOVICES:
9 – **Brown Jack** 1928; **Brown Tony** 1930; **Seneca** 1941; **Forestation** 1942; **Brains Trust** 1945; **Doorknocker** 1956; **Royal Gait** 1992; **Alderbrook** 1995; **Make A Stand** 1997

LEAST EXPERIENCED:
Seneca won on his second appearance over hurdles in 1941; **Alderbrook** on his third in 1995

MOST PERSEVERING:
Sea Pigeon won at the fourth attempt in 1980; **Salmon Spray** at the third in 1966

STILL UNBEATEN OVER HURDLES:
3 – **Seneca** 1941; **Clair Soleil** 1955; **Bula** 1971

MADE ALL:
4 – **Blaris** 1927; **Victor Norman** 1936; **Night Nurse** 1976; **Make A Stand** 1997

SHORTEST ODDS:
2/5 – **Sir Ken** 1953
4/9 – **Chenango** 1934; **Sir Ken** 1954; **Istabraq** 1999
NB: 17 odds on favourites, 6 of whom were beaten

HOTTEST LOSING FAVOURITES:
1/2 – **Free Fare** 1938 (fell)
4/7 – **Solford** 1941

LONGEST ODDS:
50/1 **Kirriemuir** 1965; **Beech Road** 1989
40/1 **For Auction** 1982

LONGEST-PRICED FAVOURITES:
6/1 – **Another Flash** 1964 (second)
5/1 – **Tokoroa 1958** (second)

MOST OFTEN FAVOURITE:
4 – **Istabraq** 1998, 1999, 2000, 2002; **Free Fare** 1936, 1937, 1938; **Sir Ken** 1952, 1953, 1954; **Another Flash** 1960, 1962, 1964; **Bula** 1971, 1972, 1973

THE CHAMPION HURDLE

RICHEST FIRST PRIZE:
£156,600 – 2002

SMALLEST FIRST PRIZE:
£340 – 1945

LARGEST FIELDS:
24 – 1964; 1991
23 – 1967; 1986

SMALLEST FIELDS:
3 – 1932
4 – 1927
NB: There have been 18 single-figure fields (8 of them postwar), the last in 1980 when 9 ran.

FASTEST TIMES:
3:48.10 – **Istabraq** 2000 (good)
3:48.40 – **Make A Stand** 1997 (good)
3:49.10 – **Istabraq** 1998 (good-soft)
NB: over 2 miles 110 yards since 1993; best at longest race distance of 2 miles 200 yards was 4:03.80 by **Persian War** in 1968 (firm).

SLOWEST TIMES:
4:41.80 **Persian War** 1969 (heavy)
4:37.60 **Insurance** 1933 (soft)
4:28.50 **Comedy of Errors** 1975 (heavy)
NB: slowest over 2 miles 110 yards is 4:03.00 by **Alderbrook** in 1996 (soft).

MOST APPEARANCES:
6 – **National Spirit** 1947–52; **Bird's Nest** 1976–81

MOST CHAMPIONS IN ONE FIELD:
5 – 1964: **Another Flash, Winning Fair, Magic Court, Kirriemuir, Salmon Spray**

CHAMPIONS FILLING ALL THE PLACES:
1964: **Magic Court, Another Flash, Kirriemuir**
1978: **Monksfield, Sea Pigeon, Night Nurse**

THE CHAMPION HURDLE

MOST OFTEN PLACED:
4 – **Persian War, Monksfield, Sea Pigeon**

SECOND TWICE WITHOUT WINNING;
5 – **Anarchist** 1941, 1942; **Quita Que** 1956, 1957; **Nomadic Way** 1990, 1991; **Oh So Risky** 1992, 1994; **Theatreworld** 1997, 1998, 1999

FOREIGN HORSES FILLING THE PLACES:
1951 – **Hatton's Grace** (Ireland), **Pyrrhus II** (France), **Prince Hindou** (France)

OLDEST RUNNER:
13 – **Mole Board** 1995

OLDEST ENTRY:
17 – **Prestidigitateur** 1973

MOST SUCCESSFUL OWNER:
4 – **Hon. Dorothy Paget** 1932, 1933, 1940, 1946

MOST SUCCESSFUL TRAINERS:
5 – **Peter Easterby** 1967, 1976, 1977, 1980, 1981
4 – **Vic Smyth** 1941, 1942, 1947, 1948

MOST SUCCESSFUL JOCKEYS:
4 – **Tim Molony** 1951, 1952, 1953, 1954
3 – **Ron Smyth** 1941, 1942, 1948
   Fred Winter 1955, 1959, 1961
   Jimmy Uttley 1968, 1969, 1970
   Steve Smith Eccles 1985, 1986, 1987
   Charlie Swan 1998, 1999, 2000

MOST APPEARANCES BY A JOCKEY:
14 – **Richard Dunwoody**
13 – **Fred Winter; Peter Scudamore**

Appendix 3

Timeform Ratings of Winners from 1962
(reproduced with kind permission)

1962 Anzio	172		**1982** For Auction	174
1963 Winning Fair	169		**1983** Gaye Brief	175
1964 Magic Court	174		**1984** Dawn Run	173
1965 Kirriemuir	166		**1985** See You Then	166
1966 Salmon Spray	175		**1986** See You Then	173
1967 Saucy Kit	166		**1987** See You Then	173
1968 Persian War	176		**1988** Celtic Shot	170
1969 Persian War	176		**1989** Beech Road	172
1970 Persian War	179		**1990** Kribensis	169
1971 Bula	176		**1991** Morley Street	174
1972 Bula	176		**1992** Royal Gait	164
1973 Comedy of Errors	178		**1993** Granville Again	167
1974 Lanzarote	177		**1994** Flakey Dove	166
1975 Comedy of Errors	178		**1995** Alderbrook	174
1976 Night Nurse	178		**1996** Collier Bay	170
1977 Night Nurse	182		**1997** Make A Stand	165
1978 Monksfield	177		**1998** Istabraq	172
1979 Monksfield	180		**1999** Istabraq	177
1980 Sea Pigeon	175		**2000** Istabraq	180
1981 Sea Pigeon	175		**2002** Hors La Loi III	161(provisional)

Appendix 4

Bibliography

Of the numerous sources consulted the following were particularly valuable:

Barnes & Alper, *The Persian War Story* (Pelham)
Bradley & Taylor, *The Wayward Lad* (Greenwater Books)
Bromley, *The Price of Success* (Hutchinson/Stanley Paul)
Brooks, *Crossing the Line* (Headline)
Clower, *Champion Charlie* (Mainstream Publishing)
Clower, *The Legend of Istabraq* (Cassell & Co.)
Curling, *The Sea Pigeon Story* (Michael Joseph)
Dunwoody, *Obsessed* (Headline)
Dunwoody & Armytage, *Hell for Leather* (Partridge Press)
Dunwoody & Armytage, *Hands and Heels* (Partridge Press)
Foley & Taub, *Danoli: The People's Champion* (Robson Books)
Gilbey, *Queen of the Turf* (Arthur Barker)
Hedges, *Mr Grand National* (Pelham)
Herbert, *Six at the Top* (Heinemann)
Herbert, *Winter's Tale* (Pelham)
Holland, *Dawn Run* (Arthur Barker)
Lyle, *Brown Jack* (Putnam)
Magee, *The Race of My Life* (Headline)
McCoy & Duval, *The Real McCoy: My Life So Far* (Hodder & Stoughton)
O'Neill & Boyne, *Paddy Mullins: The Master of Doninga* (Mainstream Publishing)
O'Neill & Richards, *Jonjo* (Stanley Paul)
Pipe & Pitman, *Martin Pipe: The Champion Trainer's Story* (Headline)
Pitman, *Good Horses Make Good Jockeys* (Pelham)
Powell, *Monksfield* (World's Work)
Rimell, *Reflections on Racing* (Pelham)
Scudamore, *Scu: The Autobiography of a Champion* (Headline)
Seth-Smith, Willett, Mortimer and Lawrence, *The History of Steeplechasing* (Michael Joseph)

THE CHAMPION HURDLE

Smith Eccles & Lee, *Last of the Cavaliers* (Pelham)
Taaffe, *My Life and Arkle's* (Stanley Paul)
Timeform, *Chasers and Hurdlers*

Pacemaker
Racing Post
Sporting Life
Stud & Stable
The Times

Index

BROADSWORD 143-4, 146, 163

Abelson, Len 47-8
ABERMAID 45
ABOVE SUSPICION 122
ABSALOM'S LADY 188-9
ACHTOI 24
Ackerman Skeaping Trophy 100, 110
Adele, Maurice 58
AFRICAN SISTER 37-40, 147
Aga Khan 47,128
Ainsworth, Sir Thomas 82
ALBERGO 76-9
Alder, Kenneth 95
ALDERBROOK 192-8
Aldsworth Hurdle 148
Alper, Henry 97-102, 104-5, 109-10
ANAGLOG'S DAUGHTER 207
ANARCHIST 40-2, 189
ANGLESEY 53
ANGLO 106
Anngrove Stud 136
ANOTHER FLASH 76-8, 83, 86, 87
Anthony, Ivor 27, 38, 50, 91
Anthony, Jack 20-1, 139, 167
Anthony, Owen 21, 36, 38-9, 139, 167
ANZIO 82-3, 86
Apperley, Charles 9
APPLE PEEL 37
APPROVAL 60
ARCTIC PRINCE 57
ARCTIC STAR 20-1, 25
ARD MACHA 37
Ardenrun Stud 79
ARDROSS 192
ARKLE 53, 84, 91, 97, 102, 119, 153, 188, 205, 214
Arkle Challenge Trophy 139
ARMOUR BRIGHT 31
Arnott, Maxie 45
AROUND THE ROSES 133
ARTISTE GAYE 145
ARTIST'S DESIGN 145
Artu, Jean-Yves 162
ASCETIC'S SILVER 16
ASSUNTO 61
ASSYNT 67
AURELIUS 93, 95-6
Austin, Willie 191
AVERAGE 55, 60

BAHUDDIN 37-9
Bailey, Kim 192-7
Balding, Toby 105, 146, 167-70, 175-6, 178, 189, 195, 199
BANDALORE 73-4, 77, 142
BARACOUDA 203
BARNBROOK AGAIN 160
BARON BLAKENEY 183
Barry, Ron 150
BEACHWAY 33
BEACON LIGHT 125, 127, 130-2
Beasley, Bobby 77, 87, 106, 114
Beaumont, Peter 188
BEAVER II 66, 84, 94
Beddington, Doreen 89
BEECH ROAD 167-71, 174-6
BELLONA 10-11
Bennett, Gil 91
Bennet, 'Tuppy' 14
Benson and Hedges Hurdle 108
Berkshire Hurdle 14, 74, 113, 143, 187
Berry, Frank 130-1
BETTY'S SECRET 206
Biddlecombe, Terry 103-4, 113, 117-18
Billywood Stud 128
BIRD'S NEST 121, 123-5, 130-2, 136-7
BLACK DUNCAN 28
Blagrave, Herbert 82
Blair, Morgan 31
Blake, Arthur and Isadore 45
Blakeley Stud 101
Blakeway 44
BLANCONA 19-20
BLARIS 13-15, 18, 22, 143, 167
BLOWING WIND 210
BLUE PRELUDE 87
BLUE ROYAL 213
BOBBY MOORE 104
Bobinski, Colonel 93
BODDAM 14-15
Bolger, Jim 205-6
BORO NICKEL 149
Bostwick, G.H. 'Pete' 27-8
BOWIE'S BRIG 109
BOWL GAME 133
BOXER 110-11
Brabazon, Aubrey 52-6, 79
Bradley, Graham 195-7, 201
BRAINS TRUST 44-5, 48
BRANTRIDGE FARMER 117
BRASHER 148
Breeders' Cup Chase 162
Briscoe, Basil 23-5, 28, 36, 139, 167

250

THE CHAMPION HURDLE

Broderick, Paddy 120, 124, 126-7, 130
Brooks, Charlie 164, 166, 195
Brooks, Vincent 107, 115
Brown, Frank 28
Brown, Harry 28, 59
Brown, Keith 170
BROWN JACK 15-18, 20, 61, 93
BROWN TONY 20-1, 99, 138
Browne, Corky 161
Browne, Dermot 156
Browne, Liam 188
BROWNE'S GAZETTE 156-7
BROWNHYLDA 40
Brueton, Horace 37
BUCK HOUSE 152
BULA 105-11, 113-15, 119, 143
Bula Hurdle 123, 132, 144, 156, 158, 169, 185, 209
Bull, Phil 48
Burrows 44
Butchers, Don 76
Byrne, John 76

CACADOR 70
CACTUS II 31
Cadogan, Lord 37
CAIRN ROUGE 144
CALIGULA 41
CALZADO 116, 118
CAMPARI 61
CANASTA LAD 110-11, 119
Cannon, Joe 10
CANTAB 66, 82-3
CAPTAIN CHRISTY 113-15, 119, 148
CAPTAIN FOX 53
CARNIVAL BOY 45
Carr, Philip 24
CARTON 39, 42
CASHEL VIEW 75
CATAPULT 66, 84-5, 93
CATTONIAN 11
Cazalet, Peter 93
Cecil, Julie 192, 194
CELTIC CHIEF 161-3, 166, 168
CELTIC CONE 161
CELTIC RYDE 143
CELTIC SHOT 161-3, 166, 168
Cesarewitch 20, 61, 88, 100, 115, 186
CHAMANNA 73

Champion Trial, Birmingham 61, 68, 78
Champion Trial, Haydock 151, 160
Chanelle, Enid 82
CHARLES I 10
CHARTER PARTY 172
CHECKTAKER 14
CHELANDRY 11
Cheltenham Trial Hurdle 113, 116
CHENANGO 27-8, 160
Chenorio, Marcel 58
CHESHAM SQUIRE 198
Chester Cup 100, 134
Chesterton Stud 79-80
Christmas Hurdle 125, 129, 132, 144, 151, 158-9, 166, 169, 212
CHUCHOTEUR 33-5, 57
Churchill, Sir Winston 65, 86
CHORUS II 100-1
CILL DARA 207
CIMA 152, 163
CISSIE GAY 76
CITY HALL 210
City Trial, Nottingham 104, 144, 146
CLAIR SOLEIL 63, 66-7, 72, 74-6, 142
CLASSICAL CHARM 163
CLAUDE LE LORRAIN 162
CLAY DUCK 164
CLEAR CASH 18-21
CLEAR CUT 164
Cloghran Stud 122
CLONAVE 10
CLOUGHTANEY 162
COCKTAIL 47-8
COLLIER BAY 196-8, 201, 209
Collins, Con 155
COLOURED SCHOOLBOY 49
Colt Sigma Hurdle 133
COMEDY ACTRESS 112
COMEDY OF ERRORS 111-19, 121-2, 124-6, 143
CONNAUGHT RANGER 135
Cook, Robert 108
COOL GROUND 167
Coolmore Stud 206, 210
CORAL DIVER 103, 110-11
CORONACH 47
Coronation Hurdle 68,78
CORPORAL CLINGER 160
Corrie, Tom 112

Corry, Bill 91
Corsa di Siepi dei Quattro Anni 156
Cotswold Chase 75
COTTAGE LASS II 187
Coulthwaite, Tom 25, 181, 202
County Hurdle 12-13, 28, 75, 78, 110
Coventry, Arthur 9
Cox, Mr J.R. 70
CREPELLO 76
CRISP 112
Crowley, Anne-Marie 205-6, 213
CRUACHAN 69
Cullinan, Tommy 20-1, 79
Cundell, Ken 94-5
Cunningham, Michael 143-4, 146
Curzon, Lady 20

Daily Express Triumph Hurdle 99, 110, 122, 129, 143, 156, 166, 183
DAIRYMAID 45
DANOLI 190-2, 196-8, 208, 211
DARING RUN 138, 142-4, 146, 148
DASHING WHITE SERGEANT 124
DATO STAR 209, 212
Davies, Colin 97, 100-1, 104-5, 109
Davis, Snowy 67, 78
DAWN RUN 147-53, 187
Dawson, Mat 10
De Selincourt, Mrs 21
De Walden, Lord Howard 115
De Vere Hotels Hurdle 159
Deal, Peter 202
DEEP RUN 147-8, 169, 186
Delaney, Brian 164
DESERT ORCHID 151-2, 156, 189, 195
DESTRIERO 175, 178
DIAMOND DO 149
Dick, Dave 72
Dick, David 94
DICK THE GEE 65
Dickinson, Michael 182, 184-6
Dickinson, Monica 156
Dillon, Dennis 54-5
DIOGENES 33
DISTEL 45-6, 48-50
Donaghue, Steve 15, 18

THE CHAMPION HURDLE

DONDIEU 108, 198
DOORKNOCKER 70, 148
Doumen, Francois 212
DRAGOON 40
DRAMATIST 90, 125-7
Dreaper, Mrs 92
DRUMIKILL 103
DRYBOB 51
DUBIAN 155
DUCKDOWN 164
DUKW 50, 54
Duller, George 12-15, 17, 19, 56
DUNSHAUGHLIN 46
Dunwoody, Richard 172-4, 188, 196-7, 199-200, 209-10
Dupre, Francois 66
Durdham Down 9
Durkan, John 207
Dutton, Billy 94
Dwyer, Mark 188-9

EASBY ABBEY 113-14
EASTER HERO 20-1
Easterby, Peter 84, 94-5, 105, 120-2, 124, 126-7, 130, 133, 135, 137, 140-1, 160, 210
EASY CHAIR 42
Ebor Handicap 134, 141
EBORNEEZER 78-80
Edwards, Roy 96-100
Edwards-Heathcote, Captain Bill 107
EGO 34
EKBALCO 142-4, 147, 151
ELCHO 91
Elsenham Stud 26
Elsworth, David 189
ENCOROLI 50
EPHORUS 40, 42
Erin Foods Champion Hurdle 125, 129, 132, 142
ESCALUS 103-4
EVEN DAWN 148
EXHIBIT A 89

Fakhouri, Tawfik 142
FANE RANGER 146
Fanshawe, James 176-9
FARE TIME 73-7, 82, 142
FARRNEY FOX 84-5
Fawley Stud 75
FELICITATION 41
FENIMORE COOPER 19, 20
FIDUS ACHATES 83
FIDWAY 179
FIFTY DOLLARS MORE 148

Fighting Fifth Hurdle 109, 112-13, 122, 124, 132, 142, 151, 156, 166, 169, 174, 212
Finn, Paddy 85
Finnegan, Paul 144
Fishback, Jerry 160
Fisher, Roger 142
Fitzgerald, Jimmy 188
FLAKEY DOVE 187-91
FLAMBETTE 27
FLAMBINO 27
FLAME GUN 75
FLAMING 26-8
FLASH BULB 76, 92
FLASH IMP 124
FLASHAWAY 76
FLATTERER 160-2
FLORENCE NIGHTINGALE 122
FLORESTAN 63
FLOWN 185-6
FLOYD 163, 166
FLUSH ROYAL 61
FLY BOOK 91
FLYINGBOLT 83, 92-3
Foley, Tom 191, 196
FOR AUCTION 143-4, 146-7
FOREST SUN 170, 192
FORESTATION 41-4
FORTUNE AND FAME 189, 191-9
Forster, Tim 174, 194
Foster, Glyn 155, 159
Francome, John 105, 116, 137-8, 157, 172, 185
FREDCOTERI 144
FREDDIE 87
FREDDY FOX 49
FREE FARE 27, 30-6, 38
French Champion Hurdle 26, 49, 78-9, 103, 135, 152-3, 160
FRENCH HOLLY 210
FRIENDLY BOY 75
Frost, Jimmy 175-6, 179
Furlong, Frank 81
Furlong, Major Noel 52

GACKO 162
GALA PERFORMANCE 128
GALATIAN 61-2
GALCADOR 60
Gallagher, Dean 196
Garratt, Alfie 16
GARNISHEE 111
GAY LIGHT 28-9
GAY SCOT 49

GAYE BRIEF 145-7, 151, 156-9, 163
GAYE CHANCE 145
GAYE LE MOSS 145
GAYE MEMORY 145
Geake, Tony 167
GENERAL PEACE 19
General Peace Hurdle 14, 17, 29-20, 25, 33, 37
Genesis Green Stud 110
Gibson, Jack 110
Gifford, Josh 199
Gilbert, Johnny 72
Gillette Hurdle 84-5
GLENCARAIG LADY 147
Gloucestershire Hurdle 11, 73, 76-7, 92, 102, 108-9
GOLDEN CYGNET 131, 148
GOLDEN MILLER 24-5, 29
GOLDHILL 94, 112
Good, Meyrick 41, 43, 46, 58
GOOD DAYS 51
Gordon, Micky 46
Gore, Bob 19
Gosden, John 207
Goulding, David 143
Graham, Clive 24
Grand Handicap Hurdle 10
Grand International Hurdle 10
Grand National 10-13, 21, 31, 167-8, 170, 174
Grand National Hurdle 10
GRANVILLE AGAIN 178-9, 185-9, 191-2, 198
GREBE 133
GREEKTOWN 84
GREEN DESERT 198
GREY OF FALLODEN 88
Grey Talk Hurdle 78
Griffin, Bob 91
Gubbins, Roderic 33-5
Guest, Richard 168, 195
Gwilt, Ted 33, 82

Haine, John 90-3
HALF FREE 148
HALKOPOUS 185-6
Hall, Charlie 69-70
Halley, John 213
Halley, Nixie 91
HAPPY VALLEY 110
HAPSBURG 27
Harding, Perry 34-5
HARLECH 54
HARPIST 14
Hartigan, Frank 14, 94
Hartigan, Jack 36

THE CHAMPION HURDLE

Hastings, Aubrey 16-17, 27
HATTON'S GRACE 51-6, 60, 154, 203, 211
Hatvany, Baron 66
HAVASNACK 75
Head, Alec 49
Head, Willie 49
Heaslips 143
HEIGHLIN 143
HEIGHT O' FASHION 84, 92, 150
HELTER SKELTER 19
HENBIT 169
Henderson, Nick 154-61, 169-70
Hern, Dick 98
HIGH HAT 86
HIGHLAND WEDDING 167
Hill, Charmian 148-53
HILL SONG 28-9, 186
Hills, Barry 169
HIS SONG 209
HIT PARADE 183
Hobbs, Bruce 30, 34
Hollins, Mrs 14
Homeau, Christian-Serge 162
Honour, Fred 59
HORS LA LOI III 211, 214
Horton, David 164
HOTEL MINELLA 196, 208
Hughes, Dessie 131, 133, 135-6
HURRY HARRIET 150

ICEBERG II 37
Imperial Cup 11-13, 19, 27-8, 48-9, 53, 68, 78, 116, 142, 167
IMPNEY 62, 67
Ingham, Staff 21, 29
INSURANCE 22, 24-7, 110, 143
INTERLAKEN 42
International Hurdle 10, 27-8, 31, 33
INTO VIEW 103, 109
Irish Cambridgeshire 36, 55, 61
Irish Cesarewitch 45, 54-5, 77, 150, 207
Irish Championship Hurdle 176, 185, 189
IRISH GAMBLE 144
Irish Lincoln 54
Irish Sweeps Hurdle 103, 110-11, 113, 116, 123, 126
Isaac, Tommy 42

ISTABRAQ 121, 154, 203-14
IVAN KING 138
IVY GREEN 75, 147

JACK DRUMMER 25
JACK OF TRUMPS 207
JACKDAW 16, 186
JAY TRUMP 106
Jenks, Bryan 103
Jennings, Tom 95
JERRY M 19
JODAMI 188
JOHNNY 149
JOHNS-WORT 92, 95
Jones, Arthur 71-2, 79, 80, 86
Jones, H.T. 100, 157
Jubilee Hurdle 10, 39
Judd, Gerry 66, 74, 76
JUVEN LIGHT 163

KATARINO 213
KELANNE 110
Kelleway, Paul 65, 106-8, 111, 115, 174
Kent, Linda 192
Keoghs 52, 55
KILLINEY 109
Kinane, Tommy 131
KING 73-5
King, Jeff 91-2, 107, 130
Kingsley, Maurice 59
KING WEASEL 135
Kingwell Hurdle 102, 110, 112, 126, 161, 166, 169, 192
Kintbury Hurdle 99
KIRRIEMUIR 86-9, 92-3, 95, 100, 142
KIWI 37
KNOCK HARD 52
KRIBENSIS 166, 168-72, 174, 176, 179, 185, 188, 192
KYBO 131-2

LABRADOR 15
LADY REBECCA 203
LAËKEN 58
LAIRD O' MONTROSE 77
LAITRON 45, 48
Lambton, George 10-11, 42
Lanark Silver Bell 112
Lancashire Chase 10
Lancashire Hurdle 27, 58, 68
LANZAROTE 111-12, 115-19, 121-2, 124-5, 137, 209
LARBAWN 91
LARGE ACTION 188-9, 192-

3, 201
Latecomers' Hurdle 110
Lawrence, John 24, 101, 174
L'ESCARGOT 102-3
LE MAESTRO 33
LE PAILLON 49-50, 93
Leader, Ted 25, 79
Lee Cooper Hurdle 161
LEMANAGHAN 41
Leyland-Naylor, David 98
LIDO LADY 82
Lillingston, Alan 84-5
LIMBER HILL 62
LIMESTONE LAD 203, 211
Lindley, Jimmy 73
Lingfield Hurdle Cup 14, 16, 21, 25, 27-8, 30-2, 33, 37
Linley, Richard 146
LION COURAGE 28-9
LITTLE OWL 139
LITTLE POLVEIR 167, 175
LIVELY LORD 62
Liverpool Hurdle 11-13, 27, 30-1, 62-3, 68, 78, 90
LOBAU 33-4, 37
LOCKYERSLEIGH 109
LONDON GAZETTE 86-8
Lonsdale Hurdle 104
Loraine, Sir Percy 45
LOTUS LAND 113
LOYAL KING 46
LUCKY BRIEF 145
LUCKY VANE 176
LUNCHEON HOUR 40, 42
Lungo, Len 183

McAlpine, Sir Malcolm 40
McCourt, Graham 179-80
McCoy, Anthony 199-202
McDonagh, Des 128-9, 131-2, 135
McGhie, James 87
McGregor, Sydney 55
Mackeson Handicap Hurdle 93, 124
McLean, James 61
McManus, J.P. 207, 209, 212, 215
MACK THE KNIFE 198
Magee, Captain 78
Magee, Sean 38
Magee, Billy 47
MAGIC COURT 86-9, 90, 92
Magnier, Clem 61, 76
Magnier, Colin 143-4
Magnier, John 206
Maguire, Adrian 199

THE CHAMPION HURDLE

Mahon, Frank 115, 155, 161
MAJOR ROSE 100, 104, 109
MAKALDAR 93-6
MAKE A STAND 200-2, 209, 211, 213
Manchester November Handicap 30-1
Mangan, Michael 121, 129
MARCO 47
MARGARET BEAUFORT 36
Marle Hurdle 44
MARLY RIVER 162-3
Marquis Cugliemi di Vulci 155
Marshall, Bryan 53
MASK AND WIG 37-8
Masson, Tom 67, 98-9
MASTER MONDAY 125
MASTER WILLIE 201
Mathet, Francois 66
MEDOC II 76
Mellor, Stan 107, 199
MELADON 138
MELODINA 155
MENTON 32-3, 36
MERRY DEAL 71-5, 79-80, 142
MERRYLAND 71
Messenger, Stuart 189
MICHELOZZO 174
MIEUXCE 71
MILK BAR 42
MILL HOUSE 53
MILVERTON 155
MIRALGO 45
MOLE BOARD 193, 197
Molony, Martin 55, 107
Molony, Tim 55-6, 59-61, 63, 66, 79, 175
MONKSFIELD 121, 123, 125-33, 135-6, 159
MON PLAISIR 116
Moore, Dan 46
Morgan, Danny 27, 49
MORLEY STREET 169, 174-6, 178-9, 185, 189, 191-2, 195
Morrow, Arthur 33
MOSS BANK 78-9
Mould, David 96
MOYNE ROYAL 108
MR DONOVAN 207
MR FRISK 194
MR MULLIGAN 202
Muir, Ian 75
Muldoon, Pat 132, 134
Mullins, Paddy 149-53, 162
Mullins, Tony 150-1

Murless, Noel 86, 88, 155
Murphy, Paddy 90-1
MUSE 189
MYSILV 193, 196-7

National Hunt Chase 11, 13, 34
NATIONAL SPIRIT 46-51, 53-6, 60
NELLA 45
Newbury Autumn Cup 100
Newbury Spring Cup 11
Newton, Emma 178
Nicholson, Clifford 70
Nicholson, David 85, 143, 174, 176, 184
Nicholson, Frenchie 32, 45, 47
Nickalls, Tom 58
Nightingall, Walter 43
NIGHT NURSE 120-31, 139-41, 158-9, 203
NOHALMDUN 160
NOHOLME 59-60, 62, 68
NOMADIC WAY 169-72, 175-6, 189
NORMANDY 104
NORTHERN TRIAL 198
November Hurdle 13-14, 68, 74
NUAGE DORE 66
Nugent, Sir Hugh 24, 158
Nugent, Sir William 10
NUPSALA 162

O'Brien, Aidan 202, 204-6, 208-13
O'Brien, Dan 36
O'Brien, Vincent 36, 51-3, 57, 61, 78, 139, 167, 204-6
OCEAN SWELL 78
ODETTE 46
OH SO RISKY 179, 189
Old, Jim 196-7, 201
OLD MULL 84
OLD TOM 94
Oliver, Anne 192
OMAHA 27
O'Neill, Danny 191
O'Neill, Jonjo 105, 120, 126, 130, 132-3, 135-7, 139, 141, 148, 151-3, 172
ORIENT WAR 104
O'Ryan, Bobby 46
Osborne, Jamie 173, 188, 196-7, 201-2
Osborne Hurdle 88

O'Sullevan, Peter 54
Oteley Hurdle 68, 72, 74-5, 77-8, 82, 88-9, 130, 134, 158, 189
OUR HOPE 32-5, 38-9
OXO 57, 163
Oxx, John 85

Page, Doug 79
Paget, Dorothy 22-6, 31-2, 36, 39, 42, 44-6, 48, 50, 59-60, 71, 82, 178
Pajgar, Dr Burjar 78
Parkhill, Marshall 178
PARNELL 45
Parvin, Billy 25-6
PAS SEUL 90
PAST GLORIES 171
PATRIMONY 39
PAWNBROKER 84-5, 124
Payne, Bill 14
PEACE RIVER 17-18
PEERTOI 21
Pellerin, Georges 32-3, 91
PENDIL 107
Perkins, Polly 139-40
Persse, Atty 33
PERSIAN GULF 98
PERSIAN WAR 97-105, 106-10, 121, 154, 203
Pick, Ernie 194, 197
Piggott, Charles 37-8
Piggott, Keith 37-8
Piggott, Lester 88
PILSUDSKI 171
Pipe, Martin 181-6, 188, 192, 198, 200-2, 208, 210
Pitman, Richard 116-18
Pitt, Arthur 109
Plaine, Michel 33-4
POETIC LICENCE 42
POLLARDSTOWN 138, 143
POMPLEMOOSE 28
PONGO'S FANCY 107
POOR DUKE 82
Porzier, Yann 162
PRECIPITATION 78
Prendergast, Patrick 189
PRESTER JOHN 37
PRESTIDIGITATEUR 114
Price, Richard 187, 190
Price, Ryan 63-7, 69, 74, 77-8, 83, 86, 94, 100, 109, 139, 167, 205
Price, Tom 187, 190
PRINCE CHARLEMAGNE 69
PRINCE FLORIMONDE 45

THE CHAMPION HURDLE

PRINCE HINDOU 55
Princess Elizabeth Hurdle 48
Princess Royal Hurdle 68, 71, 87
PRIORIT 66
PRUDENT ACHTOI 37
PRUDENT GIRL 24
PRUDENT KING 75
PYRRHUS 55
PYTHAGORAS 44

Queen Alexandra Stakes 15
Queen's Prize 11, 78
Queen's Vase 82
QUELLE CHANCE 83-5
QUERQUIDELLA 16
QUITA QUE 70, 72, 189

RADIANCE 44
RAINBOW BATTLE 124
RAINCHECK 107
Rathcoole Hurdle 52, 59
Rayson, Dennis 110
RED APRIL 44
RED DOVE 187
RED MARAUDER 168
RED RUM 147
Rees, F. B. 17, 19-20
Rees, L. B. 17
REGINA 128
REGIT 108
Reid, Don 136
RETOUR DE FLAMME 72-4, 77
Reynolds, Brayley 50
RHODES SCHOLAR 44
Richards, Sir Gordon 48, 91
Richards, G. W. 123,134
RIGHTHAND MAN 195
Rimell, Fred 44-5, 49, 73, 103, 111-14, 145, 166-7, 194
Rimell, Mercy 117, 125-6, 145, 158, 161, 174
RIO TINTO 115
Riordon, John 148
RIVER BELLE 147
RIVER CEIRIOG 160
ROBIN O'CHANTRY 15
ROBIN WONDER 157
Robinson, Willie 83
Robinson, W. E. 33
Robson, Tommy 86, 88
Rogers, Charlie 16, 20, 23, 36, 46
Rogers, M. 94
Rogersons 90, 91
Rohan, Pat 171

ROI D'EGYPTE 76
ROLIE 17, 19, 20
ROMAN HACKLE 39-40
ROSATI 72, 142
Rose of Lancashire Hurdle 67-9
ROSE OF MEDINA 155
Rosebery, Lord 11, 40
ROSEWELL 45
ROSS SEA 84
ROSYTH 65, 86
ROYAL DERBI 186
Royal Doulton Hurdle 145
ROYAL FALCON 19-20
ROYAL GAIT 105, 176-80
ROYAL GAYE 145
ROYAL OAK 60
ROYAL PALACE 155
ROYAL VULCAN 144-5
Rudkin, Edgar 122
RUSTLE 161
Ryan, Peter 128

SABIN DU LOIR 150, 158
SADLERS CLERK 149
SADLER'S WELLS 206, 210
SAFFRON TARTAN 76-7, 148
Sandeman Aintree Hurdle 152, 159, 161, 168, 174, 176
SALMON SPRAY 83, 86, 88-93, 142, 167
Sangster, Robert 169
Sardan Long Distance Hurdle 118
SARTORIUS 98
SAUCY KIT 94-6, 100
SAYPAREE 186
Scalp Hurdle 55
Scarth, Eric 186
SCEPTRE 84
Schweppes Gold Trophy 65, 86, 100, 109, 118, 142, 143-4
SCORIA 115
Scott, Brough 149
Scottish Champion Hurdle 128, 131, 170, 185
SCOTTISH UNION 48
Scudamore, Michael 163
Scudamore, Peter 105, 163-4, 172-4, 183-6, 198-200
SEA BIRD 133
SEA PIGEON 90, 93, 120-3, 125-7, 130-41, 159, 179, 191
SECRETO 206
Sedgwick, Fred 37
SEE YOU THEN 154-61, 169-70, 191, 203, 214

SEMPERVIVUM 92-3, 95, 103
SENECA 40-1, 43, 180
SEPTIME 74
SHADOW LEADER 209
Shamrock Handicap Hurdle 11
Shankhill Hurdle 55
SHAUN GOILIN 21
Sheikh Ali Abu Khamsin 146
Sheikh Hamdan Al Maktoum 207
Sheikh Mohammed 166, 171, 174, 176-7, 179
Sheppard, Jonathan 160
SHINING GOLD 53
Sievier, Robert 97
SILVER RING 12
SILVER SEA 10
SILVER THISTLE 45
SINGSPIEL 171
SIR KEN 27, 58-63, 67-70, 102, 106, 109, 116, 130, 151, 154, 203, 209, 210
Slack, George 73
Sleator, Paddy 70, 76, 83, 144
SMART WOMAN 74
Smith, Bill 90, 112-14
Smith Eccles, Steve 117-18, 157-9, 160, 170
SMOKE PIECE 65
Smurfit, Michael 174, 176, 189, 192
Smyth, Ron 40-3, 48-50, 53
Smyth, Vic 40-3, 48, 50
SNUFF BOX 82
SOLFORD 36, 38-40
SOLOMON II 104
SON AND HEIR 33
SONG OF ESSEX 24-7, 186
SOUTHPORT 42
Spa Hurdle 70, 75, 80
SPACE TRUCKER 201
SPARTAN GENERAL 89
SPECIALITY 54
Speck, Billy 15
Spencer, George 85-6
Spencer, Reg 122, 127
Sprague, Harry 70
STAN'S PRIDE 157, 190
Stephens, Mrs M. 31
Stephenson, Arthur 181
Stephenson, Willie 57-9, 61-2, 68, 164
STIRLING 84
Stott, Billy 26, 79
Stoute, Michael 166, 169,

171-2
STRAIGHT DEAL 71
STRAIGHT POINT 100
STRANFIELD 132
STROLLER 67-70
Strong, Sir Charles 79
Stroud, Anthony 178
Sturt, Wally 197, 201
Stype Wood Stud 156
SUDDEN VICTORY 170
SULA BULA 146
Sun Alliance Hurdle 145, 150, 190, 202, 208-9
SUN HAT 86-7
Sun Templegate Hurdle 147
SUPREME COURT 87
Surtees, Robert 9
Swan, Charlie 207-9, 212-13
Sweeney, Phil 145
Swift, Brian 98-9
SWIFT AND TRUE 31-2
STYX RIVER 31
SYBILLIN 192
Sykes, Elizabeth 112

Taaffe, Pat 92-3, 114
Tabor, Vic 24
TALGO ABBESS 96
TAMBARA 128
TAMBOURIN 73
TAMMUZ 118
TEAPOT II 61-2
TEES HEAD 26
TELEGRAM II 59-60
TELEPROMPTER 139
Temple Gwathmey Chase 27, 160
THE DIVER 45-6
THE ILLIAD 175
THE PARSON 190
THE REJECT 157
THE TSAREVITCH 158
THEATREWORLD 201, 208, 210-11
THERESINA 128
Thirkell, Freddie 171
Thomas, Arthur 83
Thompson, Marcus 16

THOROUGHFARE 74
TICKETS 31
TINGLE CREEK 157, 170
Tinkler, Colin 130
Todd, George 89
TOKOROA 73-5, 77
TOM SHARP 158
TOP TWENTY 75
TOUT OU RIEN 72
Tree, Jeremy 133-4
TREE TANGLE 118-19
TRELAWNY 76
TRESPASSER 11-12, 25, 31, 61
TRIONA 43-4, 49
Triumph Hurdle 66, 68, 73, 94, 113, 171
Tudor Rose Hurdle 60
Turnell, Andy 91, 123, 132
Turnell, Bob 88, 90-1, 123
TURKEY BUZZARD 14
TWILIGHT SLAVE 148
TWW Hurdle 93

Underwood, Grenville 71-2
UP SABRE 33-4
URGAY 50
URUBANDE 208
Uttley, Jimmy 99, 101, 103-4

VALFINET 185-6, 189
VARMA 110
VAULX 37
Vaux Breweries Gold Trophy 134
VERBATIM 42
VERMILION 66, 75
VIC DAY 82
Victor Ludorum Hurdle 99
VICTOR NORMAN 28, 31-3, 123
Victory Hurdle 14, 68-9, 71, 73, 75, 79
VIDI 43-4
VITEMENT 38
VULGAN 91

Walwyn, Fulke 23-4, 40, 60,
72, 81-2, 86, 88-90, 92, 117-18, 121, 139, 167, 205
Ward, Rodney 70
Warner, Ben 30, 33
WARNING 98
Warman, Mrs 73
WAYWARD LAD 195
Webb, George 16
Wernher, Sir Harold 16, 18
Welsh Champion Hurdle 37, 108-9, 111, 114, 116, 118, 157
Welsh Grand National 37, 124
Wessel Cables Champion Hurdle 144, 151, 169
WEST TIP 172
Westgate Hurdle 70
WHEATLEY 31, 36
Wheatley, Ted 113
White, Ken 118-19
WHITE PARK BAY 84-5
WILHELMINA HENRIETTA 88-9, 198
Williams-Bulkeley, Victoria 20
Williamson, Norman 188, 192-3, 195
Wilson, Gerry 28-9, 44-5, 79
WINDERMERE LADDIE 25-6
WINNING FAIR 84-6
Winter, Fred 39, 63, 65-7, 69, 72, 75, 78-9, 82, 105-7, 109-10, 112, 114-17, 121, 157-8, 161, 164-5, 167, 184, 210
Winters, Tommy 67, 75
Woods, Paddy 188
Wootton, Frank 12, 21
Wootton, Stanley 21, 59
WORCRAN 88-9, 95
WRACK 11, 27
Wright, Stan 71, 73-4

Yarborough Plate 41
YES MAN 149

ZARIB 113
ZENO 17-19
ZIMULATOR 208